WILLIAM R. FEY, OFM Cap., born in Pittsburgh, Pennsylvania, in 1942, holds a doctorate in the philosophy of religion from Oxford University and is currently assistant professor of philosophy at St. Fidelis College, Herman, Pennsylvania. In June 1975 he presented a paper before the international Newman symposium in Dublin.

FAITH AND DOUBT

FAITH

and

DOUBT

The Unfolding of
Newman's Thought on Certainty

By William R. Fey, OFM Cap.

With a Preface by Charles Stephen Dessain

PATMOS PRESS
SHEPHERDSTOWN, WEST VIRGINIA
1976

"Dominus illuminatio mea"

CONTENTS

PREFACE

In the last quarter of a century there have appeared a number of studies of Newman's defence of the certainty which leads on to faith, and they have utilised drafts and other unpublished material which he left behind. These have perhaps never been used so extensively or with such understanding as by Father William Fey in his *The Unfolding of Newman's Thought on Certainty*. By a fortunate coincidence, a volume of all Newman's more important papers on this subject is to be published at the end of this year, and Father Fey, although that was not his intention, has provided them with a useful commentary.

The Theological Papers of John Henry Newman: On Faith and Certainty (Oxford University Press) include a dozen or so of the attempts Newman made in the course of years to write what became *A Grammar of Assent*. They show him wrestling with his problem and illustrate vividly the development of his thought, and the parts played by the will or the imagination. Father Fey, who quotes from these papers, puts them in their setting and interprets them. He considers Newman's thought on certainty historically, the background of the empiricist philosophy, and discusses more fully than has been done hitherto, Newman's relationship with Locke, and indeed the whole empiricist approach to the problem. This was a study long overdue, and as Newman's own thought gradually emerges in it, the relevance of his argument to the discussion of faith among contemporary British philosophers of religion becomes clear.

Father Fey has given us a book which is valuable, both for its elucidation of Newman's views and for its contribution to the modern debate.

The Oratory, Birmingham   Charles Stephen Dessain
1 September 1975

INTRODUCTION

At the height of the Victorian era Thomas H. Huxley remarked that if he were compiling a "primer of infidelity" he would draw heavily from the writings of John Henry Newman (1801–1890).[1] He could not understand how Newman combined faith in God with sympathy for the doubting mind; or respect for intellectual inquiry with recognition of the limits of logic. Yet it was precisely these combinations which set Newman apart from other Victorian thinkers and permitted him to make a unique contribution to the defense of religious belief.

The Deists of the eighteenth century and the Evidential School of the nineteenth undertook a defense of faith in theory by constructing proofs on paper. But Newman undertook a defense of faith in practice as he found it in the religious life of individuals. "I would maintain," he wrote, "that faith must rest on reason, nay even in the case of children, and the most ignorant and dull peasant, whenever faith is living and loving . . . And my task is to elicit and show to the satisfaction of others what these grounds of reason are."[2]

On October 9, 1845, Newman became a Roman Catholic. Looking back in 1864 he wrote: "I was not conscious . . . on my conversion, of any change, intellectual or moral, wrought in my mind."[3] This claim is an exaggeration, but it must be understood in the light of Newman's remarks about development.

> There is no false teaching without an intermixture of truth; and it is by the light of those particular truths . . . that we pick our way, slowly perhaps but surely, into the One Religion which God has given, taking our certitudes with us, not to lose, but to keep them more securely, and to understand and love their objects more perfectly.[4]

He did not deny that his thought had developed. He wrote of his early sermons: "In deep subjects, which had not been fully investigated, I said as much as I believed, and about as far as I saw I could go."[5] In fact his thought gradually took shape through a life-

xi

time of dialogue with old friends and new critics. Sometimes there was a separation of distinct questions which had been confused; sometimes an awareness of new questions which had been over-looked. Although Newman discussed the one problem of faith and reason throughout his life, he concentrated on different sides of it at different times. He held that "One thing at a time is the general rule given for getting through business well . . . In a large and complicated question it is much to settle portions of it."[6]

Newman carried out his lifelong investigation on two levels. On one level he addressed his own countrymen who, he felt, generally lacked real faith. They might hold the opinion that Christianity is probably true, but for Newman religious faith must be an absolute assent to what God has revealed. "Is it possible," he asked, " . . . that faith in Revelation is nothing beyond the thought, 'Perhaps after all God may have spoken?' . . . Who would call this an act of faith? Was such Abraham's faith?"[7] Consequently he explained and defended the certainty of faith.

On a second level Newman faced a growing skepticism which de-nied the possibility of objective (certain) knowledge in general about what is the case. Consequently he explained and defended the certainty of knowledge. He described the operation of our human and often informal modes of knowing. He attempted to explain the evolution of an idea while preserving its enduring reference. Finally, he brought these investigations to bear on his perennial problem: the reasonableness of faith. The certainty of our human mode of knowing is also found in that reasoning which leads men to make a judgment that they ought to believe, which, when made with a right will and an honest hope, and prompted by divine grace, becomes both a certain and a saving act of faith.

Newman himself was especially suited to handle questions at both levels. He was deeply aware of troublesome difficulties which made him sympathize with those in doubt. But he was equally aware of mysterious facts which he could not ignore. He was certain. He had an unshakable faith in God's word. Again, he was certain. He had a convinced common sense in ordinary matters and he was certain in each case, even when he could not explain it to others, or, for that matter, to himself.

He would never be satisfied with quick solutions that left the riddle unresolved. But neither would he be satisfied with a quick retreat to feeling that resolved the issue only by abandoning it to the skeptic. Either to deny the facts or to affirm them too abruptly was unsatisfactory because it was superficial. Instead Newman sought to balance fidelity to the facts with humility before the mysteries. He sought to respect elusive truths which had become part of himself, and yet to respect honest men in doubt who so often were his friends.

My object, in this book, is to trace Newman's discussion of questions about certainty as they occurred to him. It would be logical to treat knowledge first, and faith afterwards. But life is not always logical and Newman wrote out of his life. In fact, for him, circumstances reversed the order. He was first challenged to clarify the mysterious certainty of faith before confronting the ordinary, but also mysterious, certainty of knowledge. Is the certainty of faith in God's word nothing more than an assent to a conclusion resting on personal evidence? If it is not merely the conclusion of an informal argument, what is it and how is it related to reason? And is the certainty of knowledge in matters of fact nothing more than an assent to a conclusion resting on a vast complex of premises? If it is not merely the conclusion of a complicated formal inference, what is it and how is it related to argument? In each case, how is certainty not simply an arbitrary decision to ignore counter-evidence?

But if Newman reflected out of his life, he also reflected against the background of his times. The empiricist philosophy of knowledge and belief inherited from John Locke provided the setting for his work. The questions he raised and the expressions he used were colored by that climate, a climate that continues to influence the philosophy of religion and of knowledge in the English-speaking world today. While I attempt to situate Newman within that empiricist context, my intention is not to deny his remarkable originality, but to locate precisely wherein it lies.

In the course of preparing this study I have encountered many kindnesses which I wish to acknowledge. My thanks are, first of all, due to Fr. Thomas More Janeck who, as my religious superior, initially gave me leave to pursue this study at Oxford; and to his successor, Fr. Brendan Malloy who continued to support my work. I owe special gratitude to my supervisor and friend, Professor Basil Mitchell of Oriel College, Oxford, for his advice and encouragement; and to Fr. Stephen Dessain of the Birmingham Oratory for his expert direction and kind permission to make use of previously unpublished material.

I appreciate the helpful comments of Dr. John Coulson and Fr. A. M. Allchin who read and examined this work in its original form as a doctoral dissertation. I would also like to thank Mr. Brian Wicker for permission to use parts of his unpublished thesis for the University of Birmingham. His study of Newman's empiricist background became a helpful guide in my own research.

I am, of course, most indebted to my Capuchin Franciscan brothers both in America and in England for their fraternal support throughout the original composition and more recent revision of this work. In particular, I would like to thank Fr. Peter Peacock, Fr. Cassian Reel and the entire community for their kindness during my stay at Greyfriars, Oxford. In a very special way, I wish to express thanks to Fr. Ronald Lawler, now at the Pontifical College Josephinum, who, as my own respected teacher and brother in St. Francis, provided invaluable assistance through informal conversations about the central issues of this book. Wherever I may have borrowed ideas that are his own, I wish to render due acknowledgement.

Finally, a special debt of gratitude is owed to Mary Griset Holland of Patmos Press for her careful and thoughtful editing of the manuscript; and to the Province of St. Augustine of the Capuchin Order, Pittsburgh, Pennsylvania, for a grant to facilitate its rapid and timely publication.

St. Fidelis College   William R. Fey, OFM Cap.
Herman, Pennsylvania
September 14, 1975

References

1. Thomas H. Huxley, "Agnosticism and Christianity" *Nineteenth Century* 25 (1889) 948 note 6.
2. *MS* A.30.11 ("On the popular practical personal evidence for the truth of Revelation" 5 January 1860; and "Evidences of Religion" 12 January 1860). Some of these manuscripts are partly printed in David A. Pailin, *Way to Faith* (London, 1969) Appendix ii, 202–223; many of them are now available in *The Theological Papers of John Henry Newman:*

On Faith and Certainty (ed.) Hugo M. De Achaval and J. Derek Holmes (Oxford, 1976).

   3. *Apo* 214. See Francis Bacchus and Henry Tristram, "Newman (John Henry)" *Dictionnaire de Theologie Catholique* (Paris, 1931) 11:351. But see Orestes Brownson's article, *"The Christian Examiner and Religious Miscellany* . . . March 1850" *Brownson's Quarterly Review* n.s. 4 (July 1850) 306: "We have never pretended that our conversion to Catholicity was . . . the result of a progress in our Protestant life. It was a change, and consisted not in being clothed upon, as Mr. Newman would say, with Catholic truth, but in throwing off Protestant heresy, and accepting Catholic truth in its place."

   4. *GA* 249.

   5. *Apo* 418. He was speaking of his *US*.

   6. *Prepos* x–xi.

   7. *VM* 1:86 note 6 (added 1877).

LIST OF ABBREVIATIONS

It will be noted that frequently more than one date is given in the reference citations, both in the List of Abbreviations and in the notes. Where this is the case the date (or dates) given following the title is the date of the initial writing or presentation or publication of the work cited, while the second date, given together with the place of publication, indicates the date of the published volume used by the author. The purpose of this system is to convey *biographical* information by indicating when the material cited was first written or preached. Sometimes this date of writing or preaching coincides with the initial date of publication, but in such cases no distinction is made because the purpose is merely to indicate the date of preparation or presentation. It is hoped that this departure from the usual format will be helpful to the reader, especially with regard to clarifying the chronological development of Newman's thought.

Writings of John Henry Newman

Apo—Apologia Pro Vita Sua (1864) ed. Martin J. Svaglic, Oxford, 1967.

Ari—The Arians of the Fourth Century (1833) London, 1901.

Ath—Select Treatises of St. Athanasius; vol. 1: *Newman's Translation of Selected Texts;* vol. 2: *An Appendix of Illustrations;* (1841–1844) London, 1903.

AW—John Henry Newman: Autobiographical Writings (1820–1879) ed. Henry Tristram, London, 1955.

Call—Callista: a Tale of the Third Century (1855) London, 1904.

Correspondence—Correspondence of John Henry Newman with John Keble and Others, 1839–1845, eds. Fathers of the Birmingham Oratory, London, 1917.

DA—Discussions and Arguments on Various Subjects (1836–1866) London, 1907.

Dev—An Essay on the Development of Christian Doctrine (1845) London, 1906.

Diff—Certain Difficulties Felt by Anglicans in Catholic Teaching Considered; vol. 1: *in Twelve Lectures Addressed in 1850 to*

the Party of the Religious Movement of 1833 (1850) London,
1901; vol. 2: *in a Letter Addressed to the Rev. E. B. Pusey,
D. D., on the Occasion of His Eirenicon of 1864; in a Letter
Addressed to the Duke of Norfolk on the Occasion of Mr.
Gladstone's Expostulation of 1874* (1865, 1874–1875) London,
1907.

Ess—Essays Critical and Historical (1828–1846) 2 vols. London,
1907.

GA—An Essay in Aid of a Grammar of Assent (1870) London,
1906.

HS—Historical Sketches (1833–1854) 3 vols. London, 1903–1906.

*Idea—The Idea of a University Defined and Illustrated: I. in Nine
Discourses Delivered to the Catholics of Dublin, II. in Oc-
casional Lectures and Essays Addressed to the Members of the
Catholic University* (1852, 1854–1858) London, 1907.

Jfc—Lectures on the Doctrine of Justification (1838) London, 1900.

LD—Letters and Diaries of John Henry Newman, vols. 11–22:
1845–1866, eds. Charles Stephen Dessain (Dessain and Vincent
F. Blehl, vols. 14–15; Dessain and Edward E. Kelly, vol. 21)
London, 1961–1972; vols. 23–30: 1867–1884, eds. Dessain and
Thomas Gornall, Oxford, 1973–1975.

*Letters—Letters and Correspondence of John Henry Newman Dur-
ing His Life in the English Church* (1817–1845) ed. Anne
Mozley, 2 vols. London, 1891.

LG—Loss and Gain: the Story of a Convert (1848) London, 1906.

Mix—Discourses Addressed to Mixed Congregations (1849) London, 1906.

MS—Manuscripts. References are to packet numbers at the Birmingham Oratory.

OS—Sermons Preached on Various Occasions (1850–1873) London, 1904.

PN—The Philosophical Notebook of John Henry Newman; vol. 1:
General Introduction to the Study of Newman's Philosophy by
Edward Sillem, Louvain, 1969; vol. 2: *The Text* (1859–1888)
eds. Edward Sillem and A. J. Boekraad, Louvain, 1970.

PPS—Parochial and Plain Sermons (1825–1843) 8 vols. London,
1901–1907.

Prepos—Lectures on the Present Position of Catholics in England
(1851) London, 1903.

SE—Stray Essays (1884–1886) private, 1890.

SN—Sermon Notes of John Henry Cardinal Newman 1849–1878, eds. Fathers of the Birmingham Oratory, London, 1913.

Theses—"Cardinal Newman's Theses de Fide and his Proposed Introduction to the French Translation of the University Sermons," (1847) ed. Henry Tristram, *Gregorianum* 18 (1927) 219–241.

US—Fifteen Sermons Preached Before the University of Oxford (1826–1843) London, 1906.

VM—The Via Media of the Anglican Church; vol. 1: *Lectures on the Prophetic Office of the Church Viewed Relatively to Romanism and Popular Protestantism* (1837) London, 1901; vol. 2: *Occasional Letters and Tracts* (1830–1845) London, 1901.

Writings of John Locke

Draft—An Early Draft of Locke's Essay, Together with Excerpts from His Journals, Draft A, (1671) eds. Richard I. Aaron and J. Gibb, Oxford, 1936. References in parentheses state page numbers in the Aaron-Gibb edition.

Essay—An Essay Concerning Human Understanding (1690), 2 vols. ed. Alexander C. Fraser, New York, 1959. References include the page numbers of the Fraser edition, given in parentheses.

Locke MS—Manuscripts. Lovelace Collection: Bodleian Library.

Works—The Works of John Locke (1685–1703), 10 vols. London, 1812.

* An asterisk following a quote or quotes indicates that the quoted material has been translated from Latin.

FAITH AND DOUBT

Chapter I

THE PROBLEM OF FAITH AND REASON

Newman's attack on inadequate solutions

Newman's early interest in Evangelicalism had made him distrust reason. The eighteenth-century Calvinist, Joseph Milner, maintained that in a being as corrupt as man even a rigorous exercise of reason in aid of religion would only mislead the believer.[1] It was Locke, he wrote, who "led the fashion in introducing a pompous parade of *reasoning* into religion" leading away " from evangelical simplicity."[2]

Newman reflected this attitude in an early sermon. Since the Fall "passion and reason have abandoned their true place in man's nature, which is one of subordination, and conspired together against the Divine light within him, which is his proper guide. Reason has been as guilty as passion here."[3]

When Newman was elected a Fellow of Oriel College in 1822 he joined a respected intellectual circle, the Noetic or Evidential School gathered around Richard Whately, later Archbishop of Dublin. While the Enlightenment had driven many continental Christian intellectuals into fideism or sentimentalism, it tended to advance the trend in the Church of England toward a rationalization of Christianity into those doctrines which would survive the strictest logical tests. The Noetics argued that no one has a right to believe until he has applied to his claims the same canons used by mathematicians and physicists. For logical argument is "the most appropriate intellectual occupation of MAN, *as* man,"[4] and when it is obtained it compels assent to the articles of Christian belief.[5] But by establishing a proportion between the reasonableness of one's belief and the rigour of objective proof, this school tended to reserve a well-founded faith for the scholarly few who could master technical proofs.

The Noetics deepened in Newman a desire for intellectual content as well as evangelical fervor.[6] He became suspicious of a purely emotional hold on religion. "I wish to go by reason," he wrote, "not by feeling."[7] Yet his own observation of the religious mind at work showed that the Noetic's criterion for reasonable belief is artificially narrow. Many do hold a reasonable faith and not merely an ungrounded commitment although they are not able to put their evidence into logical form.

Whately had written that *"all* Reasoning, on whatever subject, is one and the same process, which may be clearly exhibited in the form of Syllogisms."[8] But Newman's experience showed that the degree of evidence is not always proportionate to the degree of formalization. In fact the natural scientist himself must resort to a concrete logic in implicit types of reasoning about matters of fact.

The Noetics seemed to have endorsed Descartes' dogma that the clarity and distinctness of an idea is the criterion of its truth, and then concluded that truths of faith like those of mathematics should be immediately compelling to an honest mind. But Newman recognized that there is no way of coercing the assent of faith simply by presenting apologetical arguments in demonstrative form. "First shoot round corners," he challenged, "and you may not despair of converting by a syllogism."[9]

Newman attacked a variety of inadequate solutions to the problem of faith and reason under the general term "Liberalism." "Liberalism," he wrote, "is the mistake of subjecting to human judgment those revealed doctrines which are in their nature beyond and independent of it; and claiming to determine on intrinsic grounds the truth and value of propositions which rest for their reception on the external authority of the Divine Word."[10]

At first Newman found in Joseph Butler a refreshing alternative to the rationalism of the Liberal school. He agreed with Butler about the broad role of probability in that human mode of inquiry which is not governed by the rationalist alternative of having either mathematically demonstrated propositions or nothing worthy of being called knowledge. But he found here traces of a new Liberalism which was more skeptical than confident. Butler had written: "To us probability is the very guide of life."[11] But, Newman argued, "the danger of this doctrine, in the case of many minds is its tendency to destroy in them absolute certainty, leading them to consider every conclusion as doubtful, and resolving truth into an opinion, which it is safe indeed to obey or to profess, but not possible to embrace with full internal assent."[12]

In 1845 Newman described the anti-dogmatic principle which seemed to follow when men lost confidence in reason's ability to prove the mysteries of revelation.

> That truth and falsehood in religion are but matter of opinion; that one doctrine is as good as another; . . . that there is no truth; that we are not acceptable to God by believing this than by believing that; . . . that we may take up and lay down opinions at pleasure; that belief belongs to the mere intellect, not to the heart also; that we may safely trust to ourselves in matters of Faith, and need no other guide,—this is the principle of philosophies and heresies, which is very weakness.[13]

This attitude had become so pervasive among Newman's countrymen that he complained: "It is not at all easy (humanly speaking) to wind up an Englishmen to a dogmatic level."[14] For many of them "their highest opinion in religion is, generally speaking, an assent to a probability—as even Butler has been understood or misunderstood to teach—and therefore consistent with toleration of its contradictory."[15] For some of them the religious mind is "slowly and calmly . . . floated upon the open bosom of an ocean without a shore, the dead of interminable, hopeless scepticism, in which nothing is believed, nothing professed, nothing perhaps even guessed at."[16]

If this new Liberalism were accepted, he said, "the celebrated saying, 'O God, if there be a God, save my soul, if I have a soul!' would be the highest measure of devotion:—but who can really pray to a Being, about whose existence he is seriously in doubt?"[17] John Keble "met this difficulty by ascribing the firmness of assent which we give to religious doctrine . . . to the living power of faith . . . which accepted it . . . It is faith and love which give to probability a force which it has not in itself."[18] In 1844 Keble wrote to Newman: "I have always fancied that perhaps you were over sanguine in making things square and did not allow for Bp. Butler's notion of doubt and intellectual difficulty being some men's intended element and trial."[19] But Newman did admit difficulties. In

fact he often "made use" of Keble's approach. Nevertheless, he
wrote: "I was dissatisfied because it did not go to the root of the
difficulty. It was beautiful and religious but it did not even profess
to be logical."[20] Faith is not an assent of the mind to a probability.
Nor is it an adhesion of the heart to a probability. For in that
case, no matter how firm one's commitment, the truth itself remains
uncertain.

Rationalism, sentimentalism and subjectivism

On the one hand Newman rejected the indifference often engendered by a rationalist spirit. He spoke of the age of evidences as
"a time when love was cold."[21] He also rejected the sentimentalism
often engendered by a sentimental spirit. He warned against the
danger of allowing religious inquiry to be directed by sympathy
rather than reason: "religion, as a mere sentiment, is to me a dream
and a mockery."[22]

Still he came to recognize a certain bond between sentimentalism
and rationalism.

> There is a widely, though irregularly spread School of doctrine
> among us . . . which aims at and professes peculiar piety as di-
> recting its attention to the heart itself, not to anything external to
> us, whether creed, actions or ritual. I do not hesitate to assert that
> this doctrine is based upon error, that it is really a specious form
> of trusting man rather than God, that it is in its nature Ra-
> tionalistic.[23]

Newman's objection was not that sentimentalism stressed feeling,
or rationalism reasoning, but that when either personal feeling or
private judgment is made the criterion for religious truth, faith becomes subjective. Man makes himself the measure of what is revealed. But faith implies the simple acceptance upon testimony of
what reason cannot reach. Newman distinguished between objective
and subjective truth and explained: "By Objective Truth is meant
the Religious System considered as existing in itself, external to this
or that particular mind: by Subjective, is meant that which each
mind receives in particular, and considers to be such."[24]

In 1870 he turned to the problem of knowledge in general. Again
he contrasted an objective grasp of what is the case with both a rationalistic and a sentimentalist subjectivism. "This universal living

scene of things is after all as little a logical world as it is a poetical; and as it cannot without violence be exalted into poetical perfection, neither can it be attenuated into a logical formula."[25]

Newman's constant talk of man's duty to truth;[26] his description of faith as obedience to the authority of revealed truth;[27] his attack against "private judgment" of revelation;[28] his defense of dogma and creed;[29] and his defense of certain knowledge about matters of fact in general[30]—can all be understood as a defense of objective truth.

> To believe in Objective Truth is to throw ourselves forward upon that which we have but partially mastered or made subjective, to embrace, maintain, and use general propositions which are larger than our own capacity, of which we cannot see the bottom, which we cannot follow out into their multiform details; to come before and bow before the import of such propositions, as if we were contemplating what is real and independent of human judgment.[31]

Newman and Locke

One cannot fully grasp the thrust of Newman's thought without taking into account his close acquaintance with the work of John Locke (1632–1704). Nor can one fully appreciate the former's synthesis of faith and reason without reflecting on the latter's discussion of the reasonableness of faith. It was Locke's *Essay Concerning Human Understanding* rather than the works of Descartes, Kant or Hegel which Newman considered the outstanding achievement of modern philosophy. And it was his close affinity with Locke and the empiricist tradition which distinguished him from Christian thinkers more closely related to the continental rationalists.

It is not easy to determine the degree or quality of Newman's dependence on classical empiricism. When tracing the history of ideas it is always tempting to stress differences and ignore similarities. It is particularly tempting when dealing with someone of his stature to highlight peaks and forget the ordinary terrain. However, notwithstanding the remarkable originality of Newman's work, eighteenth-century English empiricism could not but set a tone, fix the terms, raise questions and suggest answers which together provided the setting for his reflections. In particular, it was Locke's work which determined the context and structure of philosophical and theological discussion in England. John Burton had taught Locke's philosophy at Oxford in the eighteenth century.[32] Richard Whately testified to Locke's enduring influence and celebrity in the early decades of the nineteenth.[33] Newman admitted that he himself was necessarily a part of this "existing system" which Locke had helped to shape; yet, he added, "there is nothing unbecoming, unmeaning, or ungrateful in pointing out its faults and wishing them away."[34]

In the *Apologia* is found an equivocal recollection: "When I was fourteen . . . I read some of Hume's Essays; and perhaps that on Miracles. So, at least I gave my Father to understand; but perhaps it was a brag."[35] With the exception of this qualified claim, Newman held that Locke was the first philosopher he seriously studied. In his *Autobiographical Memoir,* written in the third person, there is this brief entry: "In the Long Vacation of 1818 he was taken up with Gibbon and Locke."[36] This first encounter with Locke came three years before his introduction to the Oriel Noetics and two years after the "inward conversion" he described in the *Apologia:* "When I was fifteen (in the autumn of 1816) a great change of thought took place in me . . . confirming me in my distrust of the reality of material phenomena, and making me rest in the thought of two and two only absolute and luminously self-evident beings, myself and my Creator."[37] Perhaps this deeply personal experience made him uneasy when reading Locke's argument for the existence of "an eternal, most powerful, and most knowing Being; which whether anyone will please to call God, it matters not."[38]

Newman referred to Locke with respect but with reservation. During the 1850s he told a Dublin audience that "If we were to ask for a report of our philosophers, the investigation would not be . . . agreeable . . . Locke is scarcely an honour to us in the standard of truth, grave and manly as he is."[39] In 1870 he was more specific. He agreed with many of Locke's remarks on reasoning and proof. He praised Locke's character, ability and "outspoken candour." It was precisely because of his respect for the great empiricist that he found it unpleasant to be obliged to consider Locke as an opponent to views he "cherished as true with an obstinate devotion."[40] Newman certainly felt that Locke stood on more common human ground than the continental rationalists whose systems seemed extravagant and artificial. In 1860 he read *The Historical Develop-*

ment of Speculative Philosophy from Kant to Hegel by Dr. Chalybäus, Professor of Philosophy at Kiel. Newman wrote in the margin of his copy: "Do these speculations mean more than to set up a theory which *may* be true—which cannot actually be disproved or to assert a conclusion that can be demonstrated?"[41] Although Locke's "manly simplicity" seemed closer to our experience Newman had reservations.

> Whatever is to be thought of his *a priori* method and his logical consistency, his *animus*, I fear, must be understood as hostile to the doctrine which I am going to maintain. He takes a view of the human mind, in relation to inference and assent, which to me seems theoretical and unreal. Reasonings and convictions which I deem natural and legitimate, he apparently would call irrational, enthusiastic, perverse and immoral; and that, as I think, because he consults his own ideal of how the mind ought to act, instead of interrogating human nature, as an existing thing, as it is found in the world.[42]

Different authors have taken different views of Newman's relation to the empiricist tradition in general and to Locke in particular. Some have claimed to find in Newman a straightforward dependence on Locke's epistemology.[43] Others have written that any constructive influence of Locke on Newman was negligible if it existed at all, that Locke simply represented for Newman the Liberal rationalism he sought to overthrow.[44] Still others have held that Newman used classical empiricist epistemology as a model to expose the limits of human knowledge and the need for faith to supplement that deficiency.[45] And finally, others have argued that Newman, in some sense, enlarged Locke's empiricism.[46]

It was a close friend, William Froude, who told him: "You have always had . . . a special faculty of seeing *how* those [see] who see differently from yourself."[47] This "special faculty" seems to have enabled Newman to appreciate Locke's position without abandoning his own principles. "As we advance in perception of the Truth we all become less fitted to be controversialists."[48] Newman's respect for the objectivity of truth made any other attitude repugnant. Yet, paradoxically, this same respect for objectivity made him open-minded toward those with whom he disagreed. He made his own Augustine's principle that "there is no false teaching without an intermixture of truth."[49] He wrote that if those who had left the Church

had been more patient, they would have found that she would
eventually extract the "truth in the ore" of their theories.[50] He discussed the philosophical language of the Fathers of the Church in
the light of this principle.

> The reasons, which induced the early Fathers to avail themselves
> of the language of Platonism, were various. They did so, partly as
> an *argumentum ad hominem;* as if the Christian were not pro-
> fessing in the doctrine of the Trinity a more mysterious tenet,
> than that which had been propounded by a great heathen au-
> thority, partly to conciliate their philosophical opponents; partly
> to save themselves the arduousness of inventing terms . . . and
> partly with the hope, or even belief, that the Platonic school had
> been guided in portions of its system by a more than human wis-
> dom. . . . [Christian thinkers] were prompt in appropriating the
> language of philosophers, with a changed meaning.[51]

It seems fair to suggest that the same reasons which Newman felt
had led the Fathers to use the language of Plato, also led Newman
to avail himself of the language of Locke. If this parallel is correct,
he did so partly as an *argumentum ad hominem* to show that his
own position was no more mysterious than an empiricist theory of
perception, partly to conciliate his opponents, partly to avoid the
trouble of inventing new terms, and partly, perhaps dominantly, to
extract the ore of truth which was inevitably to be found there. He
would apropriate "the language of philosophers with a changed
meaning."

Newman enlarged Locke's meaning in five areas. First, he spoke
of the starting point of reasoning or experience in a broad sense.
"Empiricism" generally refers to philosophical theories which hold
that the materials of human knowledge are found in human experience; and that consequently we can never have any knowledge of
what lies beyond that experience. Of course this definition is vague
until the term "human experience" is interpreted. He felt that
Locke's interpretation was unreal, as when the latter wrote that "in
all that great extent wherein the mind wanders . . . it stirs not
one jot beyond those ideas which *sense* or *reflection* have offered
for its contemplation."[52] He seemed to suggest that we experience
ideas, not things, immediately. Sometimes Newman seems to have
said the same.[53] In 1859 he wrote in a notebook that we are not

conscious of objective reality "but of the subjective sensation or impression."[54] Earlier that year he had written on this subject at greater length.

> It is notorious we do not perceive external objects—we see them through a medium, namely in a certain idea, which is created in our minds by our senses and in other ways—as if in a mirror . . . No one whatever doubts that what the mind contemplates, at least in corporeal objects, is not the object itself, but a representation of it, which we call an idea.[55]

But in other notebook entries of the same period, Newman seems only to have meant that our experience is complex. We come to know "aspects" or "ideas" of things.[56] Yet "we begin with wholes, not with parts. We see the landscape or the mountain or the sky . . . then we take to pieces, or take aspects of, this general & vague object, which is before us."[57]

Although his private notes are ambiguous, his published work clearly begins with experience of the self existing in a world of things of which we are immediately conscious. In a sermon at Oxford he said that the beings which surround us exist independently of our own existence or awareness of them. Yet "Of the material we have direct knowledge through the senses—we are sensible of the existence of persons and things, of their properties and modes, of their relations towards each other, and the courses of action which they carry on . . . we see and hear what passes, and that immediately."[58]

Secondly, Newman and Locke both used a method which was more descriptive than ambitious or creative. Locke's "historical plain method" of analysis of the human mind in action was meant to avoid any controlling assertions about its nature. In the "Epistle to the Reader" of his *Essay*, he described himself as an "underlabourer . . . clearing away the rubbish that lies in the way of knowledge" rather than as a Cartesian master-builder.[59] He declared that his aim was "not to teach the world a new way to certainty . . . but to endeavour to show wherein the old and only way of certainty consists."[60]

Newman also sought to contemplate the mind as it is. He wrote that his object was "not to form a theory which may account for those phenomena of the intellect" which he discussed, "but to ascertain what is the matter of fact as regards them."[61] Yet he felt that Locke had distorted the facts of experience to fit his own arbitrary theory. In fact Newman's major criticism of Locke was that he is not empirical enough, not committed enough to his own method of studying the human mind in its actual operations. Instead of taking man as a pure reasoning machine, Newman recognized that man is a complex sensing, reasoning, feeling, believing and acting animal; and that this viewpoint not only stands opposed to a rationalistic theory of man, but also stands closer to our experience of man than Locke's does.[62]

Thirdly, as to the problem of knowledge Newman was led to enlarge what Locke undertook to explore. Locke had found in Descartes a fresh alternative to the obscure scholasticism he had encountered at Oxford. He wrote of Descartes: "I must acknowledge to that justly admired gentleman, the great obligation of my first deliverance from the unintelligible way of talking of the philosophy in use in the Schools."[63] But Locke became impatient with master-builders who had not first critically traced the limits of our understanding. Consequently he made epistemology the primary subject of philosophical inquiry; and wrote that the purpose of his *Essay* was to "inquire into the original, certainty, and extent of *human knowledge,* together with the grounds and degrees of *belief, opinion* and *assent.*"[64]

Newman, however, first encountered a liberal rationalism which seemed over-critical about the limits of our knowledge. He found in Butler a fresh alternative to the artificial reasoning of the Noetics, but he became impatient with unreal limitations imposed on the mind which he felt led to skepticism. Consequently he began with the genuine first-order knowledge we do in fact possess, and wrote that the purpose of his *Essay in Aid of a Grammar of Assent* was to refute "the fallacies of those who say that we cannot believe what we cannot understand . . . [and] to justify certitude as exercised upon a cumulation of proofs, short of demonstration separately."[65]

Fourthly, as to the problem of faith Newman was again led to enlarge what Locke explored. Both were concerned with the religious belief of the common man. Locke wrote that everyone "has a concern in a future life, which he is bound to look after."[66] Knowledge of such matters "cannot be looked upon as the peculiar profession of any sort of man" who can master technical arguments.[67] In fact God required no more than simple belief in divine revelation, for no matter how ignorant one might be of sophisticated demonstrations of God's existence, Scripture was both available and sufficient for him.[68]

Newman wrote that "if revelation is consequent upon *reason*, and at the same time for all men, there must be reasons" available to everyone.[69] His problem was not how the ordinary believer can have a saving faith when reason is lacking, but how his faith can be reasonable when logical demonstration is lacking. "Faith not only ought to rest upon reason as its human basis, but does rest and cannot but so rest, if it deserves the name of faith."[70]

Finally, as to the relation of faith and reason, Newman was led to enlarge Locke's approach. For Locke reason must judge, first, whether a revelation has occurred and then, whether its content is understandable. In the latter case "we must understand any proposition to which we are expected to give the assent of faith."[71] But Newman wrote that his own *Essay* began by "refuting the fallacies of those who say that we cannot believe what we cannot understand."[72] In the former case Locke implied that we cannot be certain whether a revelation has occurred. But Newman said that the second half of his *Essay* was written "to justify certitude as exercised upon a cumulation of proofs."[73]

The fact that Newman saw fit to discuss Locke's questions in reverse order would seem to imply a different view of the nature of divine faith and revelation. Supernatural faith in God's word follows the logic of testimony. And while cumulative arguments are relevant to one's coming to divine faith, faith itself is not the conclusion of an argument. Informal modes of reasoning are not related to faith in the way in which reason is related to faith on Locke's account.

References

1. Joseph Milner. *Gibbon's Account of Christianity Considered with some Strictures on Hume's Dialogues Concerning Natural Religion* (Lincoln, 1808) 218–219: "The intellectual faculty, the more . . . piercing it is, sinks only the deeper in absurdity, while it mixes itself with the mire and dirt of human depravity."

2. *Ibid.* 172, 173–174.

3. *PPS* 5:114 ("State of Innocence" 11 February 1838). On Newman and Evangelicalism see David Newsome, "The Evangelical Sources of Newman's Power" in *Rediscovery of Newman* (ed.) John Coulson and A. M. Allchin (London, 1967) 11–30; John E. Linnan, "The Search for

Absolute Holiness: A Study of Newman's Evangelical Period" *Ample-forth Journal* 73 (1968) 161–174. On the Evangelicals and the Oxford Movement see Leonard E. Eliott-Binns, *The Early Evangelicals: A Religious and Social Study* (London, 1953); Yngve T. Brilioth, *The Anglican Revival: Studies in the Oxford Movement* (London, 1925) and his *Three Lectures on Evangelicalism and the Oxford Movement* (London, 1934); R. W. Church, *The Oxford Movement* (ed.) Geoffrey Best (1891) (Chicago, 1970); Christopher Dawson, *The Spirit of the Oxford Movement* (London, 1933) 25–44; Owen Chadwick, *The Mind of the Oxford Movement* (London, 1960); David Newsome, *The Parting of Friends* (London, 1966).

4. Richard Whately, *Elements of Logic* (1826) (London, 1872) x. Newman contributed some sections to this work; see *ibid.* viii; *LD* 15:176 (10 October 1852).

5. See Whately, xx. This attitude was not new; see for example James Foster, *The Usefulness, Truth and Excellency of Christian Revelation* (London, 1731) 43: as soon as men "begin" to reason "they must be able to find" religious truth; and Mark Pattison, "Tendencies of Religious Thought in England 1688–1750" in *Essays and Reviews* (London, 1861) 269.

6. Newman wrote of Whately: "He emphatically opened my mind, and taught me to think and to use my reason," but added, "his mind was too different from mine for us to remain long on one line." (*Apo* 23). On Newman and Whately see A. Dwight Culler, *The Imperial Intellect* (New Haven, 1955) 34–45; Maisie Ward, *Young Mr. Newman* (London, 1948) 74–76, 93–95, 115–116; *PN* 1:164–170; *Letters* 1:141 (14 November 1826); Mark Pattison's *Memoirs* (London, 1885) 78; Thomas Vargish, *Newman: the Contemplation of Mind* (Oxford, 1970) 12–16.

7. *Apo* 172.

8. Whately, 151.

9. *DA* 294 ("Tamworth Reading Room" February 1841).

10. *Apo* 256; see 234 and 45: "By 'liberal' I mean liberalism in religion for questions of politics do not come into this narrative at all."

11. Joseph Butler, *Analogy of Religion* (1736) (Glasgow, 1831) 173. On Newman's relation to Butler see *PN* 1:170–183; Eamon Duffy, "Newman's Use of Butler's Maxim 'Probability is the Guide of Life' " (M.A. thesis, Hull University, 1968); J. Robinson, "Newman's Use of Butler's Arguments" *Downside Review* 75 (1958) 5–10.

12. *Apo* 30.

13. *Dev* 357–358; see *GA* 316; *DA* 129–130 (Tract 85: "Scripture in its Relation to the Catholic Creed" 21 September 1838); *LG* 70; Adrian J. Boekraad, *Personal Conquest of Truth according to J. H. Newman* (Louvain, 1955) 121–122.

14. *Apo* 185. See also *ibid.* 260–261.

15. *GA* 59–60; see *LD* 15:460 (7 October 1853).

16. *MS* A.23.1 (On opinion, belief, etc.: 30 April 1853).

17. *Apo* 30. Newman did not speak of informal proof as an alternative to formal proof of revealed mysteries or the existence of a Supreme Being. His intention was to show, not that an argument is valid, but that faith, humanly considered, is reasonable; see below 180–181.

18. *Ibid.* See John Keble, "St. Thomas' Day" in *The Christian Year* 78 (1827) (London, 1906) 213.

19. *Correspondence* 320 (12 June 1844); see 256 (4 September 1843). Keble felt that Butler's *Analogy* attempted to form the heart although the mind remains unsatisfied. See Esther Georgina Battiscombe, *John Keble: a Study in Limitations* (London, 1963) 54–55.

20. *Apo* 31. Nevertheless John Tullock understood Newman as endorsing Keble's view; see his *Movements of Religious Thought in Britain during the nineteenth century* (London, 1885) 103.

21. *US* 197 ("Faith and Reason, contrasted as Habits of Mind" 6 January 1839).

22. *Apo* 54; see 152. The sentimentalism Newman came to distrust is more closely related to Evangelicalism than to English Romanticism as he encountered it. On Newman's relation to Romanticism see Vargish, 99–108; John Beer, "Newman and the Romantic Sensibility" in *The English Mind: Studies in the English Moralists Presented to Basil Willey* (ed.) Hugh S. Davies and George Watson (Cambridge, 1964) 193–218. The Romantic Movement is amorphous (see Brilioth, *Anglican Revival* 56) and Newman's relation to it is ambiguous. He spoke favorably of Wordsworth, Coleridge and Scott as fostering a literary revival parallel to the Oxford Movement (*VM* 2:378, 386 ("Letter to Dr. Jelf" 13 March 1841); *Apo* 94). He endorsed their insistence that the whole man reasons, mind and heart (*Ess* 1:268–269 ("Prospects of the Anglican Church" April 1839)). His opposition to men such as Thomas Arnold of Rugby or Charles Kingsley has been described as "a clash, not of personalities but of traditions." (John Coulson, A. M. Allchin, and Meriol Trevor, *Newman: A Portrait Restored* (London, 1965) 28). Yet his originality should not be overlooked. He first read Coleridge only in 1834 and then was "surprised how much I thought mine, is to be found there." (*Letters* 2:39 note 1 (Chronological notes: Spring 1835); *ibid.* 2:39 (11 May 1834)).

23. *Ess* 1:95 (Tract 73: "On the Introduction of Rationalistic Principles into Revealed Religion" 2 February 1836); see Henry Parry Liddon, *Life of Edward Bouverie Pusey* (London, 1894) Appendix 3:473–480 for a list of the Tracts for the Times with dates; in *Ess* 1:ix Newman noted that he wrote Tract 73 in 1835. See David Newsome, "Newman and the Oxford Movement" in *The Victorian Crisis of Faith* (ed.) Anthony Symondson (London, 1970) 83; and Horton Davies, *Worship and Theology in England*, vol. 4: *From Newman to Martineau* (Princeton, 1962) 35–36: "Newman came increasingly to feel that the defect of Protestant worship was its subjectivity, its perpetual scrutiny of the feelings, its emphasis on our faith, not on the Object of faith, while the strength of Roman Catholic worship was its objectivity, its steady contemplation of God as revealed in the Incarnation."

24. *Ess* 1: 31, 33–34 (Tract 73: 2 February 1836); see *PN* 2:71 ("Proof of Theism" 7 November 1859).
25. *GA* 268.
26. *US* 183 ("Faith and Reason Contrasted" 6 January 1839).
27. *PPS* 3:81–87 ("Faith and Obedience" 21 February 1830).
28. *Apo* 260–261.
29. *PPS* 2:167 ("Self-Contemplation" January or February 1835).
30. *GA* 167.
31. *Ess* 1:34 (Tract 73: 2 February 1836).
32. See *The Memoirs of the Life of Edward Gibbon* (ed.) G. B. Hill (London, 1900) 80. Gibbon quoted Edward Bentham's *De Vita et Moribus Johannis Burtoni* (Oxford, 1771) 15: "Burtonus Lockium aliosque recentiores notae Philosophos in Scholas adduxit, comites Aristotele non indignos."
33. Whately, 7. See also John Yolton, *John Locke and the Way of Ideas* (Oxford, 1956) 203, and Zeno OFM Cap. *J. H. Newman: Our Way to Certitude* (Leiden, 1957) 68 note 208.
34. *US* 67 ("Usurpations of Reason" 11 December 1831).
35. *Apo* 17.
36. *AW* ("Autobiographical Memoir" 13 June 1874) 40; see R. D. Middleton, *Newman at Oxford* (Oxford, 1950) 26–27.
37. *Apo* 17–18.
38. *Essay* IV:10.6 (2:309). Sillem contrasts Newman's experience of God's presence with Locke's appeal to a Supreme Being for "intellectual moorings to adjust the course of his thinking." (*PN* 1:196). But see James Collins, *God in Modern Philosophy* (1959) (London, 1960) 97, arguing that Locke rejected the rationalistic effort to make God "serve as a deductive principle in the theory of knowledge."
39. *Idea* 319 ("English Catholic Literature" 1854–1858).
40. *GA* 162. Newman possessed a handsomely-bound three-volume set of Locke's works edited by Desmaizeaux in 1751; it is now in the Birmingham Oratory Library. The volumes bear Newman's Littlemore book-plate which indicates that they were probably brought up to Littlemore from the library Newman had built up for himself at Oriel College.
41. Marginalia in Newman's copy of Heinrich M. Chalybäus, *Historical Development of Speculative Philosophy from Kant to Hegel* (Edinburgh, 1854) 204, 349.
42. *GA* 164.
43. E.g., M. C. D'Arcy, *Nature of Belief* (1931) (London, 1945) chapt. 5.
44. E.g., Sillem. *PN* 1:202–203.
45. E.g., James M. Cameron, "Newman and the Empiricist Tradition" in *Rediscovery* (ed.) Coulson and Allchin 76–96; and his *Night Battle* (London, 1962) 219–243. See below 19–22.
46. E.g., James Collins. *Philosophical Readings in Cardinal Newman* (Chicago, 1961) 10.
47. *LD* 20:431 note 4 (25 April 1863).

48. *VM* 1:69.

49. *GA* 249; see 377–378. St. Augustine, *Confessiones* VII:15, 21 (400) in *Patrologiae Cursus Completus, Series Latina* (ed.) J. P. Migne, 221 vols. (Paris, 1844–1864) 32:744, 747–748, hereafter cited as *PL; also* St. Thomas Aquinas, *Summae Theologiae* I:17.4 ad 2: "Omne malum fundatur in aliquo bono, et omne falsum in aliquo vero" (1265–1273) in *S. Thomae Aquinatis Opera Omnia . . . (Editio Leonina),* 22 vols. (to date) (Rome, 1882–1971) 4:223, hereafter cited as *Leon.; and his Summa Contra Gentiles* 2:34 (1261–1263) in *Leon.* 13:347.

50. *HS* 3:193–194 ("Strength and Weakness of Universities" 1854).

51. *Ari* 89–90, 92.

52. *Essay* II:1.24 (1:142).

53. See *PN* 2:8–21 ("Faculty of Abstraction" 27 January 1859); 22–30 ("Elements of Thought" 24 February 1859); 78–86 ("Objects of Consciousness" 4 December 1859); 93–100 ("Formation of Mind" 3 December 1859). These notebook reflections are tentative and exploratory. On the opening page Newman added: "What I write, I do not state dogmatically but categorically, that is, in investigation, nor have I confidence enough in what I have advanced to warrant publication." (*PN* 2:6 dated 22 September 1888 indicating Newman's uncertainty about this matter even late in life). See below 76–78.

54. *PN* 2:79, 81 ("Objects of Consciousness" 4 December 1859); see 22 ("Elements of Thought" 24 February 1859).

55. *MS* A.18.11 (Notes on Logic and Philosophy: January-February 1859).

56. *MS* A.18.11 ("Questions of greater consequence" 11 January 1859).

57. *PN* 2:8 ("Faculty of Abstraction" 27 January 1859).

58. *US* 205 ("Nature of Faith in relation to Reason" 13 January 1839). Newman added to this list the "direct knowledge of . . . our own soul and its acts;" see *PPS* 4:201–202 ("Invisible World" 16 July 1837); *GA* 346. Yet in the *GA* Newman wrote that a child "instinctively interprets . . . physical phenomena, as tokens of things beyond themselves;" and that from sense impressions "we go on to draw the general conclusion that there is a vast external world." (*GA* 62–63).

59. *Essay* "Epistle to the Reader" (1:14).

60. *Works* 4:459 ("Second reply to the Bishop of Worcester" 1699); see James Gibson, *Locke's Theory of Knowledge and its Historical Relations* (1917) (Cambridge, 1968) 209.

61. *GA* 343–344.

62. See Collins, *Readings* 10.

63. *Works* 4:48 ("First letter to the Bishop of Worcester" 1697). Lady Masham gives this account from her conversations with Locke: "The first books, as Mr. Locke himself told me, which gave him a relish of philosophical things, were those of Descartes. He was rejoiced in reading these, because, though he very often differed in opinion from this writer, he yet found that what he said was very intelligible." (Lady Damaris Masham to

Jean Le Clerc, 12 January 1705 quoted in Henry Richard Fox Bourne's
Life of John Locke (London, 1876) 1:61–62. This letter is in the
Remonstrant's Library at Amsterdam).

64. *Essay* "Introduction" 2 (1:26).

65. *GA* 395–396.

66. *Works* 3:206 ("Conduct of the Understanding" 1698).

67. *Works* 6:25 ("First Letter Concerning Toleration" 1689).

68. See *Works* 7:146 ("Reasonableness of Christianity" 1695); *Essay*
IV:1.2 (2:168).

69. *MS* A.30.11 ("Evidences of Religion" 12 January 1860).

70. *Ibid.* See *Dev* 327–328. It can be argued that the simple believer is
capable neither of formal proof nor of subtle cumulative argument. But
for Newman "informal" proof is not merely a very complicated "formal"
proof. It is of a different nature entirely and is available to everyone. See
below 149–152.

71. *Essay* IV: 18.7 (2:423).

72. *GA* 495 ("Note II" December 1880).

73. *Ibid.* 496.

Chapter II

FAITH AND EMPIRICISM

Locke on faith

John Locke defined faith as "the assent to any proposition, not
. . . made out by the deductions of reason, but upon the credit of
the proposer, as coming from God, in some extraordinary way of
communication. This way of discovering truths to men, we call
revelation."[1] Locke wanted to allow for faith in this sense, but, he
insisted, it must be rational. The word of God in revelation is incontrovertible, but we must first establish that an alleged proclama-
tion is from God. We may feel most confident that it is, but objectively our faith can be no more certain than the rational arguments
which support the fact that revelation has occurred. Even were
God to immediately reveal Himself to us, "our assurance can be no
greater than our knowledge is, that it *is* a revelation from God . . .
since the whole strength of the certainty depends upon our knowledge that God revealed it."[2]

Further, "the evidence, first, that we deceive not ourselves, in ascribing it to God; secondly, that we understand it right; can never
be so great as the evidence of our own intuitive knowledge."[3] That is,
outside our intuitive knowledge of the relations between ideas, we
have, not knowledge but judgment or opinion. Since the fact of
revelation falls into this latter category, our assurance of its truth
is tempered by the limits of human knowledge in the existential
realm. If the fact of revelation is said to be revealed, one could object that this becomes circular or opens into a regress.

Locke allowed revelation to carry faith *"against the probable conjectures of reason."*[4] In this sense the content of revelation is *"above
reason."*[5] But he added, "it still belongs to reason to judge of the
truth of its being a revelation, and of the signification of the words
wherein it is delivered."[6] "Whatever God hath revealed is certainly

true: no doubt can be made of it. This is the proper object of faith: but whether it be a *divine* revelation or no, reason must judge."[7]

If one believes a revealed truth but does not rest his faith on any investigation of grounds, he is most unreasonable. In 1682 Locke wrote in his journal:

> A strong and firme perswasion of any proposition relateing to religion for which a man hath . . . not sufficient proofs from reason but receives them as truths wrought in the minde extraordinarily by god himself . . . seemes to me to be Enthusiasme . . . these illuminations . . . carry noe knowledg nor certainty any farther than there are proofs of the truth of those things that are discovered by them . . . and if there be noe proofs . . . they can passe for noething but mear imaginations of the phansy how clearly soever they appeare . . . to the minde for tis not the clearnesse of the phansy but the evidence of the truth of the thing which makes the certainty.[8]

He insisted that *"Reason must be our last judge and guide in everything,"*[9] without exception. But the result of this position is that revelation becomes secularized. Every claim to know something by revelation amounts to a conjecture that remains open to future refutation. Since a factual question about the alleged supernatural source of information can never be established by reason with certainty or even great probability, it follows that faith, untempered by judicious doubt, is never justified. While Locke does not always draw this awkward conclusion, it is implicit in his discussion from the start.[10]

Religious faith becomes one of those opinions which "make up the greater part of our concernments" where we must let "probability . . . supply the defect of knowledge."[11] If we were to wait for certainty "in the ordinary affairs of life . . . [we] would be sure of nothing in this world, but of perishing quickly."[12] Likewise if we were to wait for certainty in religious matters we would never make an act of faith.

While an objective uncertainty must remain, a subjective hesitation need not endure for "the evidently strong probability may as steadily determine the man to assent to the truth, or make him take the proposition as true, and act accordingly, as knowledge makes him see or be certain that it is true."[13] Yet no matter how strong our assent, it "excludes not the possibility that it may be otherwise."[14]

Sometimes Locke spoke of faith in stronger terms. He distinguished it from probable opinion as well as certain knowledge. Reason discovers the "certainty or probability" of propositions deduced from sensation or reflection;[15] but revelation provides a new and unique "way of discovering truths."[16] Faith "carries with it an assurance beyond doubt . . . which as absolutely determines our minds, and as perfectly excludes all wavering, as our knowledge itself."[17] The articles of faith are "as certain and infallible as the very common principles of geometry."[18]

Yet he added, "the certainty of faith has nothing to do with the certainty of knowledge . . . the assurance of faith . . . is quite distinct from . . . [and] neither stands nor falls with knowledge."[19] It is faith alone which lends assurance to what would remain opinion if subjected to reason. "Faith comes into our assistance where the light of reason fails."[20] Someone might object that reason could not certainly determine what is genuine from among competing revelations. Locke granted that prophecy and miracle are the only means God has to convince us of His words. Yet, Locke insisted, God's providence would guarantee that "we need but open our eyes to see and be sure what comes from him."[21] Only our faith that God would not mislead us moves us beyond a probable assessment of the credentials which verify that a speaker is the bearer of a divine message. Locke professed that the Scriptures would always be his guide: "I shall presently condemn and quit any opinion of mine as soon as I am shown that it is contrary to any revelation in the Holy Scripture."[22] Yet on his own account, it is difficult to see how this confident claim is not an unwarranted enthusiasm.

This inconsistency was inevitable in a believer whose firm faith refused to be shaken by the restrictions of his own philosophy. The certainty of faith in what is revealed cannot exceed our probable reasoning that a revelation has occurred. However we can consider ourselves justified in acting as if we were certain. It is clear that Locke wanted to say more than this, although his rationalism would not consistently allow it. He wanted to say that revelation provides its own certainty, that it is a new "way of discovering truth," that it is our "infallible guide."[23]

Newman, empiricism and faith

James Cameron has argued that Newman stands within the empiricist tradition but that, along with others, he gives it a dramatic

and paradoxical twist. For them "a destructive philosophical analysis is a moment in an argument designed to show that we have
no alternative to putting our trust in 'nature.' "[24] Newman differs
from his fellow empiricists only about that to which this trust com-
mits us.

Cameron described the "myth of empiricism" as a thesis about
"priorities in the enterprise of stating what is or can be known."[25]
Locke limited what can be known to ideas derived from sensation
or reflection, and added that we consider these "as distinct positive
ideas, without taking notice of the causes that produce them," that
is, "the nature of the things existing without us."[26] Hume changed
the terminology. He spoke of "those *impressions*, which arise from
the senses," adding, "Their ultimate cause is, in my opinion, perfectly inexplicable by human reason, and 'twill always be impossible
to decide with certainty, whether they arise immediately from the
object, or are produc'd by the creative power of the mind, or are
deriv'd from the author of our being."[27] However Hume also held
that self-scrutiny discloses powerful and ordinarily irresistible impulses to believe certain hypotheses about the external world. These
impulses should overcome the uncertainty which belongs to these hypotheses when they are subjected to philosophical scrutiny. "Where
reason is lively, and mixes itself with some propensity, it ought to
be assented to."[28] Skepticism about the validity of our impressions
should be reserved for the quiet of the study. It remains sovereign
but it is stripped of all practical power in the day to day activity of
human life and thought.

Cameron focused his discussion on Hume and argued that Newman used the empiricist analysis of perception as a model of religious faith. Newman would admit skepticism in matters of fact,
secular and religious, and then appeal to an "inward" propensity to
believe in Christian revelation to offset this deficiency. He would
dwell on skepticism as a polemical device to lead his listeners to seek
the vision of faith. The result of this position is that we begin from
within. The content of an inward impression gives rise to religious
utterances and provides a test of their fidelity to an outward object
of faith.[29]

It must be admitted that some of Newman's remarks provide evidence for this interpretation. In 1830 he told an Oxford congrega-
tion that "the whole revealed scheme rests on nature for the validity

of its evidence."[30] But in 1831 he began to shift his emphasis from evidence to inwardness. "Evidences . . . [do] comparatively little towards keeping men from infidelity or turning them to religious life . . . the marks of design in the creation . . . are beautiful and interesting to the believer in a God; but, when men have not already recognized God's voice within them, [they are] ineffective."[31] He made his own Hume's ironical conclusion: "Our most holy religion is founded on *Faith,* not on reason."[32]

It seemed to Newman very doubtful whether the "phenomena of the visible world in themselves" could bring one to knowledge of a Creator.[33] In fact it seemed that "the study of Nature, when religious feeling is away, leads the mind . . . to acquiesce in the atheistic theory, as the simplest and easiest."[34] In 1839 he argued that unbelief "goes upon presumptions and prejudices as much as faith does, only presumptions of an opposite nature."[35] A correct choice is guided by a proper inward disposition.

Four years later he asked: "what if the whole series of impressions, made on us through the senses, be . . . but a Divine economy suited to our need, and the token of realities distinct from themselves?" To avoid the "dreary and hopeless scepticism" which these thoughts suggest, Newman encouraged his audience to "take into account the Being and Providence of God . . . All is dreary till we believe what our hearts tell us, that we are subjects of His Governance."[36]

Cameron concluded that for Newman again and again "what is *inward* is the primary reality and saves what is *without* from absolute unintelligibility."[37] Hume ended his *Natural History of Religion* with the verdict: "The whole is a riddle, an aenigma, an inexplicable mystery."[38] According to Cameron, Newman rejected this verdict in the end, but not because he thought it unjustified. In fact Newman pronounced the same verdict when he set aside his antecedent presumption in favor of Christian faith. "It was rather that he found more in his own inwardness than Hume found in his." If religious faith offers us a certainty, Cameron added, "it is not certainty as the world understands it, but a certainty which is a mysterious fact to be taken far otherwise than the man of the world takes *his* certainties; as not certain at all by his criteria; as certainty only to those who find the certainties of the world uncertain."[39]

Notwithstanding, Newman's position cannot fairly be treated as

Cameron has suggested. For Newman, the certainty of faith is distinctive; it is "a mysterious fact." But certainty, in this context, is the same as what the world commonly understands by it. It is not merely a propensity or subjective confidence. It is an objective grasp, although in faith, of what is true.

Etienne Gilson has warned that it is a "mistake . . . in interpreting Newman's doctrine . . . to see it as a rational probabilism redeemed by a belated appeal to religious faith."[40] Cameron went further by interpreting Newman's doctrine as a rational skepticism redeemed by a belated appeal to faith. Already in 1839, however, Newman rejected the view that there is "deficiency in the power of reasoning in the multitude; and that Faith . . . is but proved thereby to be a specimen of such deficiency." In fact he emphasized that "there is no greater mistake than this."[41]

In the winter of 1846–1847 he wrote from Rome to John Bernard Dalgairns who was to supervise a French translation of the *University Sermons*. Newman recognized that some remarks in the sermons might suggest that he held skepticism in religious matters, but skepticism overcome by an inward presumption in favor of belief. He told Dalgairns it would be necessary to emphasize that the sermons dealt with the individual believer, not with faith in the abstract. When he had said that faith does not demand evidence enough for rational conviction, or that faith is sole and elementary and depends on no previous process of mind, he only meant to stress the personal nature of reasoning toward faith.[42] His emphasis on personal dispositions was not meant to displace evidence. He was not admitting skepticism and then appealing to propensities to believe what we cannot know. Often we can know what is the case although our knowing on evidence is not like mathematical reasoning from premises. Likewise we can grasp in faith what is the case on the evidence of faith itself. In both cases, skepticism is not overcome by a propensity to cling to an hypothesis. Rather ignorance is overcome by knowledge.[43]

During the 1870s Newman added notes to new editions of his works to clarify his meaning. In 1839 he had written that "it is a great question whether Atheism is not as philosophically consistent with the phenomena of the physical world, taken by themselves, as the doctrine of a creative and governing Power."[44] In 1871 he granted that we might be unable to recognize truth if physical phenomena were considered without any reference to "psychological phenomena," or to the "moral principles by which they must be interpreted." Yet proper intellectual training does wake up in the mind the idea of God. "The question is," he explained, "whether physical phenomena logically *teach* us, or on the other hand logically *remind* us of the Being of a God. In either case, if they do not *bring* us to this cardinal truth, we are, in St. Paul's words, 'without excuse.' "[45]

Where in 1841 he had written that the "one hypothesis will solve the phenomena as well as the other"[46] he added later: "This is too absolute, if it is taken to mean that the legitimate, and what may be called the objective, conclusion from the fact of Nature viewed in the concrete is not in favour of the being and providence of God."[47]

In the last University sermon he had said that we simply trust our senses and may leave the question of their substantial truth for another world. In the same way, we are impelled by an inward instinct to trust the fidelity of testimony offered for a revelation.[48] But in 1871 he added:

> The senses convey to the mind 'substantial truth,' in so far as they bring home to us that certain things are, and *in confuso* what they are. But has a man born blind, by means of hearing, smelling, taste and touch, such an idea of physical nature, as may be called *substantially* true or, on the contrary, an idea which at best is but the *shadow* of the truth? for, in whichever respect, whether as in substance or by a shadow, the blind man knows the objects of sight, in the same are those things, in 'which eye has not seen, nor ear heard,' apprehended by us now, 'in a glass darkly,' *per speculum, in aenigmate*.[49]

Whether one says that knowledge is substantially true or true in shadow, the fact is that we objectively grasp what is immediately before us or, in faith, revealed to us.

References

1. *Essay* IV:18.2 (2:416). In the winter of 1670–1671 Locke engaged in a discussion with friends about "the principles of morality and revealed religion." (See Maurice Cranston, *John Locke* (New York, 1957) 141). He recognized that these issues could not be settled without first investigat-

ing the scope of human understanding. But while working out this investigation he never lost sight of his primary objective. Although some were dissatisfied with his *Essay* Locke was convinced that it secured "all the great ends of religion and morality." (*Works* 4:33–34 ("First letter to the Bishop of Worcester" 1697)).

2. *Essay* IV:18.5 (2:420–421).

3. *Ibid.* (2:420).

4. *Ibid.* 18.8 (2:423).

5. *Ibid.* 17.23 (2:412).

6. *Ibid.* 18.8 (2:424).

7. *Ibid.* 18.10 (2:425).

8. *Locke MS* f. 6:20–22 ("Journal" 19 February 1682). See also *Essay* IV:19.3 (2:430).

9. *Essay* IV:19.14 (2:438).

10. See Paul Helm, *The Varieties of Belief* (London, 1973) 92. Also see his "Locke on Faith and Knowledge" *Philosophical Quarterly* 23 (1973) 52–66; and Daniel J. O'Connor, *John Locke* (1952) (New York, 1967) 200.

11. *Essay* IV:15.4 (2:365). See Richard Ashcroft, "Faith and Knowledge in Locke's Philosophy" in *John Locke: Problems and Perspectives* (ed.) John W. Yolton (Cambridge, 1969) 209 note 6.

12. *Essay* IV:11.10 (2:335).

13. *Works* 4:299 ("Second reply to the Bishop of Worcester" 1699). Locke added that this is "all the faith necessary to a Christian."

14. *Ibid.* See Gibson, 122–123. The Deists claimed that their position was a direct consequence of Locke's theory. It is not a necessary consequence. Locke would defend a probable assent to revealed truths which are "above reason." But the Deists were confident about rational demonstrations of revealed truths and impatient with uncertain probabilities in defense of indemonstrable revelations. They accepted Locke's principle that reason must be our guide in everything and then proceeded to reject whatever is above reason as contrary to it. The only acceptable propositions of revelation were ones which coincided with truths reached by natural modes of reasoning. On Locke and the Deists see Yolton, *Way* 170–179; Samuel G. Hefelbower, *The Relation of John Locke to English Deism* (Chicago, 1918).

15. *Essay* IV:18.2 (2:416). The difficulty is to make some sense out of talk of perceiving a "probable connexion" within Locke's account of knowledge and judgment. See O'Connor, 197.

16. *Essay* IV: 18.2 (2:416). See Ashcroft 215.

17. *Essay* IV:16.14 (2:383). But he added "*only we must be sure that it be a divine revelation, and that we understand it right:* else we shall expose ourselves to . . . enthusiasm."

18. *Works* 4:275 ("Second reply to the Bishop of Worcester" 1699).

19. *Ibid.* 146–147 ("First reply to the Bishop of Worcester" 1697). He added: "With what assurance soever of believing, I assent to any article of faith, so that I steadfastly venture my all upon it, it is still but

believing. Bring it to certainty, and it ceases to be faith . . . Whether then I am or am not mistaken in the placing of certainty in the perception of the agreement or disagreement of ideas . . . faith still stands upon its own basis, which is not at all altered by it . . . any article of faith . . . stands . . . out of reach of what belongs to knowledge and certainty."
20. *Locke MS* f. 1:420–424 ("Journal" 26 August 1676); Ashcroft, 216.
21. *Works* 9:262, 261 ("Discourse of Miracles" 1702). Ian T. Ramsey has suggested a view of Locke on faith which goes far beyond what Locke's epistemology allows. See Locke's *Reasonableness of Christianity: including Third Letter concerning Toleration and Discourse of Miracles* (ed.) Ian T. Ramsey (Stanford, 1958) 9–20.
22. *Works* 4:96 ("First letter to the Bishop of Worcester" 1697).
23. *Ibid.* 7:359 ("Second Vindication of the Reasonableness of Christianity" 1697): "I know no other infallible guide but the Spirit of God in the Scripture."
24. Cameron, *Night Battle* 223. On Newman's reading of Hume see *PN* 1:203; Vargish 16–23.
25. Cameron, *Night Battle* 225.
26. *Essay* II:8.2 (1:166).
27. David Hume, *Treatise of Human Nature* I:3.5 (1730–1740) (ed.) L.A. Selby-Bigge (Oxford, 1958) 84. George Berkeley held that our "ideas" which we call "real things" are "imprinted on the senses by the Author of Nature." *Principles of Human Knowledge* 33 (1710) in *Principles, Dialogues and Philosophical Correspondence* (ed.) Colin M. Turbayne (New York: 1965) 36–37.
28. Hume, *Treatise* I:4.7 (Selby-Bigge 270).
29. Cameron, "Newman" 82–83.
30. *US* 31 ("The Influence of Natural and Revealed Religion" 13 April 1830). Newman seems to endorse the Deist position that reason and revelation "coincide in declaring the same substantial doctrines."
31. *US* 70 ("Usurpations of Reason" 11 December 1831).
32. *Ibid.* 60. David Hume, *An Enquiry Concerning the Human Understanding* X:2.100 (1748) in *Enquiries Concerning the Human Understanding and Concerning the Principles of Morals* (ed.) L.A. Selby-Bigge (Oxford, 1962) 130.
33. *Ari* 151–152. Newman added that the tradition of God's existence "has been from the beginning His own comment upon" the evidence, "graciously preceding" human investigation.
34. *DA* 299–300 ("Tamworth Reading Room" February 1841).
35. *US* 230 ("Love the Safeguard of Faith against Superstition" 21 May 1839).
36. *Ibid.* 347–348 ("Theory of Developments in Religious Doctrine" 2 February 1843); see *ibid.* 216 ("Nature of Faith" 13 January 1839): "As Reason, with its great conclusions, is confessedly a higher instrument than Sense with its secure premises, so Faith rises above Reason, in its subject-matter." Also *Ari* 75–76: "Some philosophers" claim that sensible

phenomena are "but a divine mode of conveying to the mind the realities of existence . . . representations of realities which are incomprehensible to creatures such as ourselves." Whether "right or wrong" this theory "serves as an illustration . . . of the great truth we are considering." The mind seems "to be floated off upon the ocean of interminable scepticism; yet a true sense of its own weakness brings it back, the instinctive persuasion that it must be intended to rely on something, and therefore the information given though philosophically inaccurate must be practically certain."

37. Cameron, "Newman" 87; see *Ath* 1:168 note 6; *Apo* 216–217: "The world seems simply to give the lie to that great truth of which my whole being is so full . . . Were it not for this voice, speaking so clearly in my conscience and my heart, I should be an atheist, or a pantheist, or a polytheist when I looked into the world." He added: "I am speaking for myself only; and am far from denying the real force of the arguments in proof of a God." His emphasis on an inward disposition is closely related to his emphasis on conscience. Although not treated in this book, Newman's position on conscience is central to much of his work. See *US* 18–19 ("Influence of Natural and Revealed Religion" 13 April 1830); *PN* 2: 31–77 ("Proof of Theism" 7 November 1859); *Apo* 180; *GA* 105–118; *Diff* 2:246–261 (Letter to the Duke of Norfolk: 27 December 1874). Also Adrian J. Boekraad and Henry Tristram, *The Argument from Conscience to the Existence of God* (Louvain, 1961); J. H. Walgrave, *Newman the Theologian* (1957) (London, 1960) 342–363; Joseph Crehan, "Conscience" in *A Catholic Dictionary of Theology* (ed.) H. Francis Davis, Aidan Williams, Ivo Thomas, and Joseph Crehan, 3 vols. (London, 1961-1971) 2:99-105. See A. O. J. Cockshut, *The Unbelievers: English Agnostic Thought 1840–1890* (New York, 1966) 181 arguing that Victorians "saw the search for truth in two simple ways, first as the unbiased application of the mind to the evidence, and second, as a sacred quest in which the voice of conscience was an infallible guide." Newman held that obedience to conscience and growth in virtue do not replace evidence but purify the mind, making it a sensitive instrument for discerning truth.

38. David Hume, *The Natural History of Religion* (1749–1751) in *Hume on Religion* (ed.) Richard Wollheim (London, 1963) 98.

39. Cameron, "Newman" 94, *Night Battle* 236.

40. Etienne Gilson's introduction to the Image Books: Doubleday edition of the *GA* (New York, 1955) 15.

41. *US* 210–211 ("Nature of Faith" 13 January 1839).

42. See *LD* 12:31 (8 February 1847); *US* 187 ("Faith and Reason Contrasted" 6 January 1839).

43. See below 185–186.

44. *US* 194 ("Faith and Reason Contrasted" 6 January 1839).

45. *Ibid.* note 9 (added 1871), *Romans* 1:21. See *LD* 12:31 (8 February 1847) on this same passage advising Dalgairns to "put something . . . less strong" in its place.

46. *DA* 300 ("Tamworth Reading Room" February 1841).

47. *Ibid.* note (added 1872).

48. See *US* 349 ("Theory of Developments in Religious Doctrine" 2 February 1843).

49. *Ibid.* note 5 (added 1871); 1 *Corinthians* 13:12.

CHAPTER III

NEWMAN ON FAITH

The nature of faith

Newman did not define the nature of faith according to some *a priori* theory. He took faith as he found it—described in Scripture, lived by saints, expressed in creeds, and practiced in the Church from Apostolic times to his own day. In 1849 he told a Birmingham audience that faith has always consisted in submitting to God's word, not in judging for one's self. St. Paul insisted that "Faith is most certain, decided, positive, immovable in its assent . . . This is what faith was in the times of the Apostles . . . and what it was then, it must be now, else it ceases to be the same thing."[1]

But Newman's conviction on this point was sometimes obscured by an invective against impersonal modes of scientific inquiry, sometimes by a confusion of distinct questions. From the start he held that faith as we find it includes a variety of paradoxical properties. There are antecedent dispositions before evidence, a readiness to obey, to love and to venture everything on God's word. Faith "is a particular mode of thinking and acting,"[2] yet it is not subjective. It is entirely free, yet it is entirely reasonable. It is absolute, yet a believer may seek to uncover the grounds of his belief. It is reasonable, but not the conclusion of an argued proof.

What gradually emerged in his writing was an account of how these ingredients combine in faith.

Frequently the same set of words conceals a range of meaning. It can stand for different questions and set off different inquiries which reach different conclusions. For example, to ask "what is this cake?" can mean, to a housewife, what ingredients; to a physicist, how many atoms; to a dietician, how many calories; to an artist, what shades; and so on. Likewise to ask "what is faith?" can mean, to a preacher, what are the properties of a saving faith; or to a philosopher-theologian, what is the nature of faith, what is the logic and epistemology of faith, how is it and how is it not different from knowledge.

As a preacher Newman spoke of a saving faith which includes love of God, generous obedience to His will and continual growth in virtue. But as a philosopher-theologian he recognized with increasing clarity that, whatever else must be said, faith itself is an objective (certain) assent to God revealing some truth. Newman's capacity, in his earliest work, to identify counterfeit notions about faith enabled him to formulate, over a long period, a positive understanding of faith in this sense.

First, faith is not a mere subjective way of viewing things. He admitted that "a certain frame of mind, certain notions, affections, feelings, and tempers" are necessary ingredients in a saving faith. But, he added, "we are in danger, in this day, of making religion consist in our having what is called a spiritual state of heart, to the comparative neglect of the Object from which it must arise, and the works in which it should issue."[3]

Secondly, faith, though a presumption, is "not a mere chance conjecture." It is "a moving forward in the twilight, yet not without clue or direction." Rather it is "kept in the narrow path of truth by . . . the Light of heaven which animates and guides it."[4]

Newman's emphasis on antecedent dispositions might suggest that faith is a "conjecture" beyond evidence. The believer has his "own reasons" which are sufficient to warrant assent. When he "presumes" to frame conclusions in anticipation of a logical exposition of them,[5] this seems unreasonable to one who lacks proper dispositions.

Faith makes its own evidence, 'being the *evidence* of things not seen.' And this is . . . why Faith seems to the world so irrational . . . Not that it has no grounds in Reason, that is, in evidence; but because it is satisfied with so much less than would be necessary, were it not for the bias of the mind, that to the world its evidence seems like nothing . . . Faith . . . is created in the mind, not so much by facts, as by probabilities; and since probabilities . . . are reducible to no scientific standard, what are such to each individual, depends on his moral temperament. A good and a bad man will think very different things probable.[6]

Temperament and inclination affect our judgments in many matters. People are often ready to believe what they wish were true. They are slow to admit the failure of their own projects, or to accept disappointing news, while they "readily believe reports unfavourable to persons they dislike, or confirmations of theories of their own."[7] Some antecedent dispositions are inevitable, but they are not always reasonable. They are "inducements to belief which prevail with all of us, by a law of our nature . . . whether they are in the particular case reasonable or not."[8] They cannot be eliminated but sometimes they must be corrected.

> When the probabilities we assume do not really exist, or our wishes are inordinate, or our opinions are wrong, our Faith degenerates into weakness, extravagance, superstition, enthusiasm, bigotry, prejudice, as the case may be; but when our prepossessions are unexceptionable, then we are right in believing or not believing, not indeed without, but upon slender evidence.[9]

Newman always felt that his talk of antecedent dispositions was his most promising contribution to a realistic theory of faith. He felt that the most "original" feature of his university sermons was their insistence "that antecedent probability is the great instrument of conviction in religious (nay in all) matters."[10]

The difficulty is that his language was ambiguous. Sometimes he described antecedent dispositions as moral habits. They are correct when they are developed in obedience to conscience. In this sense they dispose one toward faith in a personal God who speaks through conscience.[11] At other times Newman seems to have meant what he later called "first principles," that is, particular aspects which determine a view of things, or implicit assumptions which guide a course of reasoning.[12] He did not clearly distinguish the various senses (moral, intellectual, supernatural) in which the expression "antecedent disposition" can be taken. He was satisfied to let his remarks remind his listeners of a sense of reasoning from experience which goes beyond the impersonal model of the mind which rationalism suggests.

Thirdly, faith, as an assent, is something other than love or obedience. In 1838 Newman noted that "Romanists" define faith as an "assent of the mind to God's word." His own homilies treat faith "practically . . . as it is in fact." But "Rome, speaking theologically, traces it to its elements." He allowed that "either notion is intelligible, whichever is the more advisable."[13] The "strict definition" of faith is as an assent. But a living and justifying faith includes trust, love, obedience and the entire complex of Christian virtues. In 1850 he told a London audience that Protestants treat faith and love as inseparable while Catholics hold that they are "simply separable, and ordinarily separated in fact." Faith does not necessarily imply love, obedience or works. "The firmest faith, so as to move mountains, may exist without love."[14] Where there is no experience of this "habit, this act of the mind" and where, nevertheless, the word "faith" is used, another meaning is found for it. It is called the "motive of obedience" or the "fervour and heartiness which attend good works." Faith is taken as "hope or it is love, or it is a mixture of the two." It is defined or determined "not by its nature or essence but by its effects." For Newman, the "certainty or spiritual sight, which is included in the idea of faith, is . . . perfectly distinct in its own nature from the desire, intention, and power of acting agreeably to it."[15] We cannot have devotion without faith, "but we may believe without feeling devotion." He compared the distinction between faith and devotion to the distinction between objective and subjective truth.[16]

In 1838 he spoke of a "priority of love to faith."[17] "Love is the parent of faith."[18] "We believe God's words, because we love it . . . we do not love because we believe."[19] He seems to have confused trust in God and belief that there is a God. We might trust God because we love Him. But to say we believe God exists because we love requires further explanation. In 1839 Newman explained that love in this sense is part of the antecedent condition which disposes a man to assess evidence and receive the gift of faith.[20] A man is inclined to accept a revelation "because he has a love for it, his love being strong, though the testimony is weak. He has a keen sense of the . . . excellence of the message . . . Thus Faith is the reasoning of . . . a right or renewed heart."[21] Most men believe "not because they have examined evidence, but because they are disposed in a certain way."[22] Newman recognized that there is a serious difficulty with this position. It could be used to justify prejudice or bigotry. But he was convinced that a right state of heart would keep faith from becoming superstition or fanaticism. Faith and love together would bring the honest man to an "apprehension of Divine

Truth without that formal intimacy . . . with the special evidence for the facts believed, which is commonly called Reasoning . . . and which results in knowledge."[23]

Newman did not want to deny that faith is reasonable, nor that it is an objective assent. He wanted to contrast faith with impersonal calculation. But his language was sometimes confusing. Later he added footnotes to distinguish the sense in which love "causes" faith and the sense in which faith "causes" love. "Whereas faith, as a disposing condition, is prior to justification, love or *charitas* is posterior to it. It is a *pia affectio* or *bona voluntas*, not *charitas*, which precedes faith."[24] When "love" is taken to denote only a desire to know and serve God, it can be said to precede religious conversion. In this case it will actually require "the presence of grounds for believing" as a necessary part of coming to faith.[25] But when it is taken in its proper sense to denote the theological virtue of charity, then "love comes *after* faith, through a distinct grace . . . it is the objects of Christian faith which cause love . . . Faith leads to love *through* meditation."[26]

Fourthly, faith is not merely a disposition to act in a certain way. In his early work Newman tended to speak of a practical decision to act on probabilities as if we were certain. Locke's favorite defense of the reasonableness of his theory of faith and knowledge was that, while it made certainty impossible, it left us with enough probability to act as if we were certain.[27] In 1824 Newman seems to have said the same.

He wrote an article on Cicero for the *Encyclopaedia Metropolitana,* where he discussed the "system of doctrine which the reformers . . . of the Academic school introduced about 300 years before the Christian era."[28] The New Academy taught with Plato that the natures of things were fixed but that it was impossible for us to grasp their eternal forms or to separate appearance from reality. "From these reasonings the Academics taught that nothing was certain, nothing was to be known . . . we must suspend our decision . . . nay . . . never even form an opinion. In the conduct of life, however, probability must determine our choice of action."[29] He distinguished this school from the Pyrrhonists: "The latter altogether denied the existence of the probable, while the former admitted there was sufficient to allow of action, provided we pronounced absolutely on nothing."[30] He ended in praise of the New

Academy which, "by allowing that the suspense of judgment was not always a duty, that the wise man might sometimes *believe* though he could not *know* . . . in some measure restored the authority of those great instincts of our nature" which the Pyrrhonists had discarded.[31]

In *The Arians of the Fourth Century* (1833) Newman applied this to faith in revelation. Our trust in God's providence assures us that revelation "is true in so full and substantial a sense, that no possible mistake can arise practically from following it." In our "practical concerns" God has provided us with an intellectual ability which enlightens our difficulties without solving them.[32] Again in his 1837 lectures at St. Mary the Virgin, Newman seems to have attributed one's readiness to act on faith to his "personal interest" in its being true. He distinguished faith from opinion in terms of the degree of importance of the propositions in question rather than in terms of the "light or darkness" under which they are perceived. "Action," he said, "is the criterion of true faith."[33] When we are personally involved in some question, slight evidence can lead to action; but when we are not, a great deal of evidence may leave us unmoved. He gave examples to emphasize his point: "Though we know for certain that the planet Jupiter were in flames, we should go on as usual; whereas even the confused cry of fire at night rouses us from our beds."[34]

His remarks sometimes suggest that faith is a firm assent only in the sense that one's personal interest disposes him to act as if he were certain. At other times they suggest that personal interest is part of a complex of antecedent dispositions which can enable one to grasp a certainty (or receive the gift of faith). But his intention was always to deflate rationalism in religion by stressing the personal nature of a man's reasoning toward faith. "Life is not long enough for a religion of inferences; we shall never have done beginning, if we determine to begin with proof."[35] Faith, after all, is a "principle of action," but action does not always allow time for sifting arguments. Faith is possible for every man. But subtle investigations can be carried out only by those who have leisure; "they are not suited to the multitude."[36]

Years later Newman made it clear that a willingness to act as if revelation were true might be part of a proper disposition before faith, but it is not faith. He criticized those who "hold not that Christian doctrine is certainly true, but that it has such a semblance of truth, it has such considerable marks of probability upon it, that it is their duty to accept and act upon it as if it were true beyond all question or doubt."[37] This is not faith. "No one would say we believed our house was on fire, because we thought it safest on a cry of fire, to act as if it was."[38] Rather, "By belief of a thing this writer understands an inward conviction of its truth."[39]

Fifthly, faith, though it implies a venture, is not a determination to risk everything on what may be false. In his early work Newman tended to stress a willingness to venture beyond the conclusions of universally compelling lines of reasoning. His words, however, sometimes suggest that faith is a venture into an uncertain area where one may be mistaken. In 1837 he complained that "Romanism considers unclouded certainty necessary for a Christian's faith and hope, and doubt incompatible with practical abidance in the truth . . . Otherwise, it is urged, what is called faith is merely opinion, as being but partial or probable knowledge."[40] He replied that "according to English principles, religious faith has all it needs . . . in knowing that God is our Creator . . . and that He *may* . . . have spoken."[41] In fact, he continued, "doubt in some way or measure may even be said to be implied in a Christian's faith . . . the greater the uncertainty, the fuller exercise there is of our earnestness in seeking the truth."[42]

A year earlier he had said that we must make "ventures for eternal life without the absolute certainty of success," adding, "that is a strange venture which has nothing in it of fear, risk, danger, anxiety, uncertainty . . . and in this consists the excellence and nobleness of *faith* . . . because its presence implies that we have the heart to make a venture."[43]

> If we insist upon being as sure as is conceivable, in every step of our course, we must be content to creep along the ground, and can never soar. If we are intended for great ends, we are called to great hazards; and whereas we are given absolute certainty in nothing, we must in all things choose between doubt and inactivity, and the conviction that we are under the eye of One who, for whatever reason, exercises us with the less evidence when He might give us the greater.[44]

Newman seems to have confused various ideas under the label

"ventures of faith." Sometimes he suggested that faith is an uncertain opinion about something of great importance but where there is an abiding risk of being completely mistaken. Sometimes he suggested that faith is a certain assent to revealed truths which are only partially understood[45] or where evidence of a revelation occurring would not warrant a certain assent according to the canons of scientific inquiry.[46] Elsewhere he suggested that a lively faith is not only an assent to God's word but is a willingness to risk inconvenience in putting it into practice.[47] We are to overcome hesitation by "striving and acting against it."[48] In this last case one could be certain of God's word but hesitant about obeying it; or one could be uncertain of God's word in the first place. Newman's language may have been ambiguous but his intention was simply to stress the personal nature of one's reasoning toward faith and one's commitment in faith, rather than to describe faith as an opinion which might be mistaken. A willingness to venture beyond the canons of scientific demonstration and to risk personal involvement, are further antecedent conditions which dispose one to assess evidence correctly and receive the gift of divine faith itself.

Where evidence is inadequate for certainty, there is a risk of error. But Newman referred to the remark in *Hebrews* that faith itself is "the warrant of things not seen."[49] The whole tenor of his sermon on the "Ventures of Faith" was not that faith involves a risk of being completely mistaken, but that a lively faith involves a willingness to make a "full sacrifice," to "give up our all"[50] in living in accordance with what we are certain is true. Such a life of complete self-denial is "an intelligible *venture,* and an evidence of faith." One who has faith "ventures something upon the certainty of the world to come."[51]

He said to his audience: "Let everyone . . . ask himself . . . what stake has *he* in the truth of Christ's promise? How would he be a whit the worse off, supposing (which is impossible), but, supposing it to fail? . . . [How would he] be worse off as to . . . [his] *present* condition?" He gave the example of St. Barnabas who left his property "for the poor of Christ . . . He did something he would not have done, unless the Gospel were true. It is plain, if the Gospel turned out a fable (which God forbid), but if so, he would have taken his line most unskilfully; he would be in a great mistake, and would have suffered a loss."[52]

Newman was urging his listeners to practice their faith, to live in such a way that they would suffer a loss if Christianity were false. His remarks might be taken to imply neither that faith is a certain assent nor an uncertain opinion. For if a man acts on the opinion that Christianity is probably true, if he lives for the "prospect of gain" it offers, then if (not surprisingly) it turned out to be false he would suffer a loss. And if a man has, in faith, a certain grasp of God as revealed and revealer and lives accordingly, then if (*per impossible*) it turned out to be false he too would suffer a loss. But this would be to misunderstand the point of Newman's sermon. He did not intend to leave open the question of certainty. He assumed that faith is certain and then told his listeners that if they know something to be true in the midst of a doubting world, they should live according to that faith. They should put everything on it.[53]

Sixthly, faith is not wishful thinking. It is not an absolute assent because one is confident of an opinion. It is an absolute assent because, like knowledge, it is, in some sense, an objective grasp of what is the case. There are places in Newman's earliest work where he was explicit on this point. Faith "is a practical perception of the unseen world."[54] "Gospel faith . . . may be called, in a special manner, knowledge . . . spiritual sight."[55] It is "an original means of knowledge . . . founded on a supernaturally implanted instinct,"[56] "an instrument of indirect knowledge concerning things external to us."[57]

Finally, faith is not an assent to the conclusion of an argument. "If after all, it turns out merely to be a believing upon evidence, or a sort of conclusion upon a process of reasoning, a resolve formed upon a calculation . . . how is it novel or strange?"[58] "Religion . . . has ever been synonymous with Revelation. It never has been a deduction from what we know . . . It has never lived in a conclusion; it has ever been a message, or a history, or a vision."[59]

In *An Essay on the Development of Christian Doctrine,* published in 1845, Newman attacked the "assertion of Locke" that what God reveals is certainly true but "whether it be a divine revelation or no, reason must judge." Newman could agree with this statement if it meant only "that proofs can be given for Revelation, and that Reason comes in logical order before Faith." But he could not agree with it in the further sense in which Locke had intended it to be understood. Locke had meant that for individuals "to make Faith a personal principle of conduct for themselves, without waiting till they have got their reasons accurately drawn out and serviceable for controversy, is enthusiastic and absurd."[60] Newman complained that this theory would "cut off from the possibility and the privilege of faith all but the educated few, all but the learned, the clear-headed, the men of practised intellects and balanced minds."[61]

Therefore, it is not "enthusiasm" to make use of "reasons" which are "implicit" and which consist of "ventures after the truth" more than "accurate and complete proofs." It is not "credulity" to "embrace as most certain" conclusions of "probable arguments" when this is "under the scrutiny and sanction of a prudent judgment."[62]

For support, he turned to the testimony of Christians "ancient as well as modern." He noted that for the Fathers of the Church "to believe on less evidence was generous faith, not enthusiasm."[63] He quoted at length and with approval from an essay on human understanding by Pierre Daniel Huet.[64] His interest in this book centered on its generous references to traditional authorities. There he found distinctions which would prove helpful in sorting out different questions, such as a distinction between natural reason and divine faith. He quoted Huet's reference to Aquinas: "No search by natural Reason is sufficient to make men know things divine."[65] He also quoted Huet's reference to Suarez: "the light of Faith is most certain, because founded on the first truth, which is God."[66]

Newman found a distinction between human certainty and the "absolute and consummate" certainty of faith. Again, quoting Huet: "Although to prove the existence of the Deity we can bring arguments which, accumulated and connected together, are . . . of entire human certainty . . . 'tis clear we cannot . . . in the natural knowledge we have of God, which is acquired by Reason . . . find absolute and consummate certainty, but only that human certainty . . . to which nevertheless every wise man ought to submit his understanding."[67]

Finally, Newman found talk of "motives of credibility" which prepare the mind to receive faith. It may be "sufficient that the motives of credibility be proposed as probable," but, whether probable or certain by themselves, they cannot make us have faith.[68] He drew the general conclusion that "Arguments will come to be considered as suggestions and guides rather than logical proofs."[69] But over the next fifteen years he applied these categories in more detail to his own discovery of antecedent dispositions and of informal reasoning toward faith.

Confrontation with Roman categories

The question, what is faith? is closely related to the question, what causes faith? But again various levels of meaning can be distinguished. Why does one believe? can mean (1) what are the reasons which justify the judgment that one ought to believe? (2) what are the moral dispositions which make this judgment plausible or certain? (3) what causes the act of divine faith itself? (4) what is the object of divine faith—what is it one believes?

A few remarks are appropriate here. In his early work Newman did not clearly ask himself the third question: what causes the act of faith itself in so far as it is distinct from a judgment of credibility? He did not at first envision the possibility, logical or real, of stopping short at such a judgment.

When someone says in faith, "I believe in God" he is not saying, "I have reached the conclusion from a process of reasoning on converging evidence that there is a God and that He has spoken." The act of divine faith is distinct from every human process of reasoning. It is a free gift of grace.

But there is another and quite different distinction; namely, that between formal and informal reasoning. When someone says, "I know from an informal use of reason that I ought to believe this," he is not saying, "I have put into syllogistic form a demonstration from necessitating evidence that it is so." There is a distinctive informal use of reason found in evaluating religious matters as well as matters of fact in everyday life, natural science and history which should be distinguished from syllogistic argument.

It seems possible to argue that Newman's early work tended to confuse these two distinctions. He spent much time marking off the second distinction, but, it can be argued, in doing this he felt he had also satisfactorily marked off the first one.[70] By showing that the mode of reasoning relevant to religious matters is distinct from syllogistic argument he might appear to have shown all that is distinctive in the act of divine faith. But in that case religious assent would remain an assent to the conclusion of an argument, although informal. In rejecting rationalism which makes faith the result of a compelling syllogism, Newman would have fallen into rationalism of another sort, an informal rationalism which makes faith the necessary outcome of a non-syllogistic process of human reasoning. In fact, for Newman the reasoning relevant to coming to faith (and the certainty which is part of it) is not distinct from informal reasoning in other disciplines, but the assent of faith itself (and the unique certainty which is part of it) is distinct from every other human assent. It is without human parallel.[71]

Two factors allowed Newman to speak as he did without necessarily endorsing an informal rationalism in religion. First, he was always interested in the concrete act of faith where grace penetrates the entire process, including the human process of informal reasoning toward faith. Secondly, his use of the expression "antecedent assumptions" was broad enough to mark off both the above distinctions at once. It could be used to describe the personal factors which distinguish informal reasoning from syllogistic argument; but it could also be used to describe the distinctive operation of grace which distinguishes the assent of faith from every human assent.[72]

He came to sort out this double reference of "antecedent assumptions" when he confronted at Rome a clear distinction between a judgment of credibility and the act of divine faith. He came to emphasize that informal reasoning alone cannot explain the distinctiveness of faith as he found it.

Four months before arriving in Rome Newman read Aquinas' description of faith as "*cogitare cum assensu.*" He noticed that this description could be used to clarify the "main distinction" he had drawn in his *University Sermons,* namely that "Protestant theories of faith" hold that "*reason comes first* and then comes the will and *faith.*" Instead he had spoken of "*presumption* supported by *will* being the proof—or cogitatio and assensus going together."[73] Divine faith is not "*cogitare ante assensum*" but "*cogitare cum assensu.*" It is not an opinion proportioned to evidence followed by a decision to hold as certain what is uncertain. But neither is it a certain assent to the conclusion of an informal argument from converging evidence. Such a certain assent to the credibility of revelation may precede divine faith, but it is not faith. It is not an assent to God grasped as revealed and revealer which is the unique gift of grace. In 1839 Newman had said that "at this day" it is usual to speak of faith as if it "depended and followed upon a distinct act of Rea-

son beforehand,—Reason warranting, on the ground of evidence
. . . that the Gospel comes from God, and *then* Faith embracing
it . . . [Instead] . . . Faith is sole and elementary and complete in
itself."[74] By 1846 he interpreted this remark as a rejection of informal as well as formal rationalism in religion.

To put it differently, his reading at this time began to affect his
answer to the fourth question about the object of divine faith. In
1837 he suggested that the fact of revelation occurring is the object
of a human analysis resulting in the opinion that God *"may* have
spoken," while the content of that revelation is the object of faith's
certain assent.[75] This is rationalism in religion; in the end, faith is
an assent to an argument, admittedly informal, that a revelation
has occurred. But now Newman confronted—and found agreeable
—the view that the object of divine faith is not the conclusion of an
argument but God Himself revealing Himself (*revelatio et res
revelata*). On rationalist principles one could distinguish an uncertain opinion about the fact of revelation from a decision to hold
this opinion as if it were certain, and so assent with confidence to
the content of that revelation. But on Catholic principles a different
distinction is drawn. There is a judgment on evidence that one
ought to believe that a revelation has occurred and that its content
is reasonable. But this is distinct from divine faith where God enables a man to grasp Himself revealing Himself. The fact and the
content of revelation can be the object, although in different ways,
of both the former human and perhaps certain judgment and the
latter uniquely certain assent.[76]

An additional observation remains to be made, not about faith
in so far as it is distinct from human reasoning, but about that
mode of human reasoning which Newman called "informal." He
discussed this in the concrete context of an individual who felt
as well as thought. Though convinced that evidence in some sense
is relevant to informal reasoning, he was also convinced that logical
demonstration alone cannot explain the distinctiveness of this reasoning as he found it. Again the expression "antecedent assumptions" was called upon to do double service. It was used to denote
the moral dispositions which seem to account for one's assent on
evidence which falls short of a compelling demonstration. But it
was also used to denote a large sense of reasoning on evidence itself.
The second use of the expression "antecedent assumptions" was

present in Newman's early sermons. Rome, however, accused him of completely discarding evidence in discussing one's reasoning toward faith, so it became necessary to stress that an emphasis on antecedent assumption did not imply the abandonment of evidence. In his early writing Newman's treatment of the first question about the evidence for a judgment that a revelation has occurred was a work in contrasts. Reasoning about religion is informal and personal in contrast with syllogistic argument. But while making this point he tended to shift to the second question about moral dispositions which prepare one to make this judgment. He seemed to be saying that the evidence relevant to informal (cognitive) reasoning is irremediably weak. It can only make probable opinion reasonable. Moral (non-cognitive) dispositions are necessary to move one beyond opinion to certain assent. Newman had to make clear that this was not his meaning. Antecedent assumptions were not called upon to move one beyond what remains opinion, but to indicate that informal reasoning relies on evidence which is in fact sufficient for certain assent.[77]

Again it was Newman's confrontation with the Roman analysis of faith which indirectly led him to sort out his own position on informal reasoning. Roman theologians distinguished faith from reasoning toward faith (credibility judgment), not because the latter is necessarily uncertain, but because it is a human process of reasoning. Divine faith is an unparalleled gift of grace which elevates even the earlier process of thought to another and supernatural level. They could allow a human certainty which is distinct from the certainty of faith. They could distinguish human evidence for a judgment of credibility from the gift of faith which, in a sense, provides its own evidence. It is significant that he found all this congenial to his earlier work, believing that he could interpret his remarks in this sense without violating his meaning.

Newman arrived in Rome on October 28, 1846, one year after his conversion. He was troubled to find Roman theologians critical of his *Essay on the Development of Christian Doctrine.* In the second edition of 1846 he added a postscript to the "Advertisement" saying that he submitted "every part of the book to the judgment of the Church, with whose doctrine . . . he wishes all his thoughts to be coincident."[78] But Roman theologians were generally unfamiliar with his terminology and unhappy with his conclusions.

As it was, they first encountered his thoughts against a background which disposed them to misunderstand it, for critical reports had already begun to reach Rome regarding the *Essay*. In America Orestes Brownson accused Newman of overthrowing rational argument by rejecting formal inference.[79] A French edition of the *Essay* was being prepared by Jules Gondon and Newman knew it would then be read more widely at Rome. He was concerned about its apparently skeptical language as regards the capacity of reason to achieve religious certainty particularly where doctrine had developed historically. On December 8, 1846, he wrote to Dalgairns who was supervising Gondon's translation: "I find the Essay is accused of denying moral certainty and holding with Hermes we cannot get beyond probability in religious questions. This is far from my meaning."[80]

George Hermes had been condemned in an encyclical published only weeks after Newman reached Rome.[81] He held that while God's authority could be a mediate foundation of faith, the ultimate motive must be evidence necessitating one to accept the fact of revelation, and that since faith is founded on rational argument which can only reach probability, there is no rational basis for certainty in religious matters.[82]

With Hermes' condemnation before them, Newman knew Romans would be scandalized by parts of his *Essay*, as, for instance, where he had written "that there is but probability for the existence of God." But, he told Dalgairns, "What I *meant* was, that the moral certainty which belief *implied* arose from probable not demonstrative arguments."[83]

> Here persons at first misunderstood me, and because I talked of 'probable arguments' they thought I meant that we could not get beyond a probable conclusion in opposition to a moral certainty; *which is a condemned proposition*—but . . . I use probable as opposed to demonstrative, not to certainty.[84]

Newman's work also looked suspect in the light of the Bautain affair of only six years before. Louis Bautain was said to have held a view which tended to downplay any significant role of reason in faith. He seemed to say that while reason could not prove God's existence, a higher faculty called "intellect" instinctively grasps it. Bautain had avoided ecclesiastical censure only by signing six amending propositions in 1840. Dalgairns, who was familiar with

Newman's line of thought, wrote to him on January 31, 1847, noting apprehensively, "it is certain that his views are very like yours."[85] Newman had to defend himself against quick identification with Bautain's fideism as well as Hermes' rationalism. His reply to Dalgairns was to the point: "I hold that reason can prove the being of a God—that such a conclusion is the legitimate result of reason well employed . . . but this is very different from saying that reason is the *mode* by which individuals come at truth."[86]

It was at this time that Newman was studying Henry Holden's *Divinae Fidei Analysis* which he considered "worth reading, though it has acknowledged faults," and also Giovanni Perrone's treatise on faith and reason which he preferred to Holden.[87] He told Dalgairns: "Perrone has written a Treatise on the connection of Reason and Faith which I like very much. I am glad to see I have no view counter to it."[88] In February, 1846, he said he was "trying to scrape acquaintance with Perrone . . . if I have an opening, I shall put before him as clearly as I can my opinions about Faith and Reason."[89] But Newman had questions in apologetics which Perrone's dogmatic treatment seemed to avoid. "In polemics he does not understand the arguments he has to deal with."[90] Three years later Newman admitted that " 'the proof of Christianity' is just the point on which polemics and dogmatics meet as on common ground." But he continued to complain about Italian writers who "think proofs ought to be convincing which in fact are not. Hence they are accustomed to speak of the argument for Catholicism as a demonstration and to . . . admit no perplexity of intellect which is not directly and immediately wilful."[91] Nevertheless he was convinced that "they *quite* recognize here the distinction between moral and demonstrative proof . . . I think they . . . take a broad *sensible* shrewd view of reason and faith."[92]

The traditional Catholic position[93] is that the act of faith is an intellectual assent to what God has revealed as true, that is, to the dogmas or creeds taught by the Church. The motive or what immediately determines the intellect to assent is not merely a desire for gain nor, for that matter, even the evidence, which supports a judgment of credibility, but the authority of God. Where faith is present it rests on the authoritative testimony of God who knows and is true. Where it is not present a judgment of credibility that one ought to believe rests on natural evidence. Faith then is essentially supernatural for one believes because God has drawn him to share personally in His own knowing.[94] The "illumination" of grace does not merely give a new dignity, but a new inner structure to the faith-knowledge of the believer. God Himself is the formal object of this Divine faith-knowledge for the believer now knows revealed truths through a unique share in God's knowledge. The act of faith is made with freedom for there is a lack of strictly necessitating evidence concerning the fact of revelation. Yet, once made, it is absolutely certain beyond all other judgments. Logical truths may be perfectly certain but the "motive" for the act of faith is more excellent than any other evidence motivating certain assent. Finally the act of faith is reasonable. It presupposes a certain perception of the credibility of the fact of revelation and of the doctrine revealed by a human process of reasoning from evidence. Faith itself is not the necessary conclusion of a logical or informal argument. Nevertheless reasoning to a judgment of credibility remains a necessary condition so that the act of faith might be placed in a way which conforms to the rational nature of man.

This is, in brief, the view which Newman found to be a "broad *sensible* shrewd view of reason and faith." But in order to make himself clear to Roman theologians he contemplated publishing a French edition of the *University Sermons,* feeling that because of their *"bearing upon* my *Essay,* viz. The question of probability, evidence, etc." they would provide a helpful introduction to readers unfamiliar with his thought.[95] They "take in the two principles which are so prominent in the Essay, that no real idea can be comprehended in all its bearings at once—that the main instrument of proof in matter of life is 'antecedent probability.' "[96]

Newman told Dalgairns that to avoid misunderstanding "a great deal depends on a clear explanation *what I mean* by reason and by faith."[97] In the sermons he had set faith and reason in opposition; but he had only meant that reason, when "not under the guidance of conscience" works against faith. He had undertaken an "investigation" of "faith and reason not in the abstract, but in the individual." Consequently he had not meant to deny "that faith is of an intellectual nature, or that reason abstractedly speaking leads to truth in morals and religion."[98] He had said that faith is "distinguished from knowledge,"[99] but now he told Dalgairns to add that "faith may be called a kind of knowledge considering its proofs to be 'the natural method given us for ascertaining' the truths of revelation."[100] He had written that if faith "turns out merely to be . . . a sort of conclusion upon a process of reasoning . . . How is it novel or strange?"[101] Dalgairns was told to add: "in other words, the 'motives of credibility,' in Perrone's words 'can never constitute the formal motive of the act of faith.' "*[102]

During 1847 Newman drew up twelve *Theses de Fide* as well as a Latin preface to the *University Sermons* to be translated into French.[103] These notes, although expressly tentative, are helpful in tracing his thought on the status of a judgment of credibility in relation to divine faith. Is the distinction between this judgment and faith only one between opinion and certainty? In this case faith would be simply a credibility judgment which is certain due to informal reasoning.[104] Or is there a distinction between reasoning to a conclusion (probable or certain) and the gift of faith which enables one to assent with a unique certainty to God as revealed and revealer?[105] Newman clearly stated that there is a difference between faith and reasoning toward faith and that divine faith is certain. "The act of divine faith is an intellectual assent to Divine Truth which is excellent, certain, obscure."*[106] But the question remains: what is the difference and why is faith certain?

In the fourth thesis Newman's words could suggest that the only difference is that the former is certain and the latter necessarily uncertain. "It ought to be obviously acknowledged, by the nature of the thing itself, that the assent of faith is certain; for if it depended entirely on a logical consideration of some natural truth, it could not be perfectly certain, since a natural light does not give that certitude."*[107] In fact he was saying that natural reason cannot give that certitude which is part of the gift of faith.

Again in the eleventh thesis he wrote that faith is a certain assent to propositions which "in proportion to the motives by which they are proved, do not have certitude, but only credibility."*[108] But in light of the preceding thesis he seems to have meant that natural reasoning reaches a credibility judgment (probable or certain) but cannot reach the "absolute and perfect certitude of divine faith."*[109]

In other places Newman asserted that a credibility judgment can be certain, writing that "credibility ought to be evident to everyone who believes, even to the simple and unlearned."*[110] He quoted

Suarez: "Although the wiser have a greater kind of human certitude, it does not go beyond a human faith."*[111] In this case a credibility judgment (human faith) would be evident and possess a "kind of human certitude." However it would still be distinct from divine faith. This cannot be because it is uncertain. It must be because its certainty is not founded, as is the certainty of divine faith, on that unique gift of grace which enables one to grasp in faith God as revealed and revealer. Human motives (reasons) which precede faith, Newman wrote, *"are not* the motives of faith, nor are they such that faith can be resolved into them, but they are the ordinary means or *condition sine qua non,* by which *a way is opened up* toward faith, (by which the object) of faith is proposed and applied to the intellect, not demonstrated."*[112] While it is a necessary condition that there be human motives (reasons) which lead one to divine faith,[113] nevertheless "The absolute and perfect certitude of divine faith, is not due to argument or to human motives, but only to that which is called God, Eternal Truth, who can neither deceive nor be deceived."*[114]

On January 12, 1847, Newman told Dalgairns that he would sketch a preface for the *University Sermons* on receiving them from England. The previous day he had jotted down a number of topics to be treated in the preface. It would be "all important" to make clear that when he had contrasted faith with reason in the sermons he was considering faith primarily *"on its human* side." He was not so much considering the act of divine faith or "the spiritual intuition of the subject matter of Faith." He was mainly concerned with "the act of accepting or *passing to* accept" a revelation as genuine. The sermons attempt to show that "reasoning on antecedent probabilities" which leads to a judgment of credibility (distinct from divine faith) is *"the highest,* as being used by the highest minds, and in the highest discoveries."[115] They do not endorse an informal rationalism.

He began the English draft of the preface:

> The act of faith, by which a man believes the word of God revealed through the Church, is of course the immediate effect of divine grace, but it may be regarded in its human aspect resulting from the *motiva credibilitatis.* When human reasonings have led to a moral certainty that God has spoken, and the will determines to accept the conclusion as absolutely true, the grace of God in-

fuses a divine certainty which admits of no doubt at all. Thus the same complex act has two aspects.[116]

The sermons attempt to show that a judgment of credibility (not faith itself) is the conclusion of reasoning *"in a large sense of that word."* Reasoning in this sense is peculiar as regards both "its grounds or principles" and "its mode of arguing." First, it is reasoning on *"religious* principles," not "worldly" ones. Religious principles might include the assertion that "God sees the heart," or that "Time is nothing to eternity." Worldly ones might include the claim that "The Maker of the World intended us to enjoy life," or that "We can fulfill our duty without special grace."[117] In either case once certain principles are admitted, logic operates as an "instrumental art"* reaching conclusions consistent with them.[118]

Secondly, this mode of reasoning has two characteristics: it is personal, that is, it operates in the context of antecedent assumptions; and it is implicit, that is, its subtleties "do not fall easily into logical forms."*[119] Newman sought to explain these characteristics by distinguishing intrinsic and extrinsic arguments. "Intrinsic ones are those which are put into words from things which really and properly pertain to the matter in question; extrinsic ones, however, are those which are obviously prior and more broadly related" to the matter in question. Intrinsic arguments "prove something as an effect establishes its cause . . . Facts, therefore, are in some sense *indices* of the thing in question."*[120] But there are degrees of probative force here. Facts "may be weak or strong, sufficient or insufficient to create certainty, but they all are of one kind, tend to certainty, and often though insufficient separately, yet create certainty when combined."[121] Informal cumulative arguments are intrinsic because they arise from the matter of fact under discussion. But extrinsic arguments "in no way arise from the thing itself, which is being treated."*[122] They amount to antecedent considerations which more or less dispose this or that individual to accept an intrinsic proof. They cannot prove the case but they can confirm or lend support to an intrinsic proof when produced. They can "make a doubtful or probable proof more probable."[123] "Principles," secular or religious, are antecedent (extrinsic) considerations which support but cannot replace a cumulative (intrinsic) proof. In the concrete there will always be a combination of intrinsic proof and extrinsic antecedents.

Newman's use of terms in this preface was often inconsistent. Sometimes he used the words *praesumptio* and *credibilitas* to denote the extrinsic and antecedent bias of the mind; sometimes to denote the concrete combination of extrinsic considerations and intrinsic proof.[124] He distinguished scientific proofs which can be reduced to laws, from presumptions which make a conclusion more or less credible to various individuals. He applied this distinction to his discussion of faith in the University sermons.

> The Author [Newman] argues that those divine principles already spoken of which grace implants in the mind of the individual are the fruitful source of a number of strong presumptions or antecedent probabilities that the Church is the organ of Divine Truth, which require very little of actual proof to produce in him a judgment that the conclusion is credible or to effect the *evidentia credibilitatis,* on which by an act of the will faith follows . . . proof, in itself perhaps but weak, leads to credibility in the conclusion; only when a person is in possession of those religious principles which a right moral state causes.[125]

It might appear that credibility denotes an uncertainty which is judged probable by one who is disposed. But Newman's intention throughout this preface was to contrast credibility, not with certainty as such, but with the evident certainty of scientific demonstration.[126] Nevertheless there are many mixed meanings which are difficult to sort out.

He felt that it is "quite consistent" to hold both that faith is a presumption "in its previous logical process," and that it is absolutely certain in itself. "Arguments in themselves but probable are sufficient under the magisterial power of the will to create a state of undoubting certainty." Faith "starts from probabilities, yet it ends in peremptory statements."[127] But it is not clear when he was speaking of divine faith or when he was speaking of a credibility judgment before faith. His emphasis on the concrete situation of an individual, on the personal nature of his reasoning, and on the enduring influence of Divine Providence, led him to overlook distinctions without necessarily denying them.

In his notes and letters during the following years, however, Newman stated unambiguously that a judgment of credibility could be certain although it is not the certainty of faith. Around Easter 1848 he wrote that "what divine faith receives as *certain*, acquisita or human faith has already received as not more than credible, because depending on the truth of certain premises and the cogency of a certain logical process."[128] That is, a judgment of credibility differs from divine faith not because the former is uncertain but simply because it depends on a logical process while divine faith is not the conclusion of an argument. It seems that as Newman came to see this more clearly he began to see that a credibility judgment could be certain without being confused with the certainty of faith itself.

In his 1848 notes he explained that "credible" does not mean "merely capable of belief, but morally (or practically) certain." The evidence does not seem sufficient because of the importance of the matter under consideration. It does not displace all "doubt or fear," but it is *"sufficient in itself"* to produce conviction. The conclusion is not logically demonstrated, but it is so thoroughly established that it ought to be believed. "A proof for credibility . . . leads the mind *prudently* to receive the conclusion for certain."[129] In other words, a "credible proof" is not "a mere proof of the greater or overbalancing probability." It is not merely a "probable argument" but one that is "in its mode of stating, and as involving other arguments implicity in itself . . . sufficient for certainty." As probabilities cumulate "the limit of increasing probabilities is credibility in the conclusion and certainty in the mind."[130]

On June 27, 1848, Newman wrote to Mrs. William Froude:

> I wish you would consider whether you have a right notion of how to gain faith. It is, we know, the Gift of God, but I am speaking of it as a human process and attained by human means. Faith then is not a conclusion from premises, but the result of an act of the *will*, following upon a *conviction* that to believe is a *duty*. The simple question you have to ask yourself is 'Have I a *conviction* that I *ought* to accept the Catholic Faith as God's Word?' if not, at least, 'do I *tend* to such a conviction?' or 'am I *near* upon it?' For directly you have a conviction that you *ought* to believe, reason has done its part, and what is wanted for faith is, not proof, but *will*.[131]

He admitted that *"We can believe what we choose."* Men hold one creed; "if they pleased" they could hold another. However he was not encouraging an act of will on insufficient grounds. "The simple question with them is which of the two creeds their *reason* tells

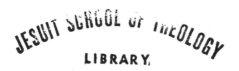

them they *ought* to believe." He later added, *"Though you can* believe what you choose, you must believe what you ought."[132]

At Rome Newman had written a novel about a young man's gradual conversion. At one point he had the young man ask, "If a man finds himself unable, though wishing, to believe, for he has not evidence enough to subdue his reason, what is to make him believe?" The priest answered, "What is to make him believe! the will, *his* will."[133] Catherine Ward read this and asked Newman, "How am I to know when I ought to believe?"[134] He replied that reason proves what ought to be believed. It does not prove what is true "as it proves that mathematical conclusions are true." There are many questions left unanswered. Yet the "grounds are sufficient for conviction." He added, "This is not the same thing as conviction . . . while there is enough evidence for conviction, whether we *will* be convinced or not rests with ourselves."[135] Later he wrote to the same correspondent about doubt before faith: "You cannot be rid of those doubts without grace; as you distinctly say, they are *not* intellectual doubts; your intellect is convinced, but in *spite* of that conviction, you are haunted with doubts."[136]

On January 27, 1850, Newman, now settled at Birmingham, wrote to J. M. Capes. Capes had published three articles in the *Rambler* under the title "Four Years' Experience of the Catholic Religion" defending his conversion as an act of "embracing the more probable of two momentous alternatives."[137] Newman told Capes that his position would be sound only if it were certain "that the *more probable* alternative is the *true* one." But this would have to be proved since it is not always or necessarily the case. In fact Capes seemed to take the "unsound position" that "it is *not certain* that Catholicism is true, only *more probable* than that it is not."[138] Credibility is not probability but neither is it the evident certainty of syllogistic reasoning. "The simple question," he wrote elsewhere, "is whether *enough* has been done to *reduce* the difficulties so far as to hinder them absolutely blocking up the way, or excluding those direct and large arguments on which the reasonableness of faith is built."[139]

The following year Francis Richard Wegg-Prosser told Newman that in so far as there are objections to the contrary, one's credibility judgment must be only a judgment about the degree of probability. Newman replied that "Unanswerable objections *need* not interfere with a moral proof." By a moral proof he did not mean "a mere balance of probabilities" where the side with "greater weight" is considered true. "On the contrary," he wrote, "a proof is something such that it can only be on *one* side." There may be many unanswered questions, but they "do not form a proof of some . . . incompatible conclusion."[140] In other words, one may grasp by an informal use of reason, what is true. He may be unable to answer difficulties, but he will be sure that they cannot prove the contrary.

In a note dated April 14, 1853, Newman attacked the view that certainty in any proper sense, is impossible in religion. When a man holding such a view

> professes to keep his mind open to change on a point if evidence comes . . . he implies that the thing in question may perhaps [turn out] in the event to be not true. And when he considers that his personal acceptance of it as true must ever be firmer or weaker with the evidence, he implies it is a question of the greater or lesser probability, that is, of lesser or greater doubt. And the anxiety of Butler to fly off to the consideration of what is *safer* . . . implies this.[141]

In October he admitted that "left to myself, I should be very much tempted" to adopt Butler's view and understand credibility as probability upon which it is safe to act.[142] But Newman was not left to himself. He read works on faith and reason written by traditional authors; he read letters written by friends struggling toward an act of faith. Together they led him to admit that a safe probability is not enough. It is not enough to say revelation is "so probable that (without deciding absolutely that it is true) . . . to act as if you believed is the safer side." It is not enough to understand "moral certainty" as "the highest step of mounting probabilities, not differing from probability in kind, but only in degree."[143] It seemed to be part of our everyday experience "that we are positively and absolutely and speculativé (not practicé only) certain of a thing by a combination of arguments, each of which is only probable."[144] What occurs in ordinary matters also occurs in religious matters. Someone might have begun with a "practical certainty," but "if this were all, there was no faith." If one is to have divine faith then "true motiva credibilitatis, leading prudentia under the guidance of pia affectio to induce the will to command the intellect to assent, would gradually be evolved."[145]

Edward Healy Thompson[146] was not satisfied with this account of the matter. He allowed that the will often commands us "to *act* on probabilities, to act, in fact, *as if* we believed," but he would not allow the will to command "*belief* itself, where the grounds are such as produce *opinion,* a probable opinion, but still opinion." He allowed that "faith corresponds to certainty," but he would not allow us to take "probabilities as certainties" by an act of will. The will could be called upon to put down fear and doubt, but only after the intellect has determined that the doubt is, in fact, "unreasonable."[147] Where it might appear that someone embraced faith without "certain intellectual evidence" Thompson suspected there existed "moral evidence . . . impossible to put into words" yet "amply sufficient." Thompson was not denying that persons may be "*bound to act on* probabilities previous to certainty. But," he added, "I believe if they did so, God would provide them with proof sufficient to produce certainty."[148]

Newman responded, "I shall be surprised if I have called, or implied, the conclusion to which human faith comes, as probable." Reason judges that a revelation is credible or "*dignum* fide" and this implies that the will, under the guidance of prudence, ought to direct the intellect to accept it as true without reservation. Moreover, " 'Probable' means that which has certain grounds, *greater* or less, to be *opined;* whereas 'credible' means that which has *sufficient* grounds to be thoroughly *believed.*"[149]

He described the two positions he meant to avoid: first, "that the conclusion of human faith was only probable" and secondly, that the will under the warrant of prudence did not "bid and gain the intellect to give an assent beyond the force of the motiva." He then explained the process of faith as he now understood it in four points. First, the object of faith's contemplation is "the Christian *doctrines,* as revealed, or the revelatio and res revelata." To believe the doctrines without accepting them "formally, as revealed" would be insufficient. To believe a revelation without accepting any definite doctrines revealed would be incoherent; "the two must be considered together."[150] Secondly, this object of faith is not strictly proved or made to appear to us true but remains "*obscure* and inevident." Thirdly, Newman asked, "If then the Revelatio and Res Revelata . . . is not to be made *evident* as true . . . what *is* to be made evident?" His answer was that "the use of arguments, the motiva is to prove evidently, not that the revelation and revealed doctrines, are true, but are credible—digna fide . . . Which arguments are in consequence called 'motiva *credibilitatis*,' not 'veritatis.' "[151] Finally,

> when the mind is convinced that the Revelatio and the res revelata are digna fide, credibilia, the prudentia sees that the intellect must fittingly, naturally, conscientiously, believe them, and the pia motio voluntatis draws the same way. Accordingly the intellect *does* assent to that as *true*, which has been evidently proved to it to be credible. And . . . it sees that if it believes at all, it cannot believe by halves—for to believe in *God's word*, which by the hypothesis it is doing, is to believe in that which claims the *firmest* and most *absolute* assent, or certainty in its highest form.[152]

Newman spent the next two months expanding this summary into a long unpublished paper entitled "On the Certainty of Faith."[153] Apparently, he was satisfied with the position in this October letter and December paper, for his private notes turn to other questions during the next few years. In any event, his friend and correspondent, William Froude, began, already in 1854, to turn his mind toward the question of certainty in our knowledge of matters of fact in general.[154]

However on September 29, 1858, J. M. Capes again brought forward the objection which Thompson had raised five years earlier. "To *act* upon an uncertainty . . . involves nothing absurd or morally false," but to force certainty is "logically absurd and morally wrong." If it can be demonstrated that Christian revelation is more probably true than false, then "it is wise to *act* on the hypothesis of its certain truth; but to profess that *one is certain that it is true*, is to utter a direct falsehood and nothing less."[155] Newman's reply reaffirmed his 1853 position, but instead of outlining his solution as he had done for Thompson, he briefly appealed to parallel cases in everyday life where "no complete proof is possible" but where we are "certain *speculativè*, not *merely practicè*," for example, that I shall die or that England is an island.[156] This in itself indicates the extent to which Froude had already begun to turn his interest toward the problem of certainty in knowledge generally.

While Newman came to stress the possibility of informal reasoning to certainty about the credibility of revelation, he never meant to adopt an informal rationalism where divine faith is simply an assent to the conclusion of such reasoning. On January 12, 1860, he wrote a paper on the "Evidences of Religion," pointing out that faith must rest on reason "as an antecedent condition in the order of nature."[157] He explained that he spoke this way because "faith itself teaches us . . . that it is a divine gift and comes from supernatural grace."[158] He wanted to limit his own discussion to the antecedent judgment of credibility, and to explore the non-syllogistic mode of reasoning on which this judgment rests and which is capable of achieving certainty although not the certainty of divine faith.

New questions

December 1859 and January 1860 mark the beginning of new ventures for Newman. On December 3rd he wrote to William George Ward: "Quite lately I have rather thought I would take up metaphysics—but I can't tell." He referred to his own growing fascination with aspects of his 1852 *Idea of a University*. "To my surprise, I find that those books on Universities have had an application and an influence which I did not expect. I find that they have removed difficulties and cleared views . . . I begin to think that I may have opened a vein of metal which others may work out after me."[159]

On December 20th he informed Charles Meynell that he was then reading Henry Mansel's Bampton Lectures on the limits of religious thought. He said that "as far as I may do so, without risk of false doctrine or temerity, I agree with [him] . . . This does not hinder me from feeling a serious objection and fear of some things which he has said."[160]

This reading of Mansel and the rereading of his own Dublin lectures seemed to raise new questions, but it was his growing correspondence with William Froude which proved most influential. On December 29th Froude sent him a long letter which contained the best statement of Froude's own skepticism. It was Froude who became for Newman the personification of Locke's position on the nature and limits of human knowledge. And it was in answer to Locke, in the person of William Froude, that Newman wrote his *Grammar of Assent* ten years later.

This significant shift of interest can be characterized in two ways. First, Newman had been attacking those who found faith irrational if it were not clearly demonstrated, and he had emphasized the personal nature of reasoning toward faith. He had explored the psychology of coming to faith—the dispositions which, taken together, become the "reason" why someone finds an informal argument cogent and forceful. But now he began to turn to the logic of informal reasoning from evidence. Whereas before he had spoken of dispositions converging into a context within which one found evidence forceful or not, now he would speak of evidence converging into a certain, although informal, proof.

Secondly, there were those who had thought Newman taught an informal rationalism in religion, where faith rests entirely on an informal argument that a revelation has occurred. He had emphasized that while informal reasoning leads to a credibility judgment (certain or probable), divine faith is distinct and possesses a distinctive certainty. But now William Froude thought Newman admitted that informal reasoning can only reach probability. He began to turn to the fact of objective (certain) knowledge of what is the case generally. This would have considerable bearing on his final understanding of divine faith as an objective (certain) grasp of God making Himself known as revealed and revealer. On January 5, 1860, Newman made the following note: "I propose to draw out the nature of the evidence or *motivum credibilitatis* . . . and to enquire what is meant by the prohibition to reexamine the trustworthiness of that *motivum*."[161]

One week later he wrote about a need to go beyond his Oxford sermons. He would build on what he had preached thirty-two years before, but he would attempt to clarify his earlier remarks. They lacked a "distinctness" of language for two reasons: "first, because I was feeling my way and had not found it; next, because conscious of this, I had not the requisite confidence in my own train of thought." He felt an urgency for clarification because "just now," he wrote, "a scepticism is on foot, which throws on the individual believer the *onus* probandi, in a way never *contemplated*, or at least recognized before."[162] He outlined the skeptic's objection, remarked on the need that it be answered, and added:

If my reading was greater, perhaps I should find that it has been sufficiently done already; but even if so, every generation has a tone and a character of its own, and if I can write with existing difficulties before my mind, I have a sufficient justification for writing which is not to be found in the teaching of former writ-ings, though good in themselves, and on the whole superior to my own attempt.[163]

He felt justified in putting forward fresh suggestions because of the "existing difficulties" of men like William Froude and the "tone" of a Lockean skepticism they expressed. Likewise we are justified in ex-ploring Newman's suggestions because the "existing difficulties" in our own day are so much like those of men such as William Froude, and the "tone and character" of our own generation, so much like theirs.

References

1. *Mix* 200–201, 195–196 ("Faith and Private Judgment").

2. *Ibid.* 193.

3. *PPS* 2:153–154 ("Saving Knowledge" January or February 1835); see *PPS* 3: 79–80 ("Faith and Obedience" 21 February 1830): Faith "is not a mere temporary strong act or impetuous feeling of the mind, an impression or a view coming upon it, but it is a habit, a state of mind, lasting and consistent." It is "lasting" not because it is a vivid feeling but because it is an objective assent to what is true.

4. *US* 249 ("Love the Safeguard of Faith" 21 May 1839).

5. *Ibid.* 234 note 3 (added 1871).

6. *Ibid.* 190–191 ("Faith and Reason Contrasted" 6 January 1839), *Hebrews* 11:1; see *LD* 11:289 (8 December 1846): "The great line of argument which produces moral certainty is not evidence but antecedent probability."

7. *US* 189 ("Faith and Reason Contrasted" 6 January 1839).

8. *Ibid.*

9. *Ibid.* 189–190.

10. *LD* 11:293 (13 December 1846); see *LD* 12:32 (8 February 1847) describing the *US* as "the best things I have written" and *LD* 15:381 (12 June 1853). Newman put the *US* on a par with his *Dev, Idea,* and *GA* as his best achievements; see *PN* 1:72–75; Duffy, 21–34.

11. On this view Newman's proof of the existence of God from con-science is closely related to his talk of antecedent dispositions.

12. *GA* 375–383; *Idea* 428–455 ("Christianity and Physical Science" November 1855).

13. *Jfc* 258, 261. What he found unintelligible was the view that justifying faith was "mere trust" without love and obedience.

14. *Diff* 1:269–270.

15. *Ibid.* 269–271.

16. *Ibid.* 2:26–28 (Letter to Pusey: 7 December 1865). The significance

of calling faith "objective" is crucial to Newman's final position on the "certainty" of faith.

17. *Jfc* 236.

18. *DA* 251 (Tract 85: 21 September 1858).

19. *PPS* 4:309–310 ("Faith and Love" 25 February 1838); see 312, 315: "Love is the condition of faith; and faith . . . is the cherisher and maturer of love; it brings love out into works . . . the substance of the works is love, the outline and direction of them is faith."

20. These remarks on "love" can be taken as pointing toward Newman's developed notion of faith as a response to God's testimony about Himself, not as the conclusion of an argument; see below 173–190.

21. *US* 203 ("Nature of Faith" 13 January 1839).

22. *Ibid.* 231–232 ("Love the Safeguard of Faith" 21 May 1839). Here (232) as elsewhere Newman tended to reinforce an appeal to what is the fact by an appeal to Providence: "this must be God's order of things."

23. *Ibid.* 239–240.

24. *Jfc* 236 note 1 (added 1872); see *US* 236 note 4 (added 1871).

25. *DA* 251 note (added 1872); however see Vargish (54–56) who argues that love for the object of faith renders it "reasonable" to assent absolutely to a probability, which, simply put, is more Keble's than Newman's view of the matter.

26. *SN* 330–331 (14 August 1858).

27. See *Essay* IV:15.2 (2:364); also Ashcroft 209; Henry G. Van Leeuwen, *Problem of Certainty in English Thought 1630–1690* (Hague, 1963).

28. *HS* 1:264 ("Marcus Tullius Cicero" Spring 1824).

29. *Ibid.* 267–268.

30. *Ibid.* 269.

31. *Ibid.* 271. Newman did not completely endorse this solution; he allowed that "in some measure" it avoided skepticism.

32. *Ari* 76.

33. *VM* 1:86–87.

34. *Ibid.* But see *US* 188–189 ("Faith and Reason Contrasted" 6 January 1839) where he suggests that personal interest makes us demand more evidence: "Did a rumour circulate of a destructive earthquake in Syria . . . we should readily credit it; both because it might easily be true, and because it were nothing to us though it were. Did the report relate to countries nearer home, we should try to trace and authenticate it. We do not call for evidence till antecedent probabilities fail."

35. *DA* 295 ("Tamworth Reading Room" February 1841).

36. *US* 188–189 ("Faith and Reason Contrasted" 6 January 1839). He added: "in truth, minute investigations have a tendency to blunt the practical energy of the mind, while they improve its scientific exactness."

37. *DA* 391 ("An Internal Argument for Christianity" June 1866). Already in 1835 Newman rejected the view that "the reasonableness of a religion . . . consists in there being a direct and natural tendency in

belief in its doctrines to form that moral character it recommends." *Ess* 1:55 (Tract 73: 2 February 1835).

38. *VM* 1:87 note 8 (added 1877).

39. *DA* 391 ("An Internal Argument for Christianity" June 1866); see *GA* 59: faith is a "real internal belief."

40. *VM* 1:85–86. Later he added: "If by 'unclouded' is meant the absence of all involuntary misgivings, or a sense of . . . incompleteness in the argumentative grounds of religion, a certitude so circumstanced is *not* (according to Catholic teacl.ing) 'necessary.'" (*VM* 1:85 note 4 (added 1877)).

41. *Ibid.* 86; but see *ibid.* note 6 (added 1877). See above xii.

42. *Ibid.* 87; but see *ibid.* note 2 (added 1877): "Faith may *follow* after doubt . . . but the two cannot co-exist." Newman criticized his former "confusion between the incomplete *notices* of truth, i.e. evidence, and that 'generous faith', which though it *might* captiously demand more evidence, is contented with what it ought to feel to be enough." (*Ibid.* 88–89 note 6 (added 1877)). "There is always in concrete matters incompleteness in the evidence." (*Ibid.* 88 note 3 (added 1877)). Consequently one with faith might admit "a recognition of the logical incompleteness of its proof" but not "a refusal to pronounce it true." (*Ibid.* 108 note 2 (added 1877)). An "unreserved faith" perfects "what reason leaves sufficient, but incomplete." (*LG* 386). See below 201 note 145.

43. *PPS* 4:296 ("Ventures of Faith" 21 February 1836).

44. *US* 215 ("Nature of Faith" 13 January 1839); see *ibid.* note 1 (added 1871): "By 'absolute certainty in nothing' is meant, as I believe, 'proofs such as absolutely to make doubt impossible;' and by 'between doubt and inactivity,' is meant, not formal doubt, but a state of mind which recognises the possibility of doubting." See also *Theses* 227 (Thesis 2) on this *US* passage; and *US* 224 ("Love the Safeguard of Faith" 21 May 1839): Faith "acts, before . . . certainty or knowledge . . . Hence it is said . . . to be a venture, to involve a risk . . . to be illogical."

45. See *VM* 1:89; and *PPS* 4:297, 304 ("Ventures of Faith" 21 February 1836): the Apostles professed a generous faith "meaning somewhat and risking much." But see *GA* 13: To assent to something, it "must be in some degree known to us." Yet we can believe what we do not understand. See below 145–146.

46. See *VM* 1:86.

47. See *PPS* 4:297 ("Ventures of Faith" 21 February 1836): "Abraham 'went out not knowing wither he went.'" *Hebrews* 11.8.

48. *VM* 1:87.

49. *PPS* 4:303 ("Ventures of Faith" 21 February 1836); *Hebrews* 11:1.

50. *Ibid.* 299.

51. *Ibid.* 303. Newman seems to have distinguished the certain hope of faith from the "prospect of gain" which a man might entertain who held the opinion that Christianity is probably true; see *ibid.* 301.

52. *Ibid.* 300–302.

53. For Newman the very nature of (objectively/certainly) knowing

something to be the case (or in faith, grasping what is the case) is to preclude the possibility of the alternative being true. There is no *decision* to rule out doubt. "We do not commonly determine not to do what we cannot fancy ourselves ever doing." (*GA* 193). Not to know, not to be certain, however, is to allow the possibility of the alternative. (See *DA* 293 ("Tamworth Reading Room" February 1841)). Consequently if what one knows (*per impossible*) would be false, rationality would be lost. If an opinion turns out to be false, rationality is not lost for the possibility of the alternative is all along admitted.

54. *PPS* 3:79 ("Faith and Obedience" 21 February 1830); see *US* 61–62 ("Usurpations of Reason" 11 December 1831); *DA* 294 ("Tamworth Reading Room" February 1841); *Diff* 1:269–271.

55. *PPS* 2:151–152 ("Saving Knowledge" January or February 1835).

56. *Jfc* 267 (1838).

57. *US* 207 ("Nature of Faith" 13 January 1839).

58. *Ibid.* 179 ("Faith and Reason Contrasted" 6 January 1839).

59. *DA* 296 ("Tamworth Reading Room" February 1841).

60. *Dev* 327.

61 *Ibid.* 328.

62. *Ibid.* 327; see below 152 on the illative sense.

63. *Dev* 329. Newman referred to the *US* and (in an 1878 note) to his *GA* for a presentation of his own alternative to Locke.

64. Pierre Daniel Huet, *The Weakness of Human Understanding* (1723) (trans.) Edward Combe (London, 1725).

65. *Dev* 332; Huet, 144 commenting on Aquinas, *Summa* II II 1.5, *Leon.* 8:16–17; and *Summa* II II 5.3, *Leon.* 8:57–58.

66. *Dev.* 333; Huet, 145 quoting Francis Suarez, "De Fide Theologica" Disputatio 6:5.2 (1621) in *Opera Omnia* 28 vols. (Paris, 1856) 12:179.

67. *Dev* 333–334; Huet, 221–222; he was referring to *Wisdom* 12 and *Romans* 1:20. For Huet (227) propositions may be certain by reason and "likewise become certain by *Faith* . . . These propositions [e.g. that Christ, as man, was "endowed with sense and life"] that I find to be certain by Reason and human Certainty, when *Faith* supervenes, become certain by a divine Certainty."

68. *Dev* 335; Huet, 229. For Huet the motives of credibility may be either probable or certain. However in the latter case such a "clearsighted" certainty "cannot make us have *Faith*, if Celestial Light does not illumine us from within."

69. *Dev* 336.

70. In *US* 202 ("Nature of Faith" 13 January 1839), Newman said that faith is distinct from the reasoning which precedes it. Sometimes he seems to have meant that divine faith is distinct from a judgment of credibility. In this case he came to emphasize this more clearly. But sometimes he suggested that faith is a decision to act on a judgment of credibility and nothing more. It remains an assent to the conclusion of an argument. In this case Newman came to make a new distinction.

71. See *LD* 12:357 (14 December 1848): "the certainty of faith is indefinitely greater than mathematical."

72. Perhaps the operation of grace aiding informal reasoning is also included. Ian Ramsey's use of the expression "disclosure" seems to be mixed in a similar way. Although Ramsey does not stress moral dispositions his language covers psychological disclosures, the epistemological recognition of truth through human reasoning, and (perhaps) the grace disclosure which is part of the traditional notion of faith as gift. See Ian Ramsey, *Religious Language* (1957) (London, 1969); also Helm, *Varieties* 53–59.

73. *MS* B.9.11 (Assent of Faith 17 June 1846). He added: "assensus does not stand for *will*, but the act of the intellectus—this act, says St. Thomas, is not determined by the cogitatio that is weak, but by the will, which obliges the assensus to *anticipate* the cogitatio, i.e. while the cogitatio is going on and the process of proof is not perfect, the will obliges the intellect to receive the conclusion." Newman is commenting on Aquinas, *Scriptum super Sententiis Magistri Petri Lombardi,* Super Lib. 3. Distinctio 23.2.2 (c. 1256) (ed.) R. P. Mandonnet, 4 vols. (Paris, 1929–1947) 3:722–729.

74. *US* 202 ("Nature of Faith" 6 January 1839).

75. *VM* 1:85–86.

76. In the *GA* Newman used his real/notional distinction to express this point; the former is a notional assent to a credibility. Its object is the proposition "I ought to believe." The latter is a real assent to a reality. Its object is *"Deus revelans et res revelata."* Sometimes however he understood the real/notional distinction as cutting across these lines.

77. In the case of divine faith, the reasoning toward faith is informal and culminates in a judgment of credibility.

78. *Dev* ix.

79. See the review of *An Essay on the Development of Christian Doctrine* in *Brownson's Quarterly Review* 3 (July 1846) 342–368; *LD* 11:228 note 1. On Newman's reception in Rome see Wilfrid Ward, *Life of John Henry Cardinal Newman* 2 vols. (London, 1912) 1:135–175; Owen Chadwick, *From Bossuet to Newman: the Idea of Doctrinal Development* (Cambridge, 1957) 164–184.

80. *LD* 11:289.

81. It was the encyclical "Qui Pluribus" (9 November 1846); see *Enchiridion Symbolorum* (ed.) H. Denzinger (Freiburg, 1965) 556–559.

82. For a summary of Hermes' position, which is close to Locke's, see J. Alfaro, *Fides, Spes, Caritas* (Rome, 1968) 81; Roger Aubert, *Le probleme de l'acte de foi* (Louvain, 1950) 103–107. Sometimes Juan De Lugo seems to have said the same in his *De Virtute Fidei Divinae* Disputatio 2(1646) (*Opera Omnia Theologica* 7 vols. (Paris, 1868) 1:202–274.). See Wilfrid Ward 1:163–164.

83. *LD* 11:291 (8 December 1846): Newman was referring to *Dev* 12.

84. *LD* 11:293 (13 December 1846); *ibid.* 11:289 note 4 where Dessain

points out that Dugald Stewart, whom Newman read, wrote of probability as "opposed not to what is certain, but to what admits of being demonstrated after the manner of mathematicians." (*Elements of the Philosophy of the Human Mind* (ed.) G. N. Wright (London, 1854) 409–410).

85. *LD* 12:34 note 5 (31 January 1847). Dalgairns admitted that for Bautain reason cannot get beyond the terrestrial, while for Newman it mounts up to the very throne of God. On Bautain see Denzinger 553–554; Wilfrid Ward 1:164.

86. *LD* 12:34 (14 February 1847). With the censures or near-censures of Hermes and Bautain in the air it is not surprising that Newman was hesitant to publish. He felt it would be unbecoming to be "the propounder of a new theory" without some indication that he was "concurring in the Roman traditions." See Wilfrid Ward 1:161, 174; *Theses* 222. Newman told Dalgairns that his preference for an argument from conscience and suggestion that one from design was not "philosophically true" did not imply that "faith and reason are contrary." He could agree with Bautain in some particulars; but his point was that the proofs of natural theology are usually the work of an inquiring believer who recognizes in their conclusion the God of his faith, much as a man might recognize footprints as made by a man with eyes and ears as well as feet. But Newman was less concerned with such proofs and more with the process which leads men to faith generally.

87. *LD* 11:293 (13 December 1846); Henry Holden, *The Analysis of Divine Faith, or Two Treatises of the Resolution of Christian Belief* (1652) (trans.) W. G. (Paris, 1658). Holden defined faith as an assent "grounded upon the testimony or authority of him who tells it." He described the certainty of faith in psychological terms: there is "no hesitation, no doubt, no wavering in his judgment, nor the least fear of being deceived." (Holden, 2, 6).

88. *LD* 11:290 (8 December 1846). Giovanni Perrone S.J. was the most respected theologian in Rome during the 1830s and 1840s. Unlike many others he had kept in touch with the Tractarian Movement in England but tended to give the foremost place to William Palmer of Worcester College. (See Perrone, *Praelectiones Theologicae* 8 vols. (Rome, 1840–1844), 2a:116 note 1). Perrone was offended by the lack of restraint in Newman's remarks about the Roman Church. (See 2a: 190–191 note 2). But in a later edition he praised much of Newman's work (see the 1897 Paris edition 4:137 note 3). Perrone's treatment of faith and reason is found in volume 2b; pars 3: "De Analogia Rationis et Fidei" 341–592. He defined faith as "that free assent which the intellect, preceded and aided by divine grace, makes to supernaturally revealed truths because of the authority of God Himself revealing." *(334). In this sense there is no medium between certain (objective) knowledge and probable opinion. He spoke of certitude not merely as a psychological state but as an objective grasp of the truth. It is "a firm and rational persuasion of the soul concerning the truth of something known." *(362). The motives of credibility may be certain before faith (418–421), but they

cannot constitute the formal motive of faith itself (500). Certainty is had or it is not had for it arises "from the very light of truth." *(362). The certainty of faith, however, is an "absolute certitude"* and rests on a unique gift in faith (372–373).

89. *LD* 12:55 (24 February 1847).

90. *Ibid.* 11: 293 (13 December 1846).

91. *Ibid.* 13:333–334 (8 December 1849).

92. *Ibid.* 12:8 (10 January 1847).

93. See G. Van Noort, *Dogmatic Theology*, vol. 3: *The Sources of Revelation. Divine Faith* (Westminster, Md., 1961); Etienne Gilson, *Reason and Revelation in the Middle Ages* (New York, 1938); Josef Peiper, *Belief and Faith* (London, 1963); Alfaro, especially his bibliography 16–27; and Aubert, especially his comments on Newman, 343–356, 468–469, 564–575, 751–752.

94. Aquinas said that the "faith of demons" is only equivocally faith. They believe not because grace gives them a share in divine knowledge but because they are rationally convinced by "signs." *Quaestiones Disputatae de Veritate* 14.9 (1256–1259), *Leon.* 22:462–464. Aquinas' classic texts on faith are *Summae* II II 1–16, *Leon.* 8:7–123; *Scriptum super Sententiis* Lib.3. Distinctio 23–25, 3:691–810; *De Veritate* 14, *Leon.* 22:435–473; *Contra Gentiles* I 3–8, *Leon.* 13:7.22.

95. *LD* 12:29 (8 February 1847).

96. *Ibid.* 5 (10 January 1847).

97. *Ibid.* 8.

98. *Ibid.* 30–31 (8 February 1847).

99. *US* 222 ("Love and the Safeguard of Faith" 21 May 1839).

100. *LD* 12:31 (8 February 1847).

101. *US* 179 ("Faith and Reason Contrasted" 6 January 1839).

102. *LD* 12:31 (8 February 1847); see Perrone, 2b:500. Vargish has written that after 1847, under pressure, Newman began to acknowledge the value of reason in religion for "an intellectual minority" but had not "modified his basic position." Reason remained "external" and unnecessary. Vargish seems to overlook Newman's careful restatement of the way in which reason is and is not external to faith (Vargish, 42).

103. For details about the four copies of these theses see *Theses* 224–226. Each thesis was followed by references to the *US* and to traditional authorities. The plan to translate the Latin preface into French was never carried out; see *Theses* 244–245.

104. This could be Locke's position. We form an opinion about the fact of a revelation, then make an "enthusiastic" (certain) assent to its content.

105. This would be the traditional position.

106. *Theses* 226 (Thesis 1). It is certain because the believer has "neither doubt nor fear" *(227).

107. *Ibid.* 228; see also 232 (Thesis 7) saying the "motives" of faith are not grasped "by their own force" but "instead and, (as it were) according to their measure, they are true arguments and tend to a conclu-

sion which they clearly do not reach, that is, they make the conclusion credible."* But Newman was not saying that such arguments take the place of the unique "motives" which cause faith, but that they have their place in establishing credibility. He quoted Aquinas, *Summa* II II 1.5.2, *Leon.* 8:17.

108. *Theses* 236–237. Newman had written that faith "is founded . . . upon the will" but later changed it to read "has its origin"* in the will. He quoted De Lugo: "Human faith and opinion . . . is by itself . . . only probable"* (239 citing DeLugo, *Opera Omnia* 1:269).

109. *Theses* 236 (Thesis 10).

110. *Ibid.* 233 (Thesis 8).

111. *Ibid.* 230. (Thesis 5). See Suarez "De Fide Theologica" Disputatio 3:8.5 (*Opera Omnia* 12:70). Suarez's text is *"Et quamvis sapientiores majorem quandam humanam certitudinem, non transcendit fidem humanam"*. Later Newman noted that such a "fides humana" need not always precede divine faith in the individual although *"in respect to the body of the Church,"** the evidence of credibility must generally precede it. *Theses* 239–240. This remark occurs only in Newman's rough draft.

112. *Theses* 229 (Thesis 5). Newman quoted Charles R. Billuart: "Devils do not believe on God's authority but only on the force of evidence . . . likewise if our assent rested solely on the motives of credibility and not on the first Truth, our faith would not be supernatural."* (230 citing Billuart "Tractatus de Fide et Regulis Fidei" Dissertatio 3:3.3, 2 (1746–1751) in *Cursus Theologiae*, 20 vols. (Paris, 1827–1831) 9:76).

113. *Theses* 231 (Thesis 6).

114. *Ibid.* 236 (Thesis 10).

115. *Ibid.* 243 (11 January 1847).

116. *MS* B.9.11 (English Draft of Preface 1847) 1.

117. *Ibid.* 2, 4. See *Theses* 250 where he included, as worldly principles, a denial of the efficacy of prayer or the possibility of miracles.

118. *Theses* 250. He added that God's grace is present in some sense "not only in the act of faith itself, but also in what precedes it"* (253). See below 179.

119. *Theses* 253. See *MS* B.9.11 (English Draft of Preface 1847) 9.

120. *Theses* 254. See *MS* B.9.11 (English Draft of Preface 1847) 8. Newman's example is a court case where blood on the clothing of the accused is intrinsic and his frequent association with murderers or his previous illegal action, extrinsic to the accusation at hand. Both examples would be circumstantial and inconclusive. But they have some value in distinguishing evidence which may be immediately related to the accusation (blood on the clothes) and evidence which is not so related but which would antecedently dispose the jury toward a conviction on less immediate grounds.

121. *MS* B.9.11 (English Draft of Preface 1847) 9.

122. *Theses* 254.

123. *MS* 2.9.11 (English Draft of Preface 1847) 9; see 10: "antecedent probability . . . effects nothing, yet it is impossible to add bounds to its

influence, in making a fact credible, or in the highest degree probable."
In *LD* 15:459 (7 October 1853) Newman used the term "verisimilitude"
to denote probable reasoning to a certainty. But elsewhere he used it to
denote extrinsic antecedents and wrote: "verisimilitudes or in-verisimili-
tudes . . . do no more than recommend or disparage the proper proof."
(*PN* 2:141 ("Whether moral objections are valid against miracles"
1860)). "There are two kinds of arguments for a fact: EIKONA and
SEMEIA . . . Verisimilitude . . . and probable reasoning to a moral
certainty . . . The personal argument is mainly founded on the former,
though of course the latter must be the direct ground of conviction, but
the former heightens even a low probability as to make it enough." (*MS*
A.30.11 27 March 1860). See H. L. Mansel's notes on εἰκός, σημεῖον, and
τεκμήριον in his edition of Henry Aldrich's *Artis Logicae Rudimenta*
(Oxford, 1856) 207–216. Newman possessed Mansel's Aldrich. See Brian
J. Wicker, "Logic and Certainty" (M.A. Thesis, University of Birmingham, 1960) 102.

124. There are two possible sources of Newman's terminology. First,
Richard Whately defined presumption as "not a preponderance of probability in . . . favour [of a supposition], but such a preoccupation of the
ground, as implies that it must stand good till some sufficient reason is
brought against it." (Richard Whately, *Elements of Rhetoric* 7th ed.
rev. (London, 1846) 72). This section did not appear in earlier editions;
however, elsewhere Whately spoke of judgments, not knowledge, "established chiefly by Antecedent-probability." (*Rhetoric* 2nd ed. 1828:77;
1846 ed.: 85). "Antecedent probability . . . by itself . . . [is] utterly insufficient to establish the Conclusion . . . But the evidences [of such
antecedents] . . . have very great weight in preparing the mind for receiving . . . other Arguments." (1828 ed: 84–85; 1846 ed: 90–91). He distinguished antecedent considerations from "arguments, the combined force
of which . . . are irresistable," (*ibid.*) "real and solid Arguments . . .
established by a *preponderance* of probability." (1828 ed: 102–103; 1846
ed: 100–101). Newman said the same. (Tristram's suggestion that for
Newman a presumption is simply a weak probability seems unjustified.
(*Theses* 246). See Duffy, 32; *LD* 15:456 (7 October 1853); and *GA* 60.)
The second source is Perrone's distinction between "the chronological
order and the logical order."* On February 8, 1847, Newman quoted
Perrone: "The chronological order of knowing truth is *relative,* since it
depends on the subject, who acquires that notion of truth, and on various
circumstances, which can be an aid or an impediment to the knowing
faculty. The logical order of truth is *absolute,* for it determines the internal relations and connections of ideas which arise from the very nature
of things."* (Perrone, 2a:374 note 1; *LD* 12:31). Perrone had also written
of "*intrinsic* . . . motives," which "demonstrate *intrinsically* the truth of
a proposition or the necessary connection between subject and predicate,"
and "*extrinsic*" ones which "present to us some certain indication or con-
notation concerning that connection, and hence concerning the truth of
that proposition," for example, authority or human testimony* (364–365).

Newman was searching at the time for whatever would prove helpful in clarifying his sense of a "moral" proof in contrast with logical "demonstration."* Sometimes he used as descriptions of the same thing the terms "antecedent probability," "chronological order," "verisimilitude," "presumption," "credibility," and "extrinsic reasons."*

125. *MS* B.9.11 (English Draft of Preface 1847) 12. Above the words "religious principles" Newman wrote "knowledge." See *Theses* 253: "The presumption of faith is of a certain truth," and "a *proof* makes something evident; a *presumption* rather makes it credible."*

126. See *MS* B.9.11 (English Draft of Preface 1847) 8, 13.

127. *Ibid.* 14; also 18: "the most cogent proofs are usually cumulative, that is, consist of a multitude of converging reasons, each with but a certain degree of probability, but strong in their union, and supported by antecedent considerations."

128. *MS* B.9.11 ("Certainty of Faith" 1848).

129. *Ibid.* Newman may be suggesting that the "doubt and fear" is not because one is uncertain but because of the "importance of the subject."

130. *Ibid.* He was not saying that while the "conclusion" is insufficient for certainty, the "mind" leaps to an unjustified certainty, as Pailin suggests. (Pailin, 161–185). Rather for Newman the "mind" assents to a "conclusion" of a moral, not demonstrative, proof which however establishes truth indirectly by establishing for certain that one *ought* to accept it.

131. *LD* 12:228 (27 June 1848). Newman was probably writing of his own conversion when he added a description of someone "convinced before his reception that he *ought* to believe, but not able to bring himself to make an act of faith" until after much prayer. "It is not often that the *will* is brought so distinctly and directly into exercise, but in reality faith is always so begun." (228–229).

132. *Ibid; ibid.* 233 (3 July 1848).

133. *LG* 383–384.

134. *LD* 12:289 note 1.

135. *Ibid.* 289 (12 October 1848). Terrence Penelhum has argued that we are always free to be irrational and reject not only informal but (perhaps) even mathematical conclusions—"things that are beyond rational doubt." (Terrence Penelhum, *Problems of Religious Knowledge* (London, 1971) 147).

136. *LD* 12:356 (30 November 1848). Newman was speaking of a credibility judgment, not divine faith. He was not endorsing an informal rationalism.

137. *Rambler* 4 (July 1849) 164.

138. *LD* 13:398 (27 January 1850).

139. *Ibid.* 14:134 (20 November 1850).

140. *Ibid.* 348 (7 September 1851). A parallel example is the common-sense certainty that man is free despite an ordinary man's inability to answer difficulties suggested by determinists.

141. *MS* A.30.11 ("Certainty of Faith" 14 April 1853).

142. *LD* 15:456 (7 October 1853). Butler meant by "credible" what is "not unbelievable." (*Analogy* 223–252). Newman wrote that, although he could agree with much of what he read, he was "going by my own ideas" and had "no reason to suppose I am following any particular school of Divines" (*LD* 15:461, 458).

143. *LD* 15:456–457. In this letter, Newman mentioned not only Butler and Keble but also Félicité de Lemennais and Louis Bautain as inclining to this view. It is perhaps debatable whether Richard Whately should be included. In an 1819 pamphlet entitled "Historic Doubts Relative to Napoleon Bonaparte" (London, 1819), especially 42, 47, 18, he followed Butler but concluded that at least in history probability legitimately induces certainty. However later he wrote that "there is no one who does not consider, among probable arguments, some to be more probable than others, and again, that three or four more probable arguments have together more weight (other things being equal) than two or one. Any conclusion [may be] rendered probable though not certain by such and such arguments." (Letter to Miss Crabtree, 4 February 1844, quoted in E. Jane Whatley, *Life and Correspondence of Richard Whately D.D.* (London, 1866) 2:51).

144. *LD* 15:457. He gave the example (459) of a man establishing from internal evidence the author of an anonymous publication and concluding, "I cannot *prove* the author, but I have *no doubt,*" although "by an hypothesis of scepticism" someone else could persist in disagreement.

145. *Ibid.* 460.

146. In *Ibid.* 11:358, Dessain identifies Edward Healy Thompson as follows: "after being at Emmanuel College, Cambridge, from 1832 to 1836 and holding several curacies, [he] became a Catholic in 1846 under Newman's influence. He devoted himself to religious, literary and translation work, helped by his wife, who was a writer on her own account. Newman put him forward as Lecturer in English Literature at the Catholic University in Dublin in 1853, but he never acted. He was uncle to Francis Thompson the poet."

147. *Ibid.* 15:464–465 (8 October 1853).

148. *Ibid.* 465.

149. *Ibid.* (11 October 1853). Above "*sufficient* grounds" Newman wrote "motiva."

150. *Ibid.* 465–466; see *MS* B.7.4 ("Object of Faith" 17 January 1854) where he enlarged on this point; see below 175.

151. *LD* 15:466 (11 October 1853).

152. *Ibid.* 466–467. He added that he had not "spoken of divine grace, where it comes in, and what it does." He must have felt it comes in at various places and does various things within this process.

153. *MS* B.7.4 ("Certainty of Faith" 16 December 1853); see below 173–175.

154. See *LD* 16:102–109 (10 April 1854).

155. *Ibid.* 18:471 note 1 (29 September 1858).

156. *Ibid.* 471 (1 October 1858). Newman told Capes that "when I

came to read Catholic theology I found" your objection "solved in a way which I felt was satisfactory."

157. *MS* A.30.11 ("Evidences of Religion" 12 January 1860). He added: "theological doctrine does not come into this discussion."

158. *Ibid.*

159. *LD* 19:251 (3 December 1859).

160. *Ibid.* 256 (23 January 1860); see Boekraad, *Argument* 7–10, on the importance of Henry L. Mansel; his discussion concerns Mansel's *Limits of Religious Thought Examined in Eight Lectures* (London, 1858).

161. *MS* A.30.11 ("On the popular practical personal evidence for the truth of Revelation" 5 January 1860).

162. *MS* A.30.11 ("Evidences of Religion" 12 January 1860). On 20 December 1859 Newman wrote that his *University Sermons* are "in parts more sceptical than now I have any temptation to approve." (*LD* 19:256).

163. *MS* A.30.11 ("Evidences of Religion" 12 January 1860).

CHAPTER IV

KNOWLEDGE AND EMPIRICISM

Locke on knowledge

Locke's intention in writing his *Essay Concerning Human Understanding* was "to inquire into the original, certainty, and extent of human knowledge, together with the grounds and degrees of belief, opinion and assent."[1] The problem of certainty arose for Locke in the context of practical considerations. Knowledge in matters of religion and morals needed to be given a sure foundation.[2] In 1671 he attacked the matter immediately, but soon became aware that related issues needed to be resolved first. When the *Essay* was published nineteen years later, the material discussed in the early draft appeared in Book Four after a long preparatory analysis of knowledge by way of ideas.

There are two tendencies in Locke's theory of knowledge which can be related to two influences on his thought. Like Descartes, Locke tended to limit genuine knowledge to what is clear and distinct and therefore abstract. Like many of his contemporaries, he tended to remain skeptical about what lay beyond our ideas. We might grasp clear truths in the abstract, but we must be satisfied with probable conjectures in the concrete. An empiricist theory of knowledge was built upon the presuppositions of Cartesian rationalism, which were not questioned. A long and unnecessary experiment in the history of philisophy was begun, leaving behind the view that the objects of our knowledge are often without clarity but are often without doubt.

Locke seldom mentioned Descartes without a word of praise,[3] although Locke himself felt there were more differences than similarities between himself and the French philosopher. It would be a mistake to attribute to Descartes' influence whatever Locke might "spin out of his own thoughts," as the result of his "reflection upon

68

his own mind and the ideas he found there."[4] But it would also be a mistake to deny that the crucial conception of clear ideas as the proper objects of knowledge is Cartesian in origin. In fact, in Book Four of his *Essay*, Locke seems to have accepted a Cartesian rationalism without significant qualification.[5]

He defined knowledge as "nothing but *the perception of the connexion of and agreement, or disagreement and repugnancy of any of our ideas.*"[6] This definition conforms to the Cartesian premise that knowledge in its proper sense is an intuition of what is clear and distinct: "With me to know and to be certain is the same thing; what I know, that I am certain of; and what I am certain of, that I know."[7] Distinguishing between knowledge, or the certain perception of relations between ideas, and judgment, or the faculty of reaching opinions in probable matters,[8] he did not hesitate to describe knowledge as intuitive.

Sometimes the mind perceives the agreement or disagreement of two ideas *immediately by themselves,* without the intervention of any other; and this . . . we may call *intuitive knowledge* . . . this kind of knowledge is the clearest and most certain that human frailty is capable of. This part of knowledge is irresistible, and, like bright sunshine, forces itself immediately to be perceived, as soon as ever the mind turns its view that way; and leaves no room for hesitation, doubt, or examination . . . *It is on this intuition that depends all the certainty and evidence of all our knowledge.*[9]

Descartes had written: "By intuition, I understand . . . the apprehension which the mind pure and attentive, gives us so easily and so distinctly that we are thereby freed from all doubt."[10] But Locke was dissatisfied with what he took to be Descartes' account. He argued that it is a mistake to talk of knowing (intuiting) "innate ideas" and consequently, to claim "to be sure without proofs, and to know without perceiving."[11] This would be to claim to settle matters of fact by "conceiving" ideas apart from experience. When there is a factual question about something, one would beg the question by arguing in this way. To avoid self-deception, he "ought to build up his hypothesis on matter of fact . . . and not presume on matter of fact . . . because he supposes it to be so."[12] Locke complained that Descartes placed certainty in the "mere conceivability" of clear and distinct but hypothetical ideas.[13] Instead Locke

would place it in the perception of relations between ideas somehow
derived from experience: "I do not suppose, that to certainty it is
requisite that an idea should be in all its parts clear and distinct."[14]
    Yet elsewhere he admitted that the relations between ideas are
part of the very nature of the ideas themselves. The agreement or
disagreement of ideas with one another depends entirely on the ideas
themselves. Reason can only observe these relations; argument can
only show them by means of an intervening idea.[15] In other words,
Locke's intuition of relations between ideas does not seem to differ
significantly from Descartes' intuition of clear and distinct ideas. In
both cases "certain knowledge" does not denote an objective grasp
of the way things are. Rather it denotes the apprehension of ideas
which may or may not coincide with reality. Already in his 1671
draft of the *Essay*, Locke wrote of the "cleare and distinct knowledg that every man hath of his owne Ideas." Such *"infallible certain
knowledg"* is the clearest we can have but it remains "internal." It
cannot "prove the existence of any thing." When we claim to possess real knowledge of things outside us, we always presume their
existence and appeal to our senses for confirmation. We do not
"demonstrate the reality of the thing but the connection or dependence of our notions or Ideas about it with themselves or other
Ideas."[16]
    A second influence on Locke came from his own countrymen.
While it has been held that he owed "little or nothing" to the greatest of his English predecessors,[17] Henry Van Leeuwen has argued
that Locke's indebtedness to Englishmen, both in religious and scientific circles, was at least as great as his indebtedness to Descartes.[18]
According to Van Leeuwen the problem of certainty first became
critical in a theological context. In seventeenth-century England,
Catholics and Protestants both claimed that their docrines alone
were necessary for salvation. William Chillingworth and John Tillotson worked out a position based on the premise that absolute certainty is rarely achieved, and yet skepticism must be avoided. A
solution was found in the ordinary life of a reasonable man who
forms a practical opinion on the basis of accumulated evidence.
Absolute or mathematical certainty is beyond us and therefore the
moral certainty of everyday life must be our guide in religious matters. This approach was then carried into science where the experi-

mental method gradually upset scientific dogmatism and encouraged a cautious assent proportioned to evidence.[19]

Van Leeuwen concluded that Locke formalised a "constructive scepticism" inherent in English thought. Its key doctrine is that while certainty is beyond us, we must be content to measure our assent according to available evidence. Our assent should be reasonably situated on a scale of "resistability," but our assent to "all general truths" is limited in principle. We can have "opinion, but not knowledge."[20] Relying heavily upon the attitude of Boyle, Newton and the British scientific school, Locke specified limits beyond which the mind cannot go. In 1671 he wrote that man can have certain knowledge only of particular propositions about existing things. "Indeed," he emphasized, "all universall propositions are either Certain and then they are only verball but are not instructive. Or else are Instructive and then are not Certain."[21] Nineteen years later Locke continued to deny our ability "to discover general, instructive, unquestionable truths concerning . . . [natural] bodies." We may be able to "advance useful and experimental philosophy in physical things," but it would be "lost labour" to seek after "a *perfect science*."[22]

Locke drew a distinction between "verbal" and "real" truth, "that being only verbal truth, wherein terms are joined according to the agreement or disagreement of the ideas they stand for; without regarding whether our ideas are such as really have, or are capable of having, an existence in nature."[23] He argued that we have no "real" and certain knowledge of "the complex ideas that our names of the species of substances properly stand for."[24] Some men might be able to carefully observe probabilities or "hints well laid together" and make a correct guess about what they have been unable to discover in experience. "But," Locke insisted, "this is but guessing still: it amounts only to opinion, and has not that certainty which is requisite to knowledge." The main difference between "*probability and certainty, faith* and *knowledge*" is that knowledge follows upon an evident intuition of what is joined to the ideas under consideration, while belief follows upon something extraneous to the ideas believed and their relations.[25] Only the evidence of clear ideas can make us certain. Experiential sensible evidence can at best persuade us to believe what we cannot know. Consequently our "general" knowledge must be "nominal" for "general certainty is never to be found but in our ideas."[26]

He allowed that "whatever simple ideas have been found to co-exist in any substance, these we may with confidence join together again, and so make abstract ideas of substances. For whatever have once had an union in nature, may be united again."[27] But having ruled out any intellectual apprehension capable of sustaining real general knowledge, Locke can only speak metaphorically about "nature's way" of making things alike. He is defenseless before Hume's remark that by "nature" is meant not an apprehended real participation of things in a similarity of kind, but only the customary drift of our thoughts.

By 1700 the main charge against Locke by his critics was that of skepticism. This was the original dispute between he and Stilling-fleet, the Bishop of Worcester.[28] But Locke remained unshaken. He felt that the only alternative to a doctrine of innate ideas is one of well-founded guesses when intuition is lacking: "Where this perception is, there is knowledge, and where it is not, there, though we may fancy, guess or believe, yet we always come short of knowledge."[29] Still, his own way of ideas inevitably led him back to the objection he had raised against an intuition of innate ideas. He wanted to "make it evident, that this way of certainty, by the knowledge of our own ideas, goes a little further than bare imagination."[30] He recognized that if all knowledge rests entirely upon our internal apprehension of ideas, then the "visions of an enthusiast and the reasonings of a sober man" would be equally certain regardless of the way things actually are. Since we do not know things immediately but only through the medium of ideas, our knowledge is real only when "there is a *conformity* between our ideas and the reality of things. But," Locke asked himself, "what shall be here the criterion?"[31]

In search of a criterion Locke reviewed the various kinds of ideas. Simple ideas are naturally produced by existing things, while complex ideas are of our own making. But our ideas of substances are of an intermediate kind. They are formed by the mind and yet they claim to refer to independent things outside the mind. Locke recognized that mere compatibility among the qualities making up the idea of a substance is not a sufficient criterion that the idea has a real reference. There is no way of settling which ideal combinations refer to really existing things; only that grouping of complex ideas which has actually been drawn from the existent thing constitutes the real idea of a substance.

Attempting to make his task simpler, he admitted that we cannot in principle determine the real reference of our certain knowledge of the relations between ideas, and concluded that "we must in many things content ourselves with faith and probability."[32]

> Most of the propositions we think, reason, discourse—nay, act upon, are such as we cannot have undoubted knowledge of their truth: yet some of them border so near upon certainty, that we make no doubt at all about them; but assent to them as firmly, and act, according to that assent, as resolutely as if they were infallibly demonstrated, and that our knowledge of them was perfect and certain.[33]

The reasonable man must inquire into the grounds of probability, "cast up the sum total on both sides" and "come to acknowledge . . . on which side the probability rests." When he does this he will find that "some proofs in matters of reason, being suppositions upon universal experience, are so cogent and clear, and some testimonies in matters of fact so universal, that he cannot refuse his assent."[34] Some matters of probability "naturally determine the judgment, and leave us as little liberty to believe or disbelieve, as a demonstration does."[35] Assent is, therefore, unavoidable.

These remarks have led some to suggest that Locke redefined his original rationalist distinction between certain intuitions and probable opinion along empiricist, subjective and psychological lines. Intuition is only "irresistible belief"[36]—that probable opinion which operates as one's last appeal. Apart from trifling tautologies, assent should be proportioned to available evidence; it will then range from certain or irresistible "intuition" to uncertain or resistible "opinion." In the former case assent is forced as in demonstration. It cannot be given or withheld as one wishes.[37] In the latter case one freely forms an opinion in the light of incomplete evidence. However both are cases of "knowledge," differing only in their degree of resistibility. In other words, knowledge is redefined as more or less justified belief.

But this interpretation is inconsistent with Locke's repeated insistence that intuition and demonstration are properly the only two degrees of knowledge. "Whatever comes short of one of these, with what assurance soever embraced, is but *faith* or *opinion*, but not knowledge."[38] Certain knowledge or intuition is not merely an irresistible opinion; it is not an opinion embraced with great assurance. "The highest probability amounts not to certainty, without which there can be no knowledge."[39] For Locke, the certainty of knowledge must be distinguished from the highest degree of assurance about a probable conviction. The distinction between knowledge and opinion is not one of degree, but of kind. When we hold an opinion, no matter how strongly, our assent "excludes not the possibility that it may be otherwise."[40] But when we know, our assent excludes the possibility both of doubt and of error.

In matters of fact we cannot know. We can only guess. However Locke was still left with the problem of explaining why some such opinions are in fact "irresistible" or "unavoidable." Appealing vaguely to "things as they really are," he wrote that "names made at pleasure neither alter the nature of things, nor make us understand them . . . by *real ideas* I mean such as have a foundation in nature; such as have a conformity with the real being and existence of things."[41] But this whole question caused him considerable embarrassment. To admit knowledge of "the real being and existence of things" is to contradict his general definition of knowledge. The existential judgment which affirms that the content of an idea represents what is actually the case cannot be explained as merely setting forth a connection between ideas. It seems that the unavoidable fact that knowledge involves an objective (certain) grasp of what is the case forced Locke into admitting what he could not permit. It forced him to speak of "sensations" which are known in a way which his own theory could not allow.

Locke spoke of a knowledge of the existence of particular external objects by means of our awareness of ideas which arise from them. He outlined "three degrees of knowledge, viz. *intuitive, demonstrative,* and *sensitive*: in each of which there are different degrees and ways of evidence and certainty."[42] Sensitive knowledge would go beyond "bare probability" but it would fall short of the perfect certainty of intuition and demonstration. At first Locke severely restricted this sort of knowledge to particular sensible things which are immediately encountered, but later he ignored this awkward addition to his theory entirely.

The mind has two faculties conversant about truth and false-hood:—First, KNOWLEDGE, whereby it certainly *perceives* . . . the agreement or disagreement of any ideas. Secondly, JUDG-MENT, which is the putting ideas together, or separating them from one another in the mind, when their certain agreement or disagreement is not perceived, but *presumed* to be so.[43]

If he is to be consistent, then he must say that even sensation is dis-tinct from the transparent assurance of intuition and demonstration. It is, in Aaron's words, simply "a conviction, a feeling which cannot be further explained."[44] And he must say that while some opinions or judgments are "irresistible," this again is nothing more than a feeling which cannot be explained.

In the end Locke's skepticism about our real knowledge of the way things are is not simply the cautious conclusion of a man who abhorred the intolerance of enthusiasts. Nor is it part of an honest admission of the fallibility of sense-perception, memory, and the testimony of witnesses. It is in fact the result of a theory of knowl-edge which ultimately fails to allow objective (certain) knowledge of the way things are in spite of the limitations of the human con-dition.[45]

To a great extent this skepticism is the product of an ambiguous use of the term "idea," which is used to stand both for the opera-tions of experiencing and for the objects immediately experienced. Ideas are treated not simply as that by which we know the world about us, but as that which we know. They may be signs of existent things, but signs that have an independent reality. An impossible theory results in which the connection between ideas and the things signified by them remains fundamentally unclarified.[46]

Newman, empiricism and knowledge

In 1870 Newman asked himself "the all important question, what is truth, and what apparent truth? what is genuine knowledge, and what is its counterfeit? what are the facts for discriminating certi-tude from mere persuasion or delusion?"[47] Locke had also sought a "criterion" for real knowledge, but Locke's problem arose within his own way of ideas. For him the immediate objects of knowledge are ideas, not things. Knowledge is "real only so far as there is a *conformity* between our ideas and the reality of things."[48]

Newman sometimes appears to have raised his question of "genuine knowledge" within the same framework. On occasion he spoke of "false certitudes,"[49] but to talk of mistaken certainty can suggest that knowledge (certainty) is properly an apprehension of ideas which may or may not represent things. He observed that when our "certainty of mind has for its subject what is true, we call it a conviction, when its subject is not true, we call it a persuasion," adding, "I know of no test sufficient in concrete matters for discriminating a conviction from a persuasion."[50]

But Newman came to realize that if this were so, we could never know or be sure of what is the case. In 1870 he put the skeptic's argument in these words: "No line can be drawn between such real certitudes as have truth for their object, and apparent certitudes . . . What looks like certitude always is exposed to the chance of turning out to be a mistake."[51] Newman's response was that to construe knowledge as an apprehension of ideas or beliefs which may or may not represent reality is to misdescribe the fact of knowledge as it occurs. "We all know," he wrote, "what is meant by saying we are sure of a thing."[52]

In 1859 he discussed whether "names or terms stand for ideas or for things," contending "there is the case in which . . . is imagined, an idea without a thing, that is, the case of Universals . . . those on the side of things against Ideas, say there are not universal ideas and a controversy ensues . . . between Nominalists, Realists, and Conceptionalists." Admitting that "my own long habit has been" to take the side of universals, yet, he added, "it certainly does seem more simple and natural to say the words stand for the things. To say the words *mean* things is incorrect for *words* can mean nothing, *I* mean." Newman went on to argue that "when you say Augustus was Emperor of Rome, are you really meaning anything short of Caesar himself?" In other words, ideas are not independent objects of knowledge. They are that by which "we mean a *thing*." When we reflect on an idea or on what we mean, "cleaning it up by definition," we still mean a thing. In this case "we define the idea in order that the word may best convey not the idea but the thing, as we rub the glass, not for the sake of the glass, but for the sake of the real objects which the glass images."[53] The definition, which has to do with ideas, is expressed in a proposition, which has to do with things. Newman's intention was to defend a direct realism against a way of ideas. Ideas are not that which we know (*quod*), but his failure to sort out how we know things by and in ideas (*quo* and *in quo*) brought him close to nominalism. The term "nominalism" generally refers to the position that denies to universals any extramental existence and substitutes for the idea of a common nature an atomistic world of particulars or individuals. Locke had argued that our general knowledge must be "nominal" when it refers to extramental reality, and at times Newman seems to have said the same. "Each thing has its own nature and its own history. When the nature and the history of many things are similar, we say that they have the same nature; but there is no such thing as one and the same nature; they are each of them itself, not identical, but like."[54] To the logician "dog or horse is not a thing which he sees, but a mere name suggesting ideas."[55]

Nevertheless when Newman's remarks are brought together they seem to express a doctrine on abstraction which, in spite of a similar wording, is not Lockean in intention.

Experience tells us only of individual things, and these things are innumerable. Our minds might have been so constructed as to be able to receive and retain an exact image of each of these various objects, one by one . . . without the power of comparing it with any of the others. But this is not our case: on the contrary, to compare and to contrast are among the most prominent and busy of our intellectual functions. Instinctively . . . we are ever instituting comparisons between the manifold phenomena of the external world, . . . criticizing, referring to a standard, collecting, analyzing them. Nay, as if by one and the same action, as soon as we perceive them, we also perceive that they are like each other or unlike, or rather both like and unlike at once. We apprehend spontaneously, even before we set about apprehending, that man is like man, yet unlike; and unlike a horse, a tree, a mountain, or a monument, yet in some, though not the same respects, like each of them . . . we are ever grouping and discriminating, measuring and sounding, framing cross classes and cross divisions, and thereby rising from particulars to generals.[56]

Newman's treatment of abstraction diverged from Locke's account in three ways. First, for Locke the word for a universal is the name of a general or collective idea. "Man" for example, does not express some grasp of the kind of being in question, but simply names the complete set of beings which, for whatever reason, are designated individually by that name. This theory ignores the important difference between the distinctive concept of a species and the set of all its members.[57] According to Newman, we give the name "man" to the "kind of common measure" between various people.[58] But he felt uncomfortable with a name theory of general ideas. In one place he wrote that the term "man" suggests "not the real being which he is in this or that specimen of himself, but a definition. If I might use a harsh metaphor, I should say he is made the logarithm of his true self, and in that shape is worked with the ease and satisfaction of logarithms."[59] The point seems to be that as logarithms have quite different mathematical properties from numbers, so universals have quite different properties from singular terms in logic. They are not names of individuals, but neither are they simply names of collections.[60]

Secondly, for Locke abstraction depends upon the observation of a recurrent similarity between many individuals. But Wicker has argued that, although he was sometimes inconsistent, Newman's intention was to defend a grasp of the universal in the single individual. "At first . . . sight of man, horse, or dog," he wrote, " . . . we are drawn to consider them the matter of *one* science respectively, viz. of the abstraction humanity, equinity, caninity . . . did we see but one horse or dog . . . we could view it under the aspects of its life, organization, structure."[61]

Finally, for Locke abstraction follows from the apprehension of individuals temporally as well as logically. We begin with individual sensations and a universal concept is formed by a subsequent mental process. Again, while Newman sometimes seems to have said the same, he contradicted this view by asserting that it is "as if by one and the same action, as soon as we perceive them [i.e. individual objects], we also perceive that they are like each other."[62]

In an important 1868 paper Newman discussed the status of "abstract truths." He wrote that "nominalists" call them " 'generalizations' from experience," while "realists" hold them as "objective." But, he asked, "What is the *object?*" When the mind contemplates an abstraction like "beautifulness" what does it see? If it is not "one of the Platonic everlasting ideas," we seem to be forced to agree "with the school of Locke and of sensible experiences." Along with Locke, Newman would not admit "abstract ideas corresponding to objective realities" in the way in which Plato understood them. But, Newman added, the situation is more complicated than either Locke or Plato seemed to allow.

> I do not pass over the experiences gained from the phenomena of mind so lightly, as I fancy the school of Locke is apt to do . . . We have a sense of duty, of virtue, of justice, of beautifulness;— Have we (what is often called) an *intuition* of these? . . . What I think our mind really has as parts of its nature is certain sensations, that is, a property of being affected in a certain way by certain sensible objects or experiences . . . Thus I get the idea of sweetness or of painfulness—it is a quality of a feeling. I do not need . . . any object which my mind sees and calls sweetness or painfulness. The idea conveyed in these words is my mode of apprehending a quality.[63]

When a word is used for an idea and not simply to denote an individual thing, then "the instrument by which it is presented to us . . . is the power of abstraction" and this use of the word is "intellectual." Yet these two uses of words, for ideas and things, correspond to notional and real apprehension which, for Newman, combine in the one complex act of knowing. He wanted to stress the "fulness of meaning"[64] gained in experience and to emphasize the importance and depth of meaning of concrete individuals over against the abstract nature of the species. Occasionally this made him fall into a nominalist form of expression, but the main train of his thought remained that of a moderate realist.[65]

Again, despite a similarity in wording, Newman's intention in discussing how we know what is real was quite different from that of Locke. Locke had argued that "the bare contemplation of . . . abstract ideas will carry us but a very little way in the search of truth and certainty."[66] Still "our knowledge cannot exceed our ideas." When "they are either imperfect, confused, or obscure, we cannot expect to have certain, perfect, or clear knowledge."[67] Newman agreed that "intuition by itself will carry us but a little way into that circle of knowledge which is the boast of the present age,"[68] but he would allow certain knowledge of what is obscure.[69]

For Locke syllogistic reasoning ultimately rests on an intuition of clear relations between ideas.[70] But he argued that such reasoning is of no use "in the advancement of science, or new discoveries of yet unknown truths."[71] Newman also found that "ratiocination . . .

restricted and put into grooves" is of little use in concrete matters.[72] "Syllogism . . . though of course it has its use, still does only the . . . easiest part of the work, in the investigation of truth, for when there is any difficulty, that difficulty commonly lies in determining first principles, not in the arrangement of proofs."[73]

Newman concluded that "for genuine proof in concrete matters we require an *organon* more delicate, versatile, and elastic than verbal argumentation."[74] Locke however concluded that in such matters "we cannot have undoubted knowledge."[75] We can only have opinion. Yet sometimes probabilities will "rise so near to *certainty, that . . .* we make little or no difference between them and certain knowledge."[76] Newman recognized that this admission was inconsistent with Locke's principles. Locke had laid down the principle that we must "proportion . . . assent to the different evidence and probability of the things," and that "no probability can rise higher than its first original."[77] Consequently Newman began his own investigation by quoting those passages in which Locke "is obliged to make exceptions to his general principle,—exceptions unintelligible on his abstract doctrine, but demanded by the logic of facts . . . he affirms and sanctions the very paradox to which I am committed myself."[78]

Locke was obliged to introduce "reason" to supplement the syllogism. God has given men "a mind that can reason, without being instructed in methods of syllogizing . . . it has a native faculty to perceive the coherence or incoherence of its ideas, and can range them right."[79] In concrete matters syllogism "comes too late" to settle what has already been discovered by "an ingenious searcher after truth," who, although "unskilful in syllogism" finds his way by reason where "others better skilled in syllogism have been misled."[80]

Locke put the question: "what room is there for the exercise of any other faculty but *outward sense* and *inward perception?* What need is there of *reason?*" His reply was that reason is necessary "for the enlargement of our knowledge, and regulating our assent."[81] "Reason" is that "faculty whereby man is . . . distinguished from beasts."[82] It includes two operations at once. By "*sagacity*" it "finds out" which intermediate ideas are relevant to the matter in question. By "*illation* or *inference*" it "orders" these ideas and discovers "what connexion there is in each link of the chain" of the deduction.[83]

In this way "reason" discovers certainty in cases of knowledge, and some degree of probability in cases of opinion. But it is an awkward addition to his theory. In the first case it is an unnecessary repetition of the intuitive perception of clear relations between ideas. Discovering "what connexion there is in each link of the chain" of an inference or arranging its premises in proper order, are just special cases of perceiving logical connections between ideas. But Locke has already explicitly assigned these tasks to the faculty of perception.[84]

Newman seems to have recognized this. In the *Grammar* he complained that on Locke's account, assent is "an idle repetition" of inference or the clear perception of relations between ideas. For Newman, "either assent is intrinsically distinct from inference, or the sooner we get rid of the word in philosophy the better. If it be only the echo of inference, do not treat it as a substantive act."[85]

In the second case, Locke's "reason" is useless in determining the right degree of probability, given his general theory of knowledge. It is useless to argue that probable knowledge is distinguished from certain knowledge in being "nothing but the appearance of such an agreement or disagreement, by the intervention of proofs whose connexion is not constant and immutable or at least is not perceived to be so."[86] For if the intuition of ideas is as Locke has defined it, then it is self-contradictory for him to allow the intuition of a certain connection which is not constant, or to speak of ideas that appear to stand in certain relations without really doing so. Locke's general theory of knowing in terms of perceiving the relations between ideas led him to talk of perceiving a probable connection between them. But he could not adequately account for such unclear knowledge without exposing the weakness of assumptions he had granted from the start.[87]

There is no doubt that Newman borrowed much of Locke's terminology here. Locke spoke of reason as a "largeness of comprehension."[88] He contrasted the "full view" of a "large, sound, roundabout sense" with the "partial views" of the narrow minded.[89] He criticized those who give themselves up "to the contemplation of one sort of knowledge" such that it becomes "everything." He wrote that the mind is best kept from such a possession "by giving it a fair and equal view of the whole intellectual world, wherein it may see the order, rank, and beauty of the whole, and give a just allow-

ance to the distinct provinces of the several sciences." The result
would be "an increase of the powers and activity of the mind, not
. . . an enlargement of its possessions."[90]

Newman also spoke of a liberal education which instills in the
student an "enlargement of mind." He warned of the danger of ex-
alting "into a leading idea and key of all knowledge" the principles
of one science. In fact "the Sciences . . . have multiplied bearings
one on another . . . and demand, comparison and adjustment.
They complete and correct each other." This is the work of an enlarged mind. The result is an acquisition of knowledge "impreg-
nated by Reason," a "comprehensive view," not merely "undigested"
data gathered by men who "load their minds, rather than enlarge
them."[91]

Again, sometimes Newman's examples of "natural inference" are
similar to Locke's examples of reasoning without syllogisms. Locke
spoke of a "country gentlewoman" and Newman of a "peasant"
predicting the weather.[92] There is a similarity in the structure of
Newman's analysis of the "illative sense" and Locke's analysis of
"reason."[93]

But the whole tenor and purpose of Newman's work was to challenge Locke's presuppositions. On Locke's theory of knowledge
"reason" is said to reach "truth in the abstract, and probability in
the concrete." But Newman wrote: "what we aim at is truth in the
concrete." He recognized that Locke's "reason" was artificially
bound by his rationalist definition of knowledge. In the end it is
identical with the clear perception of abstract relations between
ideas. But Newman complained, "arguments about the abstract
cannot handle and determine the concrete. They may approximate
to a proof, but they only reach the probable, because they cannot
reach the particular."[94]

Newman's "illative sense" does not denote the perception of relations between ideas. It stands for a complex use of reason in knowing the real, the concrete, the particular. It stands for our ability
to know, not merely claim to know or guess. It stands for our ability
to explore "aspects" of things; to know what is the case; to advance
objective knowledge; to know what is probable and to recognize
error.[95]

In the end Newman would agree with Locke that to know is to be
certain. He wrote that when an objective assent is placed "then the

assent may be called a *perception*, the conviction a *certitude*, the proposition or truth a *certainty*, or thing known, or a matter of *knowledge*, and to assent to it to *know*."[96]

Newman, however, did not mean by "certain" the clear perception of relations between ideas; he did mean an objective grasp of things as they are. Against Locke he directed his inference/assent distinction.

> When, then, philosophers lay down principles, on which it follows that our assent, except when given to objects of intuition or demonstration, is conditional, that the assent given to propositions by well-ordered minds necessarily varies with the proof producible for them, and that it does not and cannot remain one and the same while the proof is strengthened or weakened,—are they not to be considered as confusing together two things very distinct from each other, a mental act or state and a scientific rule, an interior assent and a set of logical formulas?[97]

In other words, to assent or grasp that something is the case because of a complex of evidence is not the same as inferring that something follows from premises. Some philosophers assume that experience, acted upon by syllogistic reasoning, can only result in probabilities. They conclude that "certitude is ever a mistake." In this case, our experience is made to be less than it is. Others grant the same assumption but reject the conclusion. Instead they attempt to rest the certainty of knowledge on "intuitions, intellectual forms and the like, which belong to us by nature." In this case, our experience is made to be more than it is. Newman refused to take either approach. He maintained the certainty of knowledge but rejected the assumption which forced the latter school to appeal to unjustified intuitions in its defense. "I think it enough," he wrote, "to appeal to the common voice of mankind in proof of it."[98]

In brief, Newman criticized any *a priori* rejection of the possibility of certain knowledge. Without resorting to an infallible faculty for discriminating truth from error, he simply appealed to the fact that we do know (are sure) of a great many things. He called for a reinstatement of knowledge as an objective (certain) grasp of what is the case. He was not accepting Locke's way of ideas and then calling upon illation to perceive probable relations between ideas. What he was in fact calling for was a different analysis of objective (certain) knowledge in the first place.

References

1. *Essay*, Intro. 2 (1:26); see Lord King, *Life and Letters of John Locke with extracts from his Journals and Common-place Books* (London, 1864) 106.

2. See Yolton, *Way* viii.

3. See *Works* 4:48 ("First letter to the Bishop of Worcester" 1697); see above 15–16, n. 63.

4. Gibson, 207; *Works* 4:48–49 ("First letter to the Bishop of Worcester" 1697); see James Collins, *British Empiricists* (Milwaukee, 1967) 35–36.

5. See O'Connor, 155; also 202: "The empiricist who tries to derive all human knowledge from sensation and reflection [in Book Two] becomes the rationalist who bases knowledge on the intuition of self-evident relations between ideas." But see Charlotte S. Ware, "Influence of Descartes on John Locke" *Revue Internationale de Philosophie* 4 (1950) 227: Locke's "rationalism is subordinate to his non-Cartesian empiricism." See also Richard I. Aaron, *John Locke* (1937) (Oxford, 1955) 222; and Fraser's edition of the *Essay* 2:177 note 2.

6. *Essay* IV:1.2 (2:167). The mind is concerned directly with its own ideas. For Locke these ideas are independent units synthesized in knowledge through an intuition of relations between them. While the idea is the mind's immediate object, Locke admitted that the mind is oriented mediately toward an apprehension of real being.

7. *Works* 4:145 ("First reply to the Bishop of Worcester" 1697).

8. Sometimes Locke used "judgment" for the certain act of perception; sometimes for a faculty that does not yield certain knowledge; see Collins, *Empiricists* 33; Gibson, 121–122; *Essay* IV:14.4 (2:362).

9. *Essay* IV:2.1 (2:177–178).

10. René Descartes, *Rules for the Guidance of Our Native Powers*, (1619–1628) in *Descartes' Philosophical Writings* (trans.) N. K. Smith (New York, 1958) 10. Descartes' discussion of deduction parallels Locke's on demonstration; his discussion of "sagacity" (Rule 10) is perhaps a latent source of Locke's discussion of "reason" or "illation."

11. *Essay* II:1.18 (1:137).

12. *Ibid.* 1.10 (1:129).

13. *Works* 4:362 ("Second reply to the Bishop of Worcester" 1699).

14. *Ibid.* 380; also 390; see Gibson, 214, 231–232; Ware, 226–227: "the object of Descartes' intuition is intellectual; that of Locke's is in every case a relation between ideas derived from experience . . . Moreover, his doctrine of 'lumen naturale' further illustrates this empiricism."

15. See *Essay* IV:3.29 (2:221); *Works* 4:62 ("First letter to the Bishop of Worcester" 1697).

16. *Draft* 27 (41–42). Aaron is mistaken when he says that the Cartesian notion of intuition is not present in the early draft. (Aaron, 220).

17. Gibson, 236; although he also admitted the "closest relation" between Locke's work and general movements of English thought in science, religion and politics.

18. Van Leeuwen, 121. He linked Locke's theory of knowledge to the work of William Chillingworth and John Tillotson in religion, and to the work of John Wilkins, Joseph Glanville, Robert Boyle and Isaac Newton in science. In places Van Leeuwen seems to have stretched evidence to support his thesis. For example, he quoted Boyle: "A clear light or evidence of perception, shining in the understanding affords us the greatest assurance we can have . . . of the truth of the judgments we pass upon things . . . [Reason knows] immediately and as it were, intuitively, by evidence of perception." (See Boyle's "Advices in judging of Things said to transcend Reason," (1681) in *Works of Robert Boyle* (London, 1772), 4:460–461; and Van Leeuwen 99–100. This essay was added to Boyle's "Things above Reason" (1681). Its authorship is not established; but Boyle probably approved its content.) Yet Van Leeuwen concluded: "Boyle seems . . . to recognize as a real possibility that all knowledge . . . may in fact be false." (Van Leeuwen 101).

19. Van Leeuwen 13–48 on religion, and especially 90–120 on science.

20. *Essay* IV:2.14 (2:185). Van Leeuwen borrows the term "constructive scepticism" from Richard H. Popkin, *The History of Scepticism from Erasmus to Descartes* (New York, 1961); see Van Leeuwen, 12; also 121–142 on Locke. Roger S. Woolhouse has suggested that Locke did not "rule out . . . that the . . . laws formulated in natural philosophy . . . are instructively certain." (Woolhouse, *Locke's Philosophy of Science and Knowledge* (Oxford, 1971) 25). Locke's distinction between certain knowledge and probable opinion is only one between a-priori (analytic) and a-posteriori (synthetic) knowledge (17–18). Locke is not saying we cannot be certain in the latter case, but only that we cannot be certain a-priori. Woolhouse, however, rejects this dichotomy as "rationalism" artificially distinguishing what is "true by definition" and what is "grounded in the world" (27). Instead Woolhouse rests both on linguistic convention (163–182). Much evidence in Locke, however, seems to count heavily against Woolhouse's interpretation.

21. *Draft* 29(50); also *Draft* 27(41); see Patrick Romanell, "Locke and Sydenham: A Fragment on Smallpox 1670" *Bulletin of the History of Medicine* 32 (1958) 295; also Aaron, 237.

22. *Essay* IV:3.26, 3.29 (2:217–218, 223).

23. *Ibid.* 5.8 (2:248–249).

24. *Ibid.* 6.7 (2:255).

25. *Ibid.* 6.13, 15.3 (2:263, 365).

26. *Ibid.* 6.16 (2:266); see Gibson, 134–135; also Jonathan F. Bennett, *Locke, Berkeley, Hume: Central Themes* (Oxford, 1971) 123 where he argues that Locke's discussion of "nominal" species avoids skepticism and makes room for scientific advance. But see Collins, *Empiricists* 32–33 distinguishing "the meaning of 'species' in metaphysics and in the natural sciences," and defending "the realistic claim that the

human mind can gain a minimal, essential knowledge of at least the nature of man and the broad division between the living and the non-living," while admitting that "the limitations of human intelligence and the relative opacity of material things prevent us from having a perfect vision of the structures of material things, and recommend the cultivation of the various scientific techniques of descriptive analysis."

27. *Essay* IV:4.12 (2:237).

28. See *Works* 4:184 ("First reply to the Bishop of Worcester" 1697). Other critics were Henry Lee, *Anti-Scepticism* (London, 1702); and John Sergeant, *Method of Science* (London, 1696) and his *Solid Philosophy Asserted* (London, 1697). Sergeant sent Locke a copy of *Method* on 10 May 1696 with a letter saying that the "most substantial Difference" between them was about the role of "Identicall Propositions." For Sergeant, all truths are resolved into such propositions which are "taken from the Things without us" as their *"Metaphysical Verity, or their being what they are." (Locke MS* c. 18 folio 134). Yolton noted that Sergeant tends to confuse metaphysical and logical principles while legitimately arguing that knowledge presupposes an objective (certain) grasp of what is the case. (Yolton, *Way* 74–114).

29. *Essay* IV:1.2 (2:168).

30. *Ibid.* 4.2 (2:228).

31. *Ibid.* 1.3 (2:227–228). See Bennet, 59–88 (especially section 12) arguing that Locke's appearance/reality distinction is a misuse of language. Once a "veil of perception" is set up, every effort to break through it or find a causal link begs the question for one would need independent access to empirical facts to establish a link. Bennett is employing a Humean notion of "cause" where by definition a constant conjunction can be recognized only when both terms can be independently identified. Bennett's alternative to Locke's appearance/reality distinction however is to argue that "reality is a logical construction out of appearance." (68).

32. *Essay* IV:3.6 (2:195).

33. *Ibid.* 15.2 (2:364).

34. *Ibid.* 20.15 (2:454).

35. *Ibid.* 16.9 (2:376–377); see IV:17.16 (2:409): "sometimes . . . the probability is so clear and strong, that *assent* as necessarily follows it as *knowledge* does demonstration;" see also *Draft* 34 (57–58): "These Probabilitys rise soe neare to certain knowledg . . . That they governe our thoughts as absolutely . . . as the most evident demonstration . . . We make little or no difference between these Probabilitys and certain Knowledg, and our Faith thus grounded arises to Assurance."

36. See Ashcroft, 209; but also Aaron, 245.

37. See Van Leeuwen, 135; and *Essay* IV:16.6–9 (2:375–377) on degrees of probability.

38. *Essay* IV:2.14 (2:185).

39. *Ibid.* 3.14 (2:203).

40. Gibson, 122–123, citing Locke's *Works* 4:229 ("Second reply to the

Bishop of Worcester" 1699). See also O'Connor, 202; Gibson, 2–3; and Aaron, 221, who have found Locke more rationalist than empiricist here.

41. *Essay* II:13.18 (1:299); II:30.1 (1:497); see IV:4.3 (2:228). Insofar as Locke's way of ideas renders incoherent any effort to explain how a connection could be established between ideas and the things they signify he hinted at an appeal to linguistic convention and noted that "in referring our ideas to those of other men, called by the same names, ours may be false." *Essay* II:32.10 (1:518); also II:32.12, 17, 26 (1:518, 521, 525); IV:5.8 (2:248). But linguistic convention alone cannot be a criterion of correct usage or real reference. See William C. Kneale, "Are Necessary Truths, True by Convention?" *Proceedings of the Aristotelian Society* suppl. 21 (1947) 118–133; Woolhouse, 170–171; and the discussion by R. M. Hare, S. Körner and Paul Henle, "Symposium: the Nature of Analysis," *Journal of Philosophy* 54 (1957) 741–766.

42. *Essay* IV:2.14 (2:188). Newman marked this passage in his copy.

43. *Ibid.* 14.4 (2:362).

44. Aaron, 245.

45. See Yolton, *Way* 72–114, who cited an anonymous essay explaining that, for Locke, ideas are treated as independent entities such that they "are wholly owing to the Mind, and are indeed nothing else but the natural Operations of the Mind upon the several Objects presented to it." ("A Philosophical Essay Concerning Ideas" (1705) 20, in Yolton, *Way* 97). John Sergeant wrote in the preface to his *Transnatural Philosophy or Metaphysiks* (London, 1700) paragraph 23, that "The *Way of Ideas* should be *lay'd Aside.*"

46. Collins, *Empiricists* 43. Collins noted that Locke's doctrine implicitly rebukes attempts to measure the real world by the scope of our knowledge.

47. *GA* 196.

48. *Essay* IV:4.3 (2:228).

49. *GA* 232.

50. *MS* A.30.11 (Certainty and Probable Evidence: 26 June 1865).

51. *GA* 222.

52. *MS* A.30.11 (Certainty and Probable Evidence: 26 June 1865).

53. *MS* A.18.11 (Notes on Logic and Philosophy: January-February 1859).

54. *GA* 280.

55. *Ibid.* 267; see also 22, 282.

56. *Ibid.* 30–31.

57. Brian J. Wicker, "Newman and Logic," *Newman-Studien* 5 (1962) 254.

58. See *GA* 279–283, 9–10.

59. *Ibid.* 31.

60. See Wicker, "Logic" 130–131, 53–54.

61. *PN* 2:15–17, 13 ("Faculty of Abstraction" 27 January 1859); see *GA* 62, 65, 260–261.

62. *GA* 30; see Wicker, *Logic* 132.

63. *MS* A.30.11 (Apprehension and Assent: 26 April, 5 May, 7 September 1868).

64. *GA* 32. See Collins, *Readings* 41; *GA* 75, 11; and see below 145–155.

65. See Wicker, "Logic" 122, also 134: "it seems that Newman is not clear enough in his language to be free of some remaining taint of Lockean epistemology, however right he is about the essential matters involved in his argument." See also Wicker's valuable discussion of abstraction in men with whom Newman was familiar, namely Henry Aldrich (55–71), John Hill (72–84), John Campbell (84–87), Richard Whately (88–101), and Henry L. Mansel (102–111). Also on nominalism in Newman see *PN* 1:167–170; Zeno, 64–65; Walgrave, 83–84; Boekraad, *Personal Conquest* 161–169. Boekraad seems to have gone too far in insisting that Newman never fell into a nominalist way of speaking. Also see John F. Cronin, *Cardinal Newman: His Theory of Knowledge* (Washington, 1935) 82–83, summarizing the charge that Newman was a nominalist made by French, German and English authors. Cronin concluded: "Newman was not . . . a nominalist. He explicitly makes the evidence of truth something other than the distinctness and the vividness received by sense or imagination. 'I wish to go by reason, not by feeling.' " (*Apo* 172; Cronin, 98).

66. *Essay* IV:12.9 (2: 348).

67. *Ibid.* 12.14 (2:354).

68. *GA* 227.

69. Both Locke and Newman felt that in practice life is too short to wait for demonstration, (compare *Essay* IV: 14.1 (2:360) and *DA* 295 ("Tamworth Reading Room" February 1841)), and that what is "conceivable" is not a sure test of what is true (compare *Essay* IV:10.19 (2:322) and *PN* 2:153 (7 September 1861), *Idea* 400–401 ("Form of Infidelity of the Day" 1854)).

70. *Essay* IV:7.19 (2:290).

71. *Ibid.* 7.11 (2:279); see IV:7.12–13 (2:285–287).

72. *GA* 263.

73. *Ibid.* 270.

74. *Ibid.* 271.

75. *Essay* IV:15.2 (2:364).

76. *Ibid.* 16.6 (2:376).

77. *Ibid.* 16.6 and 11 (2:377 and 378).

78. *GA* 160–161.

79. *Essay* IV:17.4 (2:391). He wrote that men must see by reason the relations between ideas "as well before as after the syllogism is made, or else they do not see it at all." (*Ibid.* (2:395)).

80. *Ibid.* (2:396–398); see *ibid.* (2:392 and 400). Locke included under syllogism any reasoning "which has at least one *general* proposition in it." (*Ibid.* 17.8 (2:404)). Newman also included under verbal argumenta-

tion "all inferential processes whatever . . . for they all require general notions, as conditions of their coming to a conclusion." (*GA* 283).

81. *Essay* IV:17.2 (2:386–387).

82. *Ibid.* 17.1 (2:386).

83. *Ibid.* 17.2 (2:387); see IV:2.3 (2:179); IV:3.18 (2:207); IV:12.7 (2:346) calling for a "sagacious and methodical application of our thoughts;" also *Draft* 39, 41 (60, 62) on the need for "skill to use the evidences . . . of probability;" and *Locke MS* f. 5:77–83 ("Journal" 26 June 1681) on "a sagacity of enquiring into probable causes." (*Ibid.* 81).

84. O'Connor, 196–197.

85. *GA* 166.

86. *Essay* IV:15.1 (2:363). Here "proofs" mean "intervening ideas" in a demonstration.

87. See O'Connor. 192, 197 and Leo W. Keeler, *The Problem of Error from Plato to Kant,* Analecta Gregoriana vol. 6 (Rome, 1934) 214–221, who argued that Locke's original distinction between knowledge and judgment "does not go far in explaining how a man can (which he admits) be firmly convinced, after deliberation, of the truth of something that is not so." (220).

88. *Essay* IV:17.7 (2:403).

89. *Works* 3:190 ("Conduct of the Understanding" 1698).

90. *Ibid.* 219–220.

91. *Idea* 106, 77, 99, 111 (1852); and *US* 286, 288–289 ("Wisdom, as Contrasted with Faith and with Bigotry" 1 June 1841). Compare *Essay* IV:3.20 (2:211) with *Idea* 474–478 ("Christianity and Scientific Investigation" 1855), and *Jfc* 189 on the need to let truth have full play.

92. *Essay* IV:17.4 (2:392); *GA* 332. Newman's examples of being certain of historical or geographical facts (*GA* 177–178) also occur in Hume: "That Caesar existed, that there is such an island as Sicily: for these propositions, I affirm, we have no demonstrative nor intuitive Proof. Would you deny that I approve their Truth or even their Certainty?" (Hume to John Stewart, February 1754, in John Y. T. Greig, *Letters of David Hume* (1932) (Oxford, 1969) 1:187); also see *Treatise* I:3.11 (Selby-Bigge 124). Similar examples are also found in John Tillotson, *Rule of Faith* (London, 1666) 117–118.

93. Compare *Essay* IV:17.3 (2:388) and *GA* 362–363.

94. *GA* 279, 278.

95. See *Ibid.* 237, 239.

96. *Ibid.* 196; see *Works* 4:145 ("First reply to the Bishop of Worcester" 1697).

97. *GA* 179.

98. *Ibid.* 343–344. Locke the empiricist would be in the first category; while perhaps, Locke the rationalist would be in the second.

CHAPTER V

NEWMAN ON KNOWLEDGE

The fact of objective (certain) knowledge

The question "what is absolute assent?" or "what is certain knowledge?", like the question "what is faith?", can have various meanings. Ultimately what one means by this question will depend on what he means by the word "certain."

In one sense "to be certain" means to be (psychologically) confident about what could be false. In this sense, certainty is a state of mind, a sense of composure, a conviction that something is indubitable or beyond reasonable doubt. Here it makes perfect sense to speak of "mistaken certainties," convictions which turn out to be false.

In a second sense "to be certain" means to know that something must be true because it is (logically) necessary. Its contrary, not only is not so, but cannot possibly be so. Here it makes no sense to speak of "mistaken certainties." To be certain is not to be mistaken.

Locke held that to know is to be certain in this second sense. Consequently "knowledge" properly denotes the perception of necessary relations between clear ideas. The rest of our so-called knowledge amounts to "judgment" or uncertain belief proportioned to evidence which provides the premises of our reasoning.[1]

Newman on occasion drew attention to a third sense of "to be certain." In this classical sense it simply means to grasp that something is the case. To know is to be certain in this sense. Here certitude about a thing means the knowledge of its truth: "Certitude . . . is the perception of a truth with the perception that it is a truth, or the consciousness of knowing, as expressed in the phrase, 'I know that I know,' or 'I know that I know that I know,'—or simply 'I know'; for one reflex assertion of the mind about self sums up the series of self-consciousnesses."[2]

Certainty in this sense has much in common with psychological certainty. It involves a "feeling of satisfaction and self-gratulation, of intellectual security." In fact, Newman wrote, "the attainment of what is true is attested by this intellectual security." But it is not the same as a psychological confidence about what could be false, for it implies "the attainment of what is true." It is not simply a subjective conviction that what could be false, is not false. Newman wrote that "prejudice" may be "indefectible," but, he added, "it cannot be confused with certitude, for the one is an assent previous to rational grounds, and the other an assent given expressly after careful examination."[3] Elsewhere he wrote, "I do not say what seems like certainty is sufficient evidence to an individual that he has the truth."[4] Indefectibility is a *"sine qua non"*[5] condition, but not an adequate description of objective knowledge.

Certainty in Newman's sense also bears some resemblance to logical certainty. "No man is certain of a truth, who can endure the fact of its contradictory existing or occurring; and that not from any set purpose or effort to reject that thought, but . . . by the spontaneous action of the intellect."[6] But to be certain in this sense is not the same as to be certain about what is logically necessary. In the latter case logical principles render the alternative impossible. But in the former case, although the alternative could be so, one knows "by the spontaneous action of the intellect" that it is not so.

Newman did not build his analysis of certainty on the fact that we experience feelings of conviction, nor on the fact that some propositions are logically necessary. He built his discussion around the fact that we do and therefore can achieve objective (certain) knowledge. Certainty in this sense involves a "careful examination" of evidence. But in the end it is not simply a conviction or feeling more or less justified by such an examination. It is not simply an opinion, a justified opinion, but nonetheless an opinion. Rather "probabilities of a special kind, a cumulative, a transcendental probability . . . carries us on to a certitude."[7] Writing elsewhere, he said, "The intellect, which is made for truth, can attain truth, and, having attained it, can keep it, can recognize it, and preserve the recognition."[8]

Newman recognized that it is not enough to argue that if a claim turns out to be false it was not a case of knowledge simply because knowledge, by definition, has truth for its object.[9] If we find we were mistaken, it is because of various reasons which are sayable in defense of our knowledge that we were wrong. But the fact of mistakes does not mean that we can never objectively know (be sure) of anything and can only make claims to know which are more or less, but never conclusively, established.[10]

His discussion of certain knowledge is closely related to his analysis of religious faith. Supernatural faith is *like* objective knowledge in so far as neither of them can be adequately described as a justified opinion. The firmness of assent given to ordinary matters of fact might be explained by the practical need to act as if one were certain. The firmness of religious assent might be ascribed to "the living power of faith." But Newman was dissatisfied with this view because "it did not go to the root of the difficulty."[11] It assumed and did not expose a confusion, first about the cognitive nature of faith, and then about the objective nature of knowledge.[12]

In order to make clear Newman's sense of certainty it is helpful to reconsider Locke's alternative. On Locke's view, outside logical necessities—that is, in ordinary matters—we do not "know" but only "claim to know." This claim is a belief, and to "know" in this improper sense is to entertain a belief which is justified and true. But what has happened? The skeptic has been given the case; that is, it is admitted that we cannot know or be certain. We can only make a claim to know which in principle cannot be completely justified for various reasons. Once we start a process of justification, a regress opens up until we arrive at "basics" of one sort or another. But even then we do not "know" these basics in the sense of simply grasping them as actual.

There are some variations on this central theme. Psychologism will argue that although we cannot be certain and therefore do not know the "basics" on which our beliefs rest, our minds are such that we cannot help taking them for granted. Often this position is accompanied by the pious advice that one should not be concerned about the skepticism this position implies, for God is good in having structured our minds as they are.

On occasion Newman seems to have adopted this approach.[13] He frequently appealed to the spontaneous action of the human mind. He wrote that our knowledge of right and wrong, our conscience, cannot be resolved "into any combination of principles in our nature, more elementary than itself;" it is simply a "law of the mind."[14] He wrote that it seemed "unphilosophical" to speak of trusting our capacity to perceive or reason. "We are what we are, and we use, not trust our faculties . . . We act according to our nature, by means of ourselves, when we remember or reason. We are as little able to accept or reject our mental constitution, as our being."[15] But he did not mean to endorse a form of theoretical psychologism.

Between 1857 and 1860 Newman made notes on logic and psychology. During his last months as rector of the short-lived Catholic University in Dublin, he began to think of returning to work on his "magnum opus." At Oxford a new era of "scientism" was gaining ground. Whately's *Elements of Logic* was replaced by John Stuart Mill's *System of Logic* which claimed to explore the evidence and inductive methods of scientific investigation. Consequently in May 1857 Newman began a fresh course of philosophical reading with a study of Mill's *Logic*.[16] In his notes on Mill, he distinguished the activity of reason in coming to know (be certain) from a psychological tendency to accept what is familiar.

Mill distinguished real and verbal propositions, a distinction which, he wrote, "corresponds to that which is drawn by Kant and other metaphysicians between what they term analytic and synthetic judgments."[17] He allowed that some real propositions reflect a regularity in experience such that we naturally (psychologically) take them for certain, although they are not certain in the (logical) sense that they must be true of all possible experience. The law of causation "stands at the head of all observed uniformities, in point of universality, and therefore . . . in point of certainty . . . being thus certain it is capable of imparting its certainty to all other inductive propositions which can be deduced from it."[18] Although Mill wanted to attribute to this law an objective certainty which could support scientific inferences, given his nominalist premises, he could give no adequate justification of this belief.[19] His justification tended toward a subjective psychologism.

Newman read Mill and noted: "Does he not . . . confuse conception with imagination? . . . there are many things which we conceive or (whatever word we use) which we hold before our intellect, which we cannot imagine. Abstract words imply conceptions which are not still imaginations."[20] Newman argued that while experience is the measure of our knowledge, "metaphysically it seems dangerous to lay no stress on the active power of the mind, to appear to resolve phenomena into passive sensation."[21] Mill seemed to take the mind as a faculty of imagination which generalized uniform patterns from passively experienced sensations. Instead, Newman would begin with various propositions about the uniformity of nature or the rightness and wrongness of action which all men hold "from the first use of reason" to be true. He would not consider "the *question of their origin,* whether intuitive, or instinctive or from experience" but would simply appeal to the fact of knowledge as it occurs.[22]

Later Newman made further notes on the faculty of reason "by which we arrive from things known to things unknown." Because we are "limited" this faculty "necessarily" results in knowledge which is certain but surprising. We can mistake imagination for reason, although they are quite distinct: "what is *strange* is to the imagination *false.*" Because of this, "strictly rational processes" are always "leading to a conclusion which we are ready to reject as irrational only because it is strange."[23] The activity of mind by which we become (epistemologically) certain of what is the case is distinct from the activity of imagination in making us (psychologically) certain of what is familiar. In 1859 Newman also distinguished it from the activity of reason by which we become (logically) certain of what is necessarily true.

In its proper sense logic is simply "the Science of Proof or Inference . . . Aristotle calls it an instrumental art . . . it is not concerned with the truth or falsity of the subject matter, but is hypothetical." But there is also a "logic improper . . . which is concerned with truth and certainty." It is concerned with the "mutual action and intercommunion" between "external objects" and the "soul itself and its faculties." It determines the "criteria by which we are certain that we have possession" of genuine knowledge and distinguishes such knowledge "from counterfeits." It discusses in detail "the origin of ideas, the certainty of the senses, the common sense of nature, the nature and grounds of faith, and all those matters which relate to the truths of the premises from which Logic proper argues."[24]

When Newman described reason as a faculty or "power of taking views or aspects"[25] he meant to draw attention to a sense of certainty, knowledge and reason which is not adequately analyzed in psychological or logical terms. A subjective empirical psychologism accepts Locke's limitation of (certain) knowledge to the perception of logical necessity. It goes on to say that every other "claim" to know is due to the structure of our minds. We become convinced that certain propositions are true, not because we grasp what is the case, but because this is our necessary way of thinking. Newman's method was quite different. It could be called an objective critical psychologism. It rejects Locke's analysis as an inadequate account of human knowledge. It invites us to look at our mind, our knowing. It points out that in a complex interchange of intellectual activity and evidence we come to know a great deal about the world. The result is not that we find support for a "claim" to know. Rather through a complex interaction with the world, we come to know what is the case.

Newman wrote that his object was "not to form a theory . . . but to ascertain what is the matter of fact."[26] His intention was not to present psychologism as a theory about how we know but to engage in a critical discussion about what it is to know. Jan Walgrave has described Newman's method as a "practical psychologism" which amounts to a proof that "if we wish to live as human beings, we must, in each act of the mind, admit implicitly that it is made for the truth, that it is, therefore, capable of truth, and that it will find truth if it makes judicious use of its possibilities." Theoretical psychologism accepts the problem of knowledge which nominalism raises, and affirms that it can be solved only by investigating human nature. The result is a distinctive metaphysics of knowledge. But Newman's intention was avowedly practical, not metaphysical. He confined himself to the mind in action, not to exalt its operations into the first principles of a special theory of knowledge, but simply to employ a method which was congenial to himself and sufficient for his purpose. He felt that this approach was the only one which would have any chance of convincing those for whom he wrote the *Grammar of Assent*.[27]

Another common variation on the Lockean theme goes by the name "phenomenalism" and is often tied to what is called a "fallibilist" theory of knowledge. Again it is argued that "knowledge" in the classical sense does not occur. It is absolutely impossible for us to know that something simply is the case. We cannot grasp in an immediate way that something is so, such that we could "know that we know" something. The phenomenalist will allow that we do "know" or objectively grasp sense-data. But the rest of our experience is a more or less workable construction from these basics. One is not sure his wife exists or his child exists while speaking with them. They are not grasped in his knowledge. He only has evidence for them from impressions received through his senses.

John Hick has argued that "it is always possible for a knowledge claim to be erroneous," so that linguistically the expression "I know" should be taken to mean "I (claim to) know."[28] In the last resort we are "thrown back upon the criterion of coherence with our mass of experience and belief as a whole." During the first months of conscious life, we gradually become aware of similarities and repetitions among the many impressions which overwhelm us. An ordered environment begins to dawn. We become conscious of relatively enduring objects and persons, a "de facto stability," which enables us to explore our world and to supplement our own experiences with the reports of others. However, Hick insisted, "no apparent de jure necessity guarantees the persisting structure of our environment." Only as long as it presents itself to our senses, responds consistently to our tests and changes in an orderly way, can we use our cognitive terms with confidence and trust our entire experience as real. "And," he added, "there is nothing to be gained by claiming to possess knowledge in some quite other, mysteriously direct and infallible sense."[29]

Anthony Quinton has argued that "some statements about material objects are basic and thus . . . we can have direct and non-inferential perception of material things."[30] We do not claim to perceive sensations but things, for "every statement must contain a general predicative term." But this remains simply a *claim* to know things. Quinton did not argue that we grasp general knowledge of things. He only argued that sense-statements require, for their meaning, that their terms be used "in accordance with rules" which go beyond what is immediately given. He attempted to enlarge a sense-data theory by appealing to the "mass of background knowledge" which provides meaning-rules that justify but do not certify our knowledge claims. Perception "claims are not, even in standard conditions, incorrigible . . . There is always a certain risk involved." Nevertheless "basic statements acquire some, perhaps small, initial probability from experience."[31]

Quinton tied this "corrigibilist theory" of knowledge to Price's doctrine of "intrinsic probability"[32] and to Ayer's "conception of meaning-rules by which experience renders basic statements probable but does not certify them."[33] He also found support in Karl Popper's remark that knowledge stands upon piles driven more or less securely into the river-bed of experience.[34] Quinton added that this theory "is entirely consistent with the fallibilist conviction that no statement of fact is ever finally and unalterably established . . . It does maintain that knowledge has foundations but it does not regard them as absolutely solid and incorrigible." The argument is that "all description transcends experience since it necessarily embodies universals which cannot . . . be constituted out of experience. Experience can, then, never certify any empirical statement."[35]

Although Quinton's discussion is more fully developed than Hick's, it is enough for our purpose to focus on the latter's brief but pointed statement of this general approach. It is argued that experience can confirm but cannot give absolute assurance about the reality of things. One does not strictly "know" other persons or other things. In a looser sense of experience, a sense which Hick described as "experiencing-as," we do experience other people and physical objects. But strictly we grasp only impressions from experience.[36] From them we make interpretations or inferences. We never simply grasp a real being as it is or directly.

Newman's general argument seems to have been an effort to show that this fundamental empiricist doctrine is false. If it is false, if in fact we do directly know something (that it is the case), then a radically different theory of knowledge becomes possible and necessary. If the nature of experience is such that it gives us an opening to the being of things and does not enclose us in our subjective apprehension of impressions, then the whole logic of our existential claims will also be radically different.

Hick insisted that "knowledge, in the sense of an infallible acquaintance with truth (reality) does not occur." Most direct realists would agree with this. To hold direct realism is not necessarily to endorse infallible intuitions. A failure to grasp this possibility has led to the construction of the phenomenalist/coherence alternative. The argument is that we make mistakes, therefore there is no infallible knowledge, therefore there is no certainty. Hick argued that "we sometimes erroneously *think* we know." There is no sharp psychological distinction between supposed-knowing which is later proved erroneous, and any of our contemporary non-knowing. Consequently any of my knowledge claims could be erroneous as well.[37] He seems to have implied that unless we have a test that works according to some *a priori* rule, by which we can sort out kinds of knowing from one another, we can never be certain of anything.

Newman was aware of the fact that we often make mistakes, that men often "change" their opinions and are "as confident and well-established in their new opinions as they were once in their old . . . They set out in youth with intemperate confidence in prospects that fail them . . . and they end their days in cynical disbelief of truth." The question arises: "How then can certitude be theirs, how is certitude possible at all, considering it is so often misplaced, so often fickle and inconsistent, so deficient in available criteria." The fact of mistakes seems to threaten the possibility of any certain (objective) knowledge. "The very possibility of certitude" would be "destroyed by the introduction of a reasonable doubt, underlying" all my assertions. They would be "nothing more to me than opinions or anticipations, judgments on the verisimilitude of intellectual views, not the possession and enjoyment of truths."[38]

However the question Newman raised is: *must* we have a universal test for sorting out all our alleged claims or otherwise be unable to be confident that in a given case we are not in error? Newman wanted to defend the direct perception of persons and physical objects without claiming to have simple, naive and absolutely general empirical ways of guaranteeing the validity of our knowledge claims. Part of his direct realism was precisely the claim that such simplistic efforts to affirm or deny direct knowledge is fruitless. If someone is certain of anything it is not because he puts an infallible faculty to work, but because a complex set of circumstances occur.

Newman argued that it is a mistake "to confuse infalliblity with certitude and to argue that since we have not the one, we have not the other."[39] The two things are quite distinct. I may remember for certain what I did yesterday although my memory is not infallible. I may be quite certain that two and two make four although I often make mistakes in long addition sums. I may be sure that a particular individual is now the head of government without claiming to be infallible. "A certitude," Newman wrote, "is directed to this or that particular proposition; it is not a faculty or gift . . . Infallibility . . . *is* a faculty or gift, and relates, not to some one truth in particular, but to all possible propositions in a given subject-matter."[40] Norman Malcolm seems to have argued in a similar way against allowing the possibility of error to undermine all certainty. In some circumstances it is very reasonable to temper our confidence by recalling that errors occur. "But," he added, "it is a mistake to suppose this to be reasonable in all circumstances." It would be "a caricature of good reasoning."[41]

Could one interpret his hearing experience incorrectly and think he hears a car when he does not? Of course. And is this not true of sight as well? Certainly. Then he could not have a direct and therefore certain grasp of reality. But why? I *know* that I have made mistakes precisely because I have checked and learned what was the case. Suppose I am walking in the moonlight and think I see a man standing in the trees. I draw closer and find for certain that what I took to be a man is but a shadow. What could it *mean* to say I might be wrong here? What future evidence could overturn that? Newman considered that the "abstract" argument that we have been mistaken in the past is "impotent when directed against good evidence lying in the concrete."[42]

Frequent error should make us cautious, but it does not undermine our ability to grasp what is the case after a careful consideration. A clock that goes wrong needs regulating but it is not to be discarded. A conscience that errs needs to be educated but it is not rendered useless once corrected. Our intellectual functions are not destroyed by occasional "disarrangements" in their operation. If they were, then we could not talk about any "normal constitution" of the mind. "If we are never to be certain," Newman wrote, "after having been once certain wrongly, then we ought never to attempt a proof because we have once made a bad one."[43]

The problem of error is not to find out whether there can be objective (certain) knowledge; but to find out how mistakes are reconcilable with it. Both Hick and Newman insisted that we have no infallible test of truth.[44] But they drew quite different conclusions.

Hick concluded that we cannot be certain of anything at all: that it is so. We can only have *evidence* that things may be so, and this evidence itself is in principle defeasible. For if we were certain we had evidence we would have directly grasped the reality of something, namely the evidence itself. Newman however concluded that we do know some things are so although we do not have clear and distinct rules to help us judge what subjective impressions are reporting realities. In fact we actually encounter, not subjective impressions or interpretations of or calculations from subjective impressions at all. "We are in a world of facts."[45] And again, "The senses . . . bring home to us that certain things are, and *in confuso* what they are."[46]

Newman made use of two dialectical arguments to support his position. First, if knowledge were always uncertain we could never be sure we were ever mistaken. But sometimes we are sure of this, not because we have put an infallible faculty to work, but because we have engaged in a complex activity which we call "knowing." Secondly, if knowledge were always uncertain we could never be sure that one opinion is closer to the truth than another opinion. But sometimes we are sure of this, again, through a complex activity by which we know what is the case.

He recognized that often the best we can achieve is a reasonable conjecture, a guess, on the basis of evidence which we know. When we do know some things, we often do not know but can only guess whether they point toward other things. Science as well as religion "opens into a large field of mere opinion." But, he added:

> In both the one and the other the . . . fundamental, cardinal truths are immutable. In human matters we are guided by probabilities, but . . . they are probabilities founded on certainties. It is on no probability that we are constantly receiving the informations and dictates of sense and memory, of our intellectual instincts, of the moral sense, and of the logical faculty. It is on no probability that we receive the generalizations of science, and the great outlines of history. These are certain truths; and from them each of us forms his own judgments and directs his own course, according to the probabilities which they suggest to him.[47]

Earlier Newman wrote that "probability does in some sense presuppose and require the existence of truths which are certain."[48] At first sight he seems to have argued that we cannot be sure that something is probable unless we can grasp that something else is so, which provides evidence that justifies our claim. Otherwise we would only be probably justified in taking the evidence as we do in the light of further evidence and so on.[49] However when Newman wrote that probability requires certainty, he was not defending infallible sense-impressions as "basics" on which we construct "hypotheses" about persons and things. Nor was he defending a priori infallible rules according to which we judge that one opinion is probable and another improbable.

C. I. Lewis has written, "If anything is to be probable, something must be certain. The data which support a genuine probability must themselves be certainties." One probable statement may support another but "such confirmation is only provisional and hypothetical, and it must have reference eventually to confirmation by direct experience."[50] Quinton rephrased Lewis' point in terms of a distinction between what Price called hypothetical and categorical probability.[51] The statement: "If John caught the train, he will probably be home by six," is a hypothetical probability. The statement: "Since John has caught the train, he will probably be home by six," is a categorical probability. Lewis was then saying that any belief which is actually and categorically rendered probable and justified presupposes some such "since clause" or grasp of evidence which is not itself justified by further evidence into a regress.

Quinton objected to Lewis' argument on the grounds that "certainty is as much relevant to evidence as probability." If Lewis "admits that experience can certify our terminal empirical beliefs why should he not allow that it could support them partially or render them probable as well?" Quinton argued that Lewis had only shown that there must be an experiential foundation for our probable knowledge—a foundation which for Quinton is never certain in the sense of incorrigible, but only certain in the sense of being beyond reasonable doubt for the time being.[52]

Whether or not Quinton was correct when he said that for Lewis "certainty and incorrigibility are one and the same,"[53] Newman explicitly distinguished certainty (objective knowledge) in his sense from infallibility.[54] Consequently when he wrote that probability presupposes certainty he seems to have meant simply that probability presupposes, in some large sense, an objective grasp of reality gained through a complex of "informations and dictates of sense

and memory, of our intellectual instincts, of the moral sense, and of
the logical faculty."[55] In such cases we are sure of a great many
things. Further we are sure that some other things are possible
while others are not possible. It is because of this complex background of objective (certain) knowledge that we can make reasonable conjectures about what we do not know.

Hick insisted that there is no paradox involved in a fallibilist
theory which claims that we cannot know anything in the traditional sense Newman defended. Hick recognized that it would be
necessary "to meet the familiar charge that such a denial is self-
refuting, on the ground that 'only by knowledge can we know
whether there is such a thing as knowledge.' "[56] That is, the question remains: how do we *know* that we cannot know anything? The
answer cannot be to line up the logical and epistemological arguments employed. For if we knew we did not know, if we were sure
we could not be sure, if we were sure we were mistaken in thinking
we could be sure, we would contradict ourselves. So Hick provided
a humbler statement. He wrote that he was but recommending "a
general abandonment of the infallibilist standpoint . . . *All* our
cognitions . . . are fallible."[57] He insisted that there is no "circular-
ity" or "inconsistency" in holding this belief. But he offered the
recommendation confidently as if, behind it all, there were some line
of full assurance that knowledge claims cannot be valid: that no one
knows things as they are.[58]

Newman's reaction to these various maneuvers was that they are
hypothetical and out of touch with our experience. They are interesting theories, but the fact is that people are sure (in the classical sense) of a great many things. He gave a wide range of examples.

> We all believe, without any doubt, that we exist; that we have
> an individuality and identity all our own . . . that we have a
> present sense of good and evil, of a right and a wrong, of a
> true and a false . . . We have an absolute vision before us of
> what happened yesterday or last year . . . We are sure that of
> many things we are ignorant, that of many things we are in
> doubt, and that of many things we are not in doubt . . . We are
> sure beyond all hazard of a mistake, that our own self is not the
> only being existing; that there is an external world . . . that the
> future is affected by the past . . . that the earth . . . is a globe

. . . that there are vast tracts on it of land and water; that there are really existing cities on definite sites, which go by the names of London, Paris, Florence, and Madrid . . . We laugh to scorn the idea that we had no parents . . . that we shall never depart this life . . . that we are able to live without food . . . that a world of men did not live before our time, or that that world has had no history.[59]

There may be many problems. Often we are not sure and do not know, but we can know (be sure) of this. Often we are mistaken, but we can know (be sure) of this. Often we can only guess, but we can know we are guessing and we can know what is a good guess. In fact we are far more sure of a great many things than we are of phenomenalism or psychologism or any philosophical theory.

Hick argued that there is no self-authenticating, self-guaranteeing intellectual vision.[60] It would seem that he had in mind something like Cartesianism. He seems to have meant that there is no special *kind of knowing*, for example, by clear and distinct ideas and deductions from them, such that by investigating the properties of this kind of knowing one could be sure that the object of knowledge exists. Newman would agree with this. His direct realism does not appeal to such an argument. If a man says that the daughter with whom he is now speaking is a "real, live girl," it is not because he inspects his mode of knowing and the proposition in question, and then applies the general rule that all cognitions of this type are valid. The causes of his certainty are complex, some obvious, some elusive. But he is far more certain that she exists than he is of any theory of knowledge.

Newman occasionally spoke of "intuition" but it is necessary to sort out the various senses in which he used the term. Sometimes he used it to denote an *a priori* self-authenticating intellectual vision such as Descartes seemed to defend. Newman would not allow intuition in this sense. He criticized those who assume that experience cannot bring us to objective (certain) knowledge and then "in order to vindicate the certainty of our knowledge . . . have recourse to the hypothesis of intuitions, intellectual forms, and the like."[61] Such thinkers assume (with Locke) that knowledge strictly denotes the perception of logical relations between clear ideas. But instead of (with Locke) relegating all existential knowledge claims to judgment or opinion, they posit infallible and unsupported intuitions. Newman argued that it is a false dilemma to say we must either adopt a fallibilist theory of knowledge which denies that we can ever be sure of anything, or posit infallible intuitions. Newman wrote of the latter horn of this false dilemma: "What is this but to say that nothing in this world is certain but what is self-evident? that nothing can be absolutely proved?"[62] He refused to defend the being of God by appeal to a "religious sentiment" which, he wrote, "will commonly be *considered* intuition. Yet surely it can be justified by . . . argument. Again there are writers who hold that our knowledge of the uniformity of the operations of nature is intuitive, yet they know well that others consider it is learned from experience."[63]

Newman's own position was that sometimes we do come to know (are sure) through a complex activity of the mind whose exercise is specified or shaped by experience. On the one hand, this is non-inferential. Experience does not support our coming to know in the way premises support the conclusion of an inference. On the other hand, to defend direct realism in this sense is not to endorse Cartesian intuitions. It appears to be such only to those who have assumed that experience cannot bring us to an objective (certain) grasp of the way things are.

In 1833 Newman criticized neo-Platonists who disdained "the calculations of a tedious and progressive reason" and appealed to an "internal vision of the truth." But he qualified his meaning. He meant to reject "the unreal and almost passive illumination" of neo-Platonic theory, not an immediate grasp of existing reality which is part of his own position.[64] He rejected intuition when it is introduced as a substitute for the complex activity of reason in confrontation with experience which is "knowing" in the classical sense. He did not mean to deny that we can and do know in this way.

It is true that Newman was not always clear or consistent. Sometimes he spoke as if all rational activity follows the pattern of formal inference although sometimes the inference is too long and complex to be easily verbalized, and so is called "informal" or even "intuitive." At other times he used the term "intuition" simply to emphasize the spontaneous and personal nature of much of our reasoning.[65]

In 1859 he wrote of an ability in some to "see the truth all of a heap, by one act . . . These truths . . . are *aspects* of objective facts, and may occur to this or that person as naturally as seeing likenesses between persons . . . It is a kind of intuition."[66] Eleven years later he described "natural inference" as "intuition," "genius," or "instinct," "a perception of facts without assignable media of perceiving." Again informal reasoning was described as a "spontaneous perception of truth," "a peculiar and personal mode of abstraction," a "power of looking at things in some particular aspect, and of determining their internal and external relations thereby . . . light breaks in upon us, and our whole judgment . . . is changed."[67]

Newman might appear to have meant that a long inference of converging reasons leads us to a point where we jump to a conviction, where we decide to be certain. There is no direct grasp of the being of things. "Intuition" (in an empirical and non-Cartesian sense) simply denotes our tendency to take basic statements as more or less justified in practice, in terms of the conventions of language and so on.[68]

Informal inference might be merely an implicit, imperfect, and inchoate formal inference. But Newman emphasized that formal and informal inference are irreducible.[69] Informal inference rests on the native power of the mind to grasp directly, in a complex of circumstances, that something is the case. Experience specifies the activity of the mind when it assents to what is objectively (certainly) known. But experience does this in a way which is not reducible to the way in which premises lead to a conclusion in formal inference, articulated or unarticulated. "When the assent which I give to a truth . . . is simple and absolute, I shall call it an intuition, as being an insight into things as they are."[70]

What is the content of this "insight into things as they are?" Newman wrote: "By instinct I mean a realization of a *particular;* by intuition, of a *general* fact—in both cases without *assignable* or *recognizable* media of realization."[71] But Charles Meynell complained that he seemed to deny "the doctrine of immediate perception" or the fact that "we come into immediate contact . . . with *something which resists.*"[72] All we grasp are sense impressions (instinct) and some general principles to guide argumentation (intuition). Meynell was afraid that Newman would be accused of being a "hypothetical realist." He might be taken to mean that we only perceive our own subjective sensations and then postulate an external object as an hypothesis to account for them. A hypothetical realist holds that we cannot prove that such an object exists but conjecture that it does. "A natural realist," Meynell argued, "believes that we immediately perceive the object, and therefore it requires no proof."[73] Newman wrote back that he did not intend to say "that I know . . . by an *argument* from impression on my senses." He meant to say that "I perceive by instinct . . . without *argumentative* media, *through* my senses, but not logically *by* my senses, that there is a thing . . . we do not *prove* external individual objects but *perceive* them."[74] The content of our direct knowledge is not merely a set of sensations from which we argue to general knowledge.[75] In 1860 he had written, " 'There is an unseen world' this I cannot *deny, for the phenomena of sense, of which I am conscious, imply something beyond the object of sense.*"[76] This is not a Cartesian intuition without experiential support. It is not a decision consequent upon a long formal inference from a multitude of converging sensations. Newman called it an "assent upon a condition." In his example, it is an assent upon the "condition" that *"the phenomena of sense . . . imply something beyond the object of sense."*[77]

He recognized that many would reject the possibility of such a mode of reasoning or "insight into things as they are."[78] He had been studying Kant[79] and noted that the analytic/synthetic distinction seemed to assume that there could be no use of reason in confrontation with experience which reaches general objective (certain) knowledge. "I am disposed," he wrote, "to question whether such a distinction between necessary truth and induction or empirical truth is possible in fact, tho' Kant makes it the starting point of his treatise."[80] In writing of an "insight into things as they are" he meant to attack this assumption. We do not merely grasp impressions and make inferences from them. We grasp (are sure) that some things are so. And we know this in such a way that we can reflect further and come to know new truths about the world of our experience.

> If we are to advance conclusions of any kind and extend the range of our knowledge, we are obliged to recognize certain assents . . . as self-evident . . . They are present to our natural discernment . . . though they were simply barren and nothing

came of them. This is the obvious argument for the existence of Intuition.[81]

Objective (certain) knowledge, "deliberate assents . . . convictions or certitudes" are distinct from "prejudices, credulities, [or] infatuations," because the former involve "full consideration" and "examination of rational grounds."[82] But this informal examination can be called intuitive (in a realist and non-Cartesian sense) because it is personal, spontaneous and direct. Professor Aaron has defended an intuition that "pervades the empirical field, giving us . . . not merely certain knowledge of the existence of physical objects, but also certain knowledge of some of the structural features and relations within that physical world, so that we are entitled to think and reason about it."[83] Newman could accept this description of the content of our (certain) knowledge. He wrote that certitude or objective knowledge "follows on investigation and proof . . . is accompanied by a specific sense of intellectual satisfaction and repose, and . . . is irreversible."[84] Yet it is not merely an assent to the conclusion of an inference, a psychological confidence about an opinion, or a decision to be certain. He introduced the expression "illative sense" to denote, not a mysterious infallible faculty, but the complex of intellectual activity by which we come to know. As he wrote to Charles Meynell, "You will be sadly disappointed in my 'illative sense'—which is a grand word for a common thing."[85]

Newman recognized that "truth lies in a well . . . *prima facie* representations . . . do not reach to the real state of things, or put them before us simply as they are."[86] But his point was that *coming to know* in the sense of coming to grasp "the real state of things" is not at all like *justifying a claim to know* by appealing to better known claims which lead to this claim in the way that premises lead to a conclusion. The regress of purely inferential justifications of beliefs (opinions) should not make us seek incorrigible "basics" or self-evident intuitions from which all our knowledge is deduced. It should not make us resort to corrigible "basics" which are more or less self-supported in the practice of life and language. Such maneuvers often amount to what David Braine has called a "dogmatic irrationalism." Braine criticized "the effective abandonment of justification involved in this approach, and the tendency to make all justification depend on inference which leads to it." The foundations of knowledge are placed "beyond the reach of rational support."[87] Instead the regress of inferential justifications should make us recognize that knowledge is not always or necessarily a matter of beliefs justified by other beliefs more sure than themselves.

Critical of a man who kept running back to his arguments and "strengthening the evidence . . . as if our highest assent were only an inference,"[88] Newman noted that William Chillingworth assumed that "certain proof requires another previous proof and that again another and so on *ad infinitum*" unless we reach "something evident of itself."[89] But he argued that this regress only shows that formal "inference comes short of proof in concrete matters." It does not lead us back to "premises which are undeniable" but to what, in a loose sense, might be called "the recondite sources of all knowledge." However these "sources" cannot be isolated as basic statements or principles which provide "an interior, immediate test, sufficient to discriminate" genuine knowledge from any contemporary non-knowing. "Such a test is rendered impossible from the circumstance that, when we make the mental act expressed by 'I know,' we sum up the whole series of reflex judgments which might, each in turn, successively exercise a critical function towards those of the series which precede it."[90]

Newman concluded that "the sole and final judgment" of our knowledge rests with "the personal action of the ratiocinative faculty . . . there is no ultimate test of truth besides the testimony born to truth by the mind itself."[91] But in saying this he did not mean to abandon all justification for our knowledge. He knew it would be "quibbling" to urge that (certain) knowledge has truth for its object, so that when a belief is exposed as erroneous, knowledge did not occur.[92] There must be some sayable "reasons" or "arguments" which, in a very wide sense, can be called upon in defense of our knowledge.[93] "No one will with justice consider himself certain of any matter, unless he has sufficient reason for so considering."[94] But it is a mistake to assume that these reasons must be "basic" evidence or "undeniable" premises from which our knowledge is inferred.

It is also a mistake to seek "basic" *a priori* principles about the reliability of the senses, memory and reason which can be used to derive the rest of our knowledge from immediate sense impressions. The Cartesian empiricists sometimes seems to seek principles or rules

which give one a "right to be sure," principles which are discovered
by introspecting one's mind. These are then made the criteria of
genuine knowledge. But this becomes circular. For if someone wants
to determine in a rational way whether or not he knows or remem-
bers something, he must determine whether it is the case.[95] He
cannot first determine rules that assure the valid operation of his
faculties. "The mind is like a double mirror, in which reflexions of
self within self multiply themselves till they are undistinguishable,
and the first reflexion contains all the rest."[96]

The question arises: how can Newman say both that one must
have "sufficient reasons" for considering himself certain, and that
there is "no ultimate test of truth" besides the testimony of the
mind?[97]
   In the course of his long career he advanced a variety of possible
"tests" of certain truth. In 1850 he wrote that one test of the truth
of an idea is its "being received by others."[98] This is a valuable criterion in religion where divine revelation is given to a community
of believers with a guarantee of its preservation. Deeply struck by
Augustine's words, "the judgment of the whole world is secure,"*[99] he
wrote: "in religious . . . matters we gain truth *not without* devotion and social interchange of thought . . . availing ourselves of
the judgment of the wise and waiting for the consent of the many,
i.e. the consent of the doctors and the sensus fidelium."[100]
   But Newman recognized that, by itself, past tradition and present
universal acceptance by others are inadequate tests of truth. In 1851
he wrote, "tradition is of great and legitimate use as an *initial*
means of gaining notions about historical and other facts . . . to a
certain point. [But] . . . it is *not* sufficient in reason to make us
sure."[101]
   In 1860 he argued that if "truth is irresistible to the human
mind" then universal acceptance might be a sufficient test, for the
acceptance of an idea would "arise from the force with which it
addresses itself to the human mind, considered in its very nature."
But he noted the disagreements among men. He noted that some
philosophers even deny "the being of anything external to their own
minds." He noted that there are truths about which he would remain convinced "though every man I met assured me of the contrary." Moreover, he argued that a lack of agreement might well

be due to "a deficit in intellectual capacity" among certain individuals. Consequently he concluded that "universality of reception not only need not be, but never can be, a property of intuitive truth . . . Mere insensibility to an intuition is not a denial of it."[102]

He suggested that another "test is the *continuance* of an idea upon the mind as true."[103] Again he found this particularly relevant in matters of revelation. "Corruption cannot . . . be of long standing; and thus *duration* is another test of a faithful development" of revealed truth.[104] He often advised prospective converts to "fix a time and observe whether your conviction lasts through it and how it stands at the end of it." For, he wrote, time "solves all doubt; by bringing Truth, his glorious daughter out."[105] Even in secular matters Newman advised the scientist to "be patient" when confronted with what "appears to be contradictory" to what is known to be true. For "like other delinquents" error has a "strong suicidal propensity." The reasonable man will "commit the matter to reason, reflection, sober judgment, common sense; to Time, the great interpreter of so many secrets."[106]

But then the question arises: *why* is continuance in time a test of truth? There is no divine guarantee of endurance in truth in matters of science. Newman suggested that continuance in time provides an indirect guide to truth by revealing the flexibility, utility and coherence of an idea.

Especially in religious matters he noted that it is a "great characteristic" of revealed truth that "it can afford to be . . . free and spontaneous, to vary its aspects, to modify, enlarge, and accommodate itself to times and places without loss of principle."[107] "A power of development is a proof of life . . . for a mere formula either does not expand or is shattered in expanding."[108] He criticized theoretical innovations "on paper" and defended true and living principles on the grounds that they "have been longer in the world; they have lasted longer, they have done harder work, they have seen rougher service."[109] Yet he seems to have been over confident that in science error will, in time, "become but a great bubble, and burst" because it lacks the flexibility and endurance of truth.[110]

Especially in disciplines where one proceeds by way of theory-construction and experimentation, an hypothesis might endure because of its utility in advancing technology, or its ability to account for empirical data. But by themselves these factors are insufficient. Two incompatible theories might both account for data without either one being, in fact, true.[111]

Experience often forces us to submit "to undeniable incompatibilities, which we call apparent, only because, if they were not apparent but real, they could not coexist."[112] In such cases we know that "truth lies in a well,"[113] that "truth cannot be contrary to truth."[114] But we may still not know what is the truth. We may know that a particular theory is safe to act upon, but this is not to know that it is true. "No one would say we believed our house was on fire, because we thought it safest, on a cry of fire, to act as if it was."[115]

Again, a particular theory might endure because it displays a certain internal coherence. But again this is insufficient. Newman criticized those who make "internal consistency stand in the place of external proof."[116] An individual might be unable to be "formally refuted" because he is "fertile in hypotheses in subservience to his main theory, as expedients for successive emergencies."[117] But this is no guarantee of truth. "Logic . . . does not really prove . . . it maps out for us the lines of thought . . . [But] it is neither the test of truth, nor the adequate basis of assent."[118] Or a theory might endure because it is "conceivable" in the light of accepted beliefs and habitual experience. But this, by itself, is also insufficient. Habitual experience has "real force . . . upon the imagination, not upon the reason." Newman argued that it might make something "unlikely" yet what appeared unlikely has often turned out to be true: "Therefore the conceivable is not the same as the true."[119]

He wrote that "when I assent to a proposition, I ought to have some more legitimate reason for doing so, than the brilliancy of the image of which that proposition is the expression."[120] I must rest my assent on experience which provides the "source . . . rule and limit" of the "creations" of science. The philosopher in particular "has special need of a large mind" to keep himself "within the bounds of experience."[121] But this original use of reason in discovering an intelligibility within experience should not be confused with the "ingenuity" of men who make consistency with empirical data the "test" of the truth of their conjectures. Newman warned that "for one happy conjecture and correct conception, there are a hundred false

ones, as we learn from the history of speculations in every kind."[122]
Consistency with habitual experience may be a *prima facie* evidence
of truth, but

> that quality of an hypothesis, even in matters of scientific research
> . . . could hardly suffice, without further reasons, as a demon-
> stration of its being objectively true. As more keys than one may
> open the same lock, so one consistency may be more perfect than
> another, and the most perfect of all may be as yet unimagined.[123]

Thus he admitted that "consistency in a theory so variously tried
and exemplified"[124] might go "a certain way" towards establishing
its truth,[125] but it "is not always the guarantee of truth."[126]

Newman at times confused the methods of experimental science,
metaphysical philosophy and dogmatic theology when speaking of
"tests" of truth, and he sometimes failed to distinguish the different
role such "tests" might play in these quite different disciplines. The
growth of experimental science is not the same as the development
of philosophical insight. And the growth of both scientific and philosophical thought is different again from the development of doctrine in the Church, given a divine guarantee of the preservation
of what has been revealed.

When he discussed objective (certain) knowledge itself, however,
he recognized that here it would be misleading to speak of a "test"
of truth, for this would suggest that our knowledge is always mediated through theoretical constructs, that it does not put us in direct
touch with reality. If this were admitted a regress of justifications
would place the foundations of knowledge beyond rational support.
We would be confined to subjective impressions. We would have
"guesses and imaginations, not . . . knowledge."[127] In the classical sense knowledge is an immediate grasp that something is the
case. Experience as known cannot be a "test" of truth mysteriously
independent of our knowledge of experience itself. Yet it remains,
in some sense, the "sufficient reason" for our knowing (being sure)
that certain things are so. "From the nature of the case," he wrote,
"certainty is its own criterion, for it is mere ascertainment and testimony to a fact, viz. to our apprehension. It is an act of consciousness."[128] Later he wrote, "The truth has a witness to itself in the
mind of man . . . it is congenial to our nature."[129] And still later,
"The sole and final judgment . . . in concrete matter is committed

to the personal action of the ratiocinative faculty . . . and I own I do not see any way to go farther than this."[130]

In 1870 he described the line of thought which brought him to this position. He began with the fact that "the peculiarity of our nature, in contrast with the inferior animals" is that man "is a being of progress with relation to his perfection and characteristic good." This law of progress is carried out "by means of the acquisition of knowledge, of which inference and assent are the immediate instruments." But when he set aside every "antecedent theory" and investigated "the acquisition of knowledge" as it occurs, he discovered a paradox. "The course of inference is ever more or less obscure, while assent is ever distinct and definite." Assent is "in its nature . . . absolute," but it "follows upon what in outward manifestation is . . . complex, indirect, and recondite." These facts brought Newman to conclude that we have no alternative "but to take things as they are." Instead of pretending to possess some sure science that compels us to assent in concrete matters, we are led to admit that "there is no ultimate test of truth besides the testimony born to truth by the mind itself." No matter how perplexing this might be, he added, it is "a normal and inevitable characteristic of the mental constitution of a being like man on a stage such as the world."[131] He found that a similar line of thought brought Aristotle to speak of "*phronesis,* or judgment . . . in matters of conduct." Inference "bids us avoid extremes; but it cannot ascertain for us . . . the golden mean. The authoritative oracle which is to decide our path . . . is seated in the mind of the individual." In practical and speculative matters Newman asked "whither can we go but to the living intellect?"[132]

He began with a fact "the existence of which we cannot deny,"[133] namely, that we do know (are sure) of a great many things. Our knowledge is not a matter of *a priori* intuitions, but neither is it a matter of "guesses and imaginations,"[134] beliefs and opinions, more or less justified by "basic" sense impressions. There is much we do not know. Often we must resort to probable conjectures and theories, but we can know we are guessing. We can know that an opinion is mistaken. We can know that one opinion is closer to the truth than another opinion, and this is possible only because we do know that certain things are so. Again, sometimes we can reflect directly on the knowledge we do possess and arrive at a further understanding of the way things are. "The intellect admits of an education; man is a being of progress."[135]

Newman recognized that our (objective) knowledge cannot be adequately described as an assent to the conclusion of an inference, that something more must be said to explain the certainty of our knowledge. But sometimes he seems to have adopted Locke's epistemology and then argued merely that Locke did not go far enough in allowing a complexity of inferential reasoning which grounds our assent. When he saw that more than this is necessary to account for the certainty (objectivity) of our assent in knowledge, he seems to have drifted into a "voluntarism" where, after a complex and persuasive inference, we decide to be certain.[136] At other times, however, he spoke of an insight or grasp of an intelligibility within a complex of circumstances. In this case he was pointing toward an explanation of knowledge as direct and objective—an explanation which Locke's epistemology could not sustain. In his notes on certainty from 1853 to 1868 Newman fluctuated between voluntarism and direct realism.

As early as 1849 he recognized that (certain) knowledge is "not the mere perception of a conclusion, for then it would vary about with the strength of the premisses—but it is a state, which follows on a conclusion." He recognized that one could know (be sure), for example, that his wife is not an automaton, although there might be "objections in *reason*" which he could not answer. In fact one might *"refuse* further proofs" and say " 'Take them away, my mind is made up, is clear.' "[137] But sometimes Newman described this refusal as if it were nothing more than a decision. In 1853 he wrote that "the belief that a fact or truth is really such" is "not destroyed by objections" but only "by an act of the will."[138]

Recognizing that (certain) knowledge admits of no degrees in its assent, in 1870 he wrote: "We might as well talk of degrees of truth as of degrees of assent."[139] But in 1853 he spoke as if the absolute assent of (certain) knowledge was nothing more than a decision. In fact he called certainty proper "subjective certainty" in contrast with an assent to a conclusion which "admits of degrees" in proportion to the force of the premisses. "Certainty proper" appears to be a decision to be certain about what could be mistaken.[140]

Different words were used to denote the terms of his distinction between knowing and merely concluding. The former was sometimes called "certainty,"[141] "subjective certainty," or "certainty proper."[142] The latter was sometimes called "belief proper,"[143] "conviction,"[144] or "objective certainty."[145] By 1870 he settled on the terms "assent" and "inference" to mark this distinction, and used the term "informal inference" to denote the unique interaction with experience which shapes our knowing. But in 1858 he had spoken as if he were distinguishing a decision to adopt a state of mind, from an assent to the conclusion of an inference resting on premises provided by experience. Certainty, he wrote, "is a state of mind . . . without any sort of fear of mistake, that the proposition in question is true. At the same time . . . that state of mental certainty depends ultimately on the will."[146]

In 1865 he held that "certitude is not the compulsory effect of any process of argument as its proper cause," concluding instead that it is "a free act (to speak generally), just as the acts of conscience are free and depend upon our will . . . While certitude has truth for its object what we thus take to be truth, may be falsehood . . . since no direct available test exists by which we can at once discriminate between truth and falsehood." But Newman hesitated to conclude further that "we ought in all concrete matters to cherish a reserve of doubt . . . speaking, as it were, under correction."[147] Any inference may be "strengthened without limit" but (certain) knowledge is "already a full assent" and cannot be "anything beyond it." It is "created and maintained, not without the exercise of the reasoning faculty, but still (undeniably) not by it alone."[148]

He seems to have accepted that the only possible "exercise of the reasoning faculty" in concrete matters is one of drawing probable conclusions from inferences. In this case, the only thing further that could establish certainty must be a decision to be certain. The individual "makes himself certain." His state of mind "cannot be immediately dependent on the reasons which are its antecedents, and cannot rightly be referred back to them as its producing cause."[149]

But there are also important anti-voluntarist elements in Newman's notes. In fact he compared the "free act" of (certain) knowledge to one's freedom to exercise his conscience in properly evaluating practical questions. One's decision is not independent of evidence. It is made in response to a "duty to be certain," a duty to use one's practical or speculative reason properly in confrontation with experience in a large sense.[150]

In 1853 he distinguished a "conviction" or "opinion" about the conclusion of an inference from "the mental recognition of an alleged fact or truth."[151] While the absolute assent of (certain) knowledge "naturally follows on a conviction," it does not follow "by a mere act of the will." He put it at the head of a number of "postures of mind towards, or modes of receiving, a true proposition," which are "according to nature." It "presupposes as a sine qua non an antecedent act of reason of a definite kind." It is not "simply created by an act of the will."[152] Instead, Newman held that a true proposition "in its own nature" calls for an absolute assent. If we admit that there are objective facts which can be grasped as existing, "it stands to reason that nothing but the loss of our mental powers can hide them . . . from us." For example, we may be aware that "a living, thinking being is with us in the house, is our companion, converses with us, advises, comforts and supports us." As long as we have not lost our minds, nothing could conceal this fact from us. He spoke of a "logical determination of this or any other fact," a "decisive judgment, formed on sufficient proof" which is "irreversible."[153] But knowledge is not simply an irreversible decision following a complex and persuasive inference.

> Before an inference of whatever kind, there is a natural spontaneous act of the mind towards it . . . which I have above expressed under the word 'Assent' . . . So when the reason has drawn an inference the mind at once takes it up and adopts it, and enters it on its catalogue of knowledge . . . And if the inference be . . . a conviction, then a very special acceptance or recognition of it will take place, sui generis, or different from anything else . . . which acceptance is called certainty.[154]

Viewed as "a subject of conviction," an "objective fact" is "relative to premisses" which admit of degrees, but "viewed as a subject of certainty," it is considered simply "in the luminousness of its proof or what is called evidence." When something is objectively (certainly) known to be so, it "stands absolute and as a first principle," it becomes a "starting point" for further reflection. But whether taken as a starting point for reflection or simply in the "luminousness" of its own evidence, "it is simply perceived by the mind."[155]

Newman attempted to clarify the relation of will to knowledge in this sense. "The will cannot hinder an inference from premisses when the premisses are clearly perceived, for that inference is of a necessary character." But "it can hinder" the acceptance of what is known to be true. "The will cannot absolutely create" objective (certain) knowledge "for it is the natural and direct result of conviction, but the will can hinder that direct result from taking place." Objective (certain) knowledge is ultimately "a making up the mind that a thing is true which is proved and therefore is under the control of the will."[156] He compared our freedom to reject the dictates of reason with our freedom to reject mathematical proofs,[157] to ignore a well-formed conscience, or even to suspend our breathing.[158] We are free, after all, to be irrational.

In December 1853 he developed earlier remarks about the "reflex" nature of (certain) knowledge; that is, our self-conscious ability to know that we know what is the case. Again this could be interpreted as an ability to decide that we know (are sure).[159] But this is not what Newman was saying. If I insist that "I met so-and-so today," and someone objects that "it is impossible, for he is out of the country," I might reconsider, go back and speak again with "so-and-so" and say I am sure I am not mistaken; I know I know. Objective (certain) knowledge is "an assent of the mind to an apprehension of a truth with a reference to the grounds or motivum of that apprehension."[160] The mind "contemplates and recognizes the truth in its formal proof."[161]

Certainty is an act . . . of the intellect reflecting on, recognizing, and ratifying its existing apprehension of a truth. Since . . . certainty is a judgment, and a judgment is the assent of the intellect, and again, an apprehension of a truth is a judgment and assent, therefore certainty is the judgment of a judgment, or an assent of the intellect to an assent.[162]

It is clearly not a decision. The irreversible character of such objective (certain) knowledge, the refusal to admit degrees in such an assent, is not due to a decision. It is due to the fact that we have recognized or grasped that something is true and truth does not allow of more or less. There may be varying degrees of the quality or force of evidence which brings one to grasp that certain things are so—that two and two are four or that I am now sitting on a chair. "It follows," Newman asserted, "that though we cannot be more or less *certain* of the truth, we can be certain of it with more vigour, keenness, and directness according to the quality of the motiva/evidentia in the particular case." He continued, "The same certainty may vary in its evidentia and consequent vigour."[163] A person may now have new and perhaps more compelling evidence about a fact of which he was all along certain.[164]

When we objectively grasp that something is so, we reject "the faintest chance of our being mistaken."[165] If we cannot know in this sense, if we can only claim to know, then this attitude could only be due to an obstinate decision to ignore difficulties. But if we can and do come to know that something is the case, if there is "a recognition of an apprehension of a truth,"[166] then even "indissoluble difficulties" which "we cannot answer"[167] leave us unshaken "for we cannot apprehend falsehood."[168]

In 1865 Newman put the question to himself: if we say that the absolute assent of objective (certain) knowledge is not "immediately dependent on the reasons which are its antecedents . . . as its producing cause," is it then an "arbitrary" act (decision) or "in any way directed by reason" (insight)?[169] He answered by saying that the certain assent of knowledge amounts to the recognition of what is true.

> What is brought home to the mind in whatever way as having an objective existence, this it elevates (whatever it is) unto a higher order of thought. It gives it, as it were, an *imprimatur,* or accords it a registration on the catalogue of things which are to be taken for granted. Or to keep close to the word itself, the act of certitude is a *certifying* it or giving a *certificate* which henceforth will be its passport and protection . . . When I make an act of certitude . . . I am contemplating a fact in itself . . . apart from the means by which I gained it. Sense, logic, authority, testimony belong to the process; the result is beyond them and independent of them, and stands by itself, as long as I choose, created and dependent on myself as an individual and free agent.[170]

The intellect asserts "that what it is contemplating subjectively has an existence outside of me . . . Moreover, the act of mind in certitude is reflex; for as being the assertion of a correspondence between what is without and what is within me, it involves a recognition of myself." The result is a "speculative certainty . . . relating to truth and falsehood." It is a "real mental attainment and conscious attainment of what is true."[171]

Continuing his argument he held that we do in fact know (are sure) of many things in this way. If some men deny the existence of certitude it is because they define it otherwise or "consider we never really have grounds which are sufficient for being certain of the truth of a thing and that therefore, though we may think and call ourselves certain, we really are not."[172] They insist that we never know; we only claim to know. They argue that we cannot know (be sure) of anything unless we have an infallible test for discriminating true and false impressions. They argue that in concrete matters we cannot get beyond a degree of probability proportioned to the arguments in favor of a knowledge claim.

> I have no direct and sufficient answer to give to this objection, but, whatever be . . . the proper solution of it, I consider it is overset by the common sense and universal practice of men . . . In spite of the absence of a decisive test between conviction and persuasion, in spite of the merely probable character of the evidence . . . nevertheless mankind at large cannot help entertaining a certainty of the truth of things, which they are unable to demonstrate, a certainty not merely practical but really speculative, so absolute that they even think it would be absurd in them not to entertain it.[173]

It seems warranted to conclude that Newman sought to portray a realistic epistemology where we come to know (are sure) of what is the case, not by way of a complicated inference followed by a decision, but through a complex intellectual activity which is immediately shaped by experience.

While on holiday in Switzerland in the summer of 1866, Newman discovered what he later called "a key to my own ideas."[174] It was that "certitude is only a kind of assent," that he should begin "with contrasting assent and inference."[175] Though this provided him with the approach he would take in the *Grammar of Assent,* the contrast between assent and inference and its bearing on the question of knowledge generally had already taken definite shape in his notes and letters. In 1868 he summarized his conclusions, stating that "inference, explicit or implicit" precedes but does not compel assent. It is "accommodated" to the concrete "with greater or less accuracy" and thus reaches "conclusions . . . more or less probable." But assent "does not admit of more or less." Further, inference

> as being independent of the concrete, has no need . . . of an intelligent apprehension . . . of any subject matter whatever, being only concerned with the correlation of propositions; but on the contrary an act of Assent cannot be made without a given subject matter nor without some direct intelligent apprehension of the proposition to which Assent is given . . . the former . . . is mainly an act of pure intellect, the latter an act of experience present or past, and of memory in aid of experience.[176]

Earlier he had included "imagination," "minute logical processes," an "association of ideas . . . in a large sense of the words," and "other acts of the mind," in the complex intellectual act whereby "a large body of thought is . . . obtained for us . . . which is thus attested to be true and trustworthy," and which "may be brought under the notion of experience."[177]

In the end, then, Newman recognized that knowledge is not adequately described in Locke's terms—as an assent to a conclusion proportioned to better known premises. Our intellectual activity is not always or only *reasoning* in that sense. Sometimes it is a "direct intelligent apprehension" that something is so through a complex set of intellectual activities by which we are put in immediate contact with experience. In so far as his empiricist and nominalist tendencies could not allow such a direct grasp of the being of things, he tended toward voluntarism. Yet sometimes his inference/ assent distinction is meant to mark a distinction, not between proof and decision, but between what the traditional view of knowledge called *"ratio"* and *"intellectus."* In fact, from the tenor of Newman's writing, this seems to have been his intended meaning despite his inconsistencies.

According to the classical view of knowledge, understanding as *"ratio"* is the power of logical, discursive thought. It is the power of examining, deducing, interpreting, defining and drawing conclusions. Understanding as *"intellectus"* is the capacity of simple intuition. It is the power of grasping, apprehending a truth which offers itself to the understanding, like a landscape to the eye. The faculty of man's knowledge includes both of these at once. It is simultaneously *"ratio"* and *"intellectus,"* and the process of knowing is the action of the two together. The result is that discursive thought is always accompanied and penetrated by an effortless awareness, an activity by which a man conceives the intelligible extra-mental reality while perceiving it.[178] Knowledge, then, is not a matter of subjective impressions, opinions and beliefs apart from evidence which more or less justifies them. It is a unique relation between knower and thing known. It is an immanent activity of an intelligent being which is wholly specified by the rich complexity of his experience.[179]

The point of Newman's inference/assent distinction can be made with the help of a simple example. When astronomers reason from a vast complex of calculations, hints, previous knowledge, unformalized pieces of data and so on, to the conclusion that there must be a new planet "x"—their assent to that conclusion is just *that,* an assent to a conclusion and nothing more. After all, they may be mistaken. But if they should see the planet, land on it, explore it and so on, this would be something else entirely. They would know (be sure) there is a planet the way we know (are sure) there are trees and tables and other persons.

In other words, when the ambiguities are sorted out, the point of Newman's inference/assent distinction is not that, after a cumulative case, we decide to hold a conclusion as certain; or that a cumulative case gives us confidence about what might be mistaken. Rather the point is that within a vast and complex intellectual activity we sometimes grasp the way things are. We are sure even if we cannot explain ourselves or if some of our "reasons" are later called into question.

To defend direct realism in this sense is not to make knowledge or perception any less complex than it is. "On the contrary," Newman wrote, "we have rather added to the obscurity of the problem." For our coming to know remains wholly dependent on experience, evidence, or "premisses"—but now premisses "carried out into the realities of life . . . being instinct with the substance and the momentum of that mass of probabilities, which, acting upon each other in correction and confirmation, carry . . . [the mind] home definitely to the individual case, which is its original scope."[180]

I cannot say that I am sure that there is a chair over there, or that you are not an automaton, just because I am sure. I must and can give reasons. At first, perhaps I might have been deceived. You might have been a robot or that chair might have been an illusion. But I spoke with you and so on; I felt the chair and so on—and now I am sure I am sure. I know I know. In a sense, the vast combination of reasons, obvious and elusive, are more sure and provide a "test." But once one perceives or knows, he perceives or knows not only these reasons but something else. The reasons remain a part of his knowing or being sure about something else. That is, perceiving or knowing is complex; but it is really *perceiving or knowing,* grasping, that "this is so" in some sense apart from the reasons given in its defense.

Newman's empiricist tendencies may have led him to speak in voluntarist and nominalist terms, but he saw clearly the futility of first establishing the possibility of knowledge in the classical sense, the possibility that I might be sure there is a chair here and not there, and then concluding that it is so. He began with the fact of knowledge as it occurs. He recognized that Locke's account could not explain this fact, so he began to make, admittedly halting and often ambiguous, efforts to outline an alternative.

The development of knowledge

Quite early in his career Newman was struck by the complexity of reality. He attacked all efforts to make "this universal living scene of things" fit neatly into arbitrary and limited categories.[181] "The human mind is below truth, not above it," he said, "and is bound, not to descant upon it, but to venerate it."[182] Consequently we must "begin with investigation, to the exclusion of fanciful speculation." Theories "invented almost without data" could hardly be expected to "harmonize with the numberless and diversified phenomena of the world." The complexity of reality should teach us to avoid "excessive attachment to system" and instead to practice "modesty, patience, and caution . . . in philosophical inquiries."[183] It should also teach us patience and caution in communicating what we discover. Because "Truth is vast and far-stretching," because "its separate doctrines" depend "on the combination of various, delicate and scattered evidences . . . it can scarcely be exhibited in a given number of sentences." When this is attempted one is often "unable to exhibit more than a fragment of the whole." He "must round off its rugged extremities, and unite its straggling lines." But then his arguments and exhibitions on paper have nothing "of a personal nature" and appear "complete in themselves;"[184] they can mislead one who is not patient enough to read between the lines. Our ability to apprehend exceeds our ability to exhibit, or, as he put it: "The human mind in its present state is unequal to its own powers of apprehension; it embraces more than it can master."[185]

Newman's position on this point is closely related to his reflection on the development of revealed doctrine. In 1837 he defended "the middle path adopted by the English Church," but at the same time he hesitated to say that a middle way is necessarily the right way. "A mean system really is often nothing better than an assemblage of words; and always looks like such, before it is proved to be something more."[186] His dissatisfaction with hypothetical middle positions grew in time, for he later explained that "he found in early history a veritable *Via Media* in both the Semi-Arians and the Monophysite parties, and they, as being heretical broke his attachment to middle views."[187] After all, a *"Via Media,* a possible road, lying between a mountain and a morass" might be nothing but the "dressing up of an hypothesis" with patches to serve "as expedients for successive emergencies."[188] It might be nothing but "a receding from extremes . . . intelligible and consistent . . . [but] not as yet objective and real."[189] Something more is necessary if one is to know what is "objective and real."[190] As in the last section, the question arises: is this "something more" a decision to accept an hypothesis as true, or the faithful development of an insight into what we know to be the case?

During the 1840s Newman continued to speak of a progressive balancing of extremes. However, he argued, in the Church this is not a hypothetical "receding from extremes." It is a progressive understanding of what has been grasped as revealed.[191] "The sacred ideas which are the objects of our faith" are expressed in "particular propositions," but

> Dogmatic statements . . . however multiplied, cannot say more than is implied in the original idea, considered in its completeness, without the risk of heresy. Creeds and dogmas live in the one idea which they are designed to express, and which alone is substantive; and are necessary only because the human mind cannot reflect upon that idea, except piecemeal.[192]

In the course of the Church's reflection on the object of her faith, doctrines have evolved with "effort, hesitation, suspense," with "many swayings to the right and to the left," yet with a "certainty of advance," with "precision in its march," and with "ultimate completeness . . . till the whole truth 'self-balanced on its centre hung,' part answering to part."[193] On this point he argued that "the Truth only is a *real* doctrine, and therefore stable . . . Hence so much is said in the Fathers of orthodoxy being a narrow way . . . Heresies run into each other, (one may even say,) logically."[194] They are "partial views of the truth, and are wrong not so much in what they say, as in what they deny."[195] Hence, in order to safeguard the whole truth, the Fathers used various terms, for example, of Christ. For if any one of them is used "exclusively of Him, it tends to introduce wrong ideas respecting Him." However "their respective imperfections, as lying on different sides, when used together correct each other."[196] Through "the fiercest controversies" dogmatic theology has moved steadily "from implicit belief to formal statements,"—statements which "alternate between the one and the other side of the theological dogma in question, as if fashioning it into shape by opposite strokes."[197] We are left with a series of statements "strengthening, interpreting, correcting each other, and with more or less exactness, approximating, as they accumulate, to a perfect image."[198]

If this is to be something more than a hypothetical "receding from extremes" there must be a real grasp of the object of faith, or of the object of knowledge, which sets the balance and leaves us with no option. "You must accept the whole or reject the whole; attenuation does but enfeeble, and amputation, mutilate."[199] "All disquisitions, which contemplate things as they are, more or less destroy [hypothetical] middle Views as unreal and untenable."[200] But the development of doctrinal definitions "under the exigency of successive events, such as heresies," is not "unreal." "It is conducted upon laws" according to which the object of faith "vouchsafed to us" is safeguarded. Newman explained that "it was gradually brought home to me . . . that the decrees of later Councils . . . were but instances of that very same doctrinal law which is to be found in the history of the early Church."[201] Others might conjecture hypothetical middle views, but "the Church must be the guardian of a fact."[202]

Newman seems to have first recognized a "law" of progressive balancing of extremes to safeguard revealed truth. He then reflected that "a law implies a law-giver."[203] That is, these qualifications are not hypothetical conjectures but are guided by the Church's grasp of the object of her faith with a divine guarantee that this objective revelation would endure in her authoritative teaching. Then, he later explained, "I was led to apply" this law of balancing extremes to safeguard an objective fact which is apprehended, "to the Evidences of religion," and to our natural knowledge of God as well.[204] Through an "endless qualification" we "set right one error of expression by another" and so "steady our minds, not so as to reach their objects, but to point them in the right direction."[205] Eventually he turned this "law" into a general principle of human knowledge. "I saw that [it] . . . not only accounted for certain facts" in the history of Christian doctrine, "but was in itself a remarkable philosophical phenomenon."[206] He went on to examine the "concatenation of argument,"[207] the "first principles, sentiments and tastes," the "mode of viewing the question and of arguing," which "normally" and "naturally" constitute *the organum investigandi* given us for gaining" the truth and leaving us with no alternative but to embrace it.[208] That is, Newman seems to have turned this law of doctrinal development into a general principle that almost all truth "lies in a well," is implicitly apprehended, but is capable of being explored and made explicit.[209]

He had come to recognize both the certainty and obscurity of our knowledge. I might have a "direct insight . . . into things as they are." But my knowledge is limited and open to development. I might possess a "vision, analogous to eyesight," of reality which arises "from the original, elementary sympathy or harmony between myself and what is external to myself."[210] But this vision is not a matter of clear and distinct intuition. In 1860 he argued that the very "nature of man" involves a "process of change" or a growth, analogous to other growths, that is, an internal development of powers, appropriating and turning to account what is external."[211] What man's intellectual nature "starts with . . . is the matter and substance of what it will terminate in."[212] Yet "its whole complete nature is best seen in its termination." Newman added that this "enlarged view" of man's intellectual nature and its "intuitions" implies "a corresponding largeness in our view of the things which are their object." For example, "pride, vulgarity, the prudent . . . are real things contemplated by the mind as such," but they are embedded in the "created universe," in "the constitution of society and its variations." The objects of man's knowledge, then, are grasped both "in the abstract" and "in all the details" of their individual existence.[213]

It was this which led Newman to speak of the "tacit understandings" of the illative sense,[214] and of the "development of an idea" from implicit apprehension to explicit statement.[215]

Newman did not mean merely that a psychologically latent idea can become conscious (explicit), but that by reflecting on our experience the logical and ontological implications of what we know to be the case can themselves become known (explicit).[216]

He noted that it is often impossible to quickly represent "the outline and character, the hues and shades, in which any intellectual view really exists in the mind,"[217] or "to master and express an idea in a short space of time."[218] However we can reflect on our ideas and illustrate their significance. "One proposition necessarily leads to another, and a second to a third; then some limitation is required; and the combination of these opposites occasions some fresh evolutions from the original idea."[219] In the development of revealed doctrine, the object of faith requires this "limitation" and directs this "evolution." In the growth of secular knowledge, the limitation and direction come from "objects themselves . . . forcing on us a persuasion of their reality."[220] In each case, "the development of an idea is a deduction of proposition from proposition." It is not a matter of "drawing mere logical inferences." Rather it is a matter of "illustrating one existing idea." The various "propositions are ever formed in and around the idea itself (so to speak), and are in fact one and all only aspects of it."[221]

Newman gave a variety of examples of instances where words only "approximate" the ideas they express. When teaching children, describing color to a blind man, translating languages, writing an historical narrative, or formulating the principles of a political party —we must adapt our words to express the original idea.[222] The "principles of philosophy, physics, ethics, politics admit both of implicit and explicit statement,"[223] for example, "the doctrine of the divine right of kings, or of the rights of man . . . or utilitarianism, or free trade."[224] He spoke of "children who at first do not know that they are responsible beings; but by degrees not only feel that they are, but reflect on the great truth, and on what it implies."[225] He wrote of the philosophy of Zeno or Pythagoras, Plato or Epicurus where a "certain mode of viewing things" is eventually constructed into an explicit system.[226] He discussed at length the development of Aristotelian philosophy when implications are drawn and new questions answered on Aristotle's principles. "A learned Aristotelian is one who can answer any whatever philosophical questions in the way Aristotle would have answered them . . . although they be questions which could not occur in Aristotle's age."[227] Futher, he noted that in the case of Aristotelian philosophy or Christian theology, the development of an idea is not simply a calculation "on paper." Rather, "it is carried on through and by means of communities of men."[228]

It is . . . sometimes said that the stream is clearest near the spring . . . This does not apply to the history of a philisophy or a belief, which, on the contrary is more equable, and purer, and stronger when its bed has become deep, and broad, and full . . . Its vital elements need disengaging from what is foreign and temporary . . . It changes . . . in order to remain the same.[229]

In his long correspondence with William Froude, Newman tended to apply this general approach to the methods of empirical science.

His closest friend in the Tractarian Movement had been Richard Hurrell Froude who died prematurely in 1836. William, his younger brother, entered Oriel College in 1828 and there began a lifelong friendship with Newman. William eventually gained professional recognition in hydrodynamics research with the Royal Navy. His wife and four of their children became Catholics, largely through Newman's influence, but William remained agnostic. From 1844 until his death in 1879 he corresponded regularly with Newman giving him first-hand information about trends in nineteenth-century science, at the same time confronting him with the fallibilist outlook accepted by many scientists of the day.[230] Froude maintained that anyone who sought intellectual integrity must withhold certain assent in religious matters since they must be qualified as tentative and revisable in the same way that scientific statements must be qualified as open to change.

In 1850 Newman told Henry Wilberforce that the difficulty in answering Froude was "first his vagueness, and next his difference in first principles."[231] He criticized Froude's "extravagant" attempt to treat "moral proofs as if they were mathematical."[232] Froude often spoke of the demands of *"inexorable* logic." But while, in one sense, mathematical demonstration is "inexorable," Newman argued that, in a larger sense, "inexorable" is "a mere *name* fastened on a good argument" of any sort.[233] Froude would have to be turned away from general theories, brought "down to particulars," and made "to view things *really."*[234] For when things are viewed "really," it should become obvious that "persons may have very good reasons, which they cannot bring out into words" that amount to a logically compelling argument.[235]

In an undated memorandum, perhaps written in the winter of 1855, Newman began with the principle "that almost all truth 'lies in a well,'" and added that this implies "1. that it is hard to find, yet 2. that it may be found." He argued that one should not *a priori* rule out the possibility of this being the case "in religion" as well as "in other subject matters." In fact it should seem "likely" to be so in religious matters "inasmuch as the difficulty of arriving at truth seems to vary with the preciousness and refinement of its kind." The *"prima facie* incompleteness . . . of the arguments" for religion which count against certainty, should be balanced by the *prima facie* probability in favor of an ability to attain religious truth "arising from the 'certainty'" of actual believers. In religion as well as in mathematics, when we find "educated persons" who are certain of what we are ignorant, our initial reaction should be that truth is attainable, "though *we* had not attained it." After all, frequently a long "preparation of mind of a particular kind is indispensable for successful inquiry." He concluded: "That religious truth is an obscure subject is granted; but that does not prove that we cannot find its roads and their termination."[236]

Froude, however, was not merely assuming that religious certainty is impossible because it is obscure and its arguments incomplete; he was arguing that all certainty is impossible because, as in science, all knowledge is mediated through conjectures and theories more or less justified, but never absolutely certified by experience. He told Newman, that on no subject whatever—distinctly not in the region of the ordinary facts with which our daily experience is consonant—distinctly not in the domain of history and of politics, and yet again a fortiori, not in that of Theology, is . . . the mind of any human being, capable of arriving at an absolutely certain conclusion. That though of course some conclusions are far more certain than others, there is an element of uncertainty in all.[237]

One might have a "duty to *act as if*" he were absolutely certain. But at the same time he has a "duty to keep before his eyes his knowledge of the fallibility of his processes of thought." Even "the highest attainable probability" would not justify "discarding the residuum of doubt." Froude accepted the dictum that "probability is the guide of life." Consequently one should always keep an open mind and say, "I think I see my way clearly, it is nevertheless possible that I may be wrong."[238] He endorsed the principle: "Ever learning and never able to come to a knowledge of the Truth."[239] Furthermore, he claimed that the remarkable progress of physical science was due to "the wider and freer scope of action which this principle has conquered for itself."[240] This "fundamental principle of universal doubt" was beginning to make its way into politics. "By and Bye," Froude wrote, "I hope it will master men's minds in the province of Religion" as well. For even if one became convinced of the "probability of the truth of every proposition" of the Creed, a "universal scepticism" should qualify his assent.[241]

Newman replied that Froude's argument seemed to be "a sophism . . . much lies in the meaning of the words certainty and doubt."[242] When Froude asked whether he thought it a sophism "in reference to the pursuit of truth generally or only in reference to the pursuit of Religious Truth,"[243] Newman explained: "I do not mean that there is anything sophistical in the principles on which non-religious truth is pursued at present, but . . . I think there is a sophism in considering the certainty of secular science so far superior to the certainty or persuasion, as you would call it, of the personal evidence for Christianity."[244] The personal "way of arriving at certainty in Christianity" is "as logical" as the "scientific methods" employed to reach certainty "in subjects non-religious," such as "that we have an Indian Empire or that the earth goes round the sun."[245]

Froude complained that Newman seemed to "attribute to scientific proof a cogency and completeness of conviction, which in the domain of 'science' . . . none of the higher minds which occupy that domain, attribute to such proofs."[246] No scientist would consider that, for example, the Newtonian system was "established beyond the possibility of confutation or of change." Someone might say: "I always will hold to this" theory, but he would be making a personal claim, a decision, out of proportion to available evidence. Despite its limitations, Froude preferred "scientific proof," because "personal certainty" resting on a *"sensation* of personal conviction" seemed so very prone to error.[247]

Newman replied that he also had "no faith in 'sensations.' " He admitted that the term "personal certainty" is misleading. "I meant to have said 'personal *proof.'* "[248] If science's way of conjecture and experimental confirmation is the only sort of "proof" available to us, then of course the only justification of certainty would be an appeal to a decision or a sensation. But the question is whether we can come to know what is the case in another and immediate way. Newman wrote that he never "fancied that Newton's theory was certain in every point of view," but he was surprised to hear that scientists generally "allowed it to be uncertain." However, he added, "I thought . . . that, in spite of all the uncertainties of scientific conclusions, all persons allowed that there were some things actually demonstrated, that there had been an *advance* in real absolute knowledge."[249]

On December 14, 1860, Froude visited Newman at the Birmingham Oratory. Later Newman recorded the essentials of their conversation. Froude "maintained that every additional piece of evidence made a man *more certain,* i.e. (absolute certainty being impossible)." To this Newman argued that while a man might rejoice to find further confirmation, sometimes, *"in fact"* he is *"not* more certain, if he had 12 witnesses than if he had 11."[250] Froude maintained that in science nothing is proved, but Newman held "that such ἐποχὴ "[251] is only "part of the *calculus* as it were of science . . . a rule of the game." Science might nourish "scepticism" but only as an "expedient," or "necessary" excercise "of reason in those processes which were peculiar to itself."[252] Froude insisted that "no truth has been arrived at without this habit of sceptical caution—it was the parent of discovery." To which Newman replied that "no great thing was done without the reverse habit, viz. that of conviction and faith . . . *devotion* cannot exist without it—nor can any sustained course of action."[253]

While Newman found in the *"advance"* of science an argument that at least something is allowed to be certain, Froude found in that same *"advance"* an argument for "sceptical caution . . . the parent of discovery." In 1864 he told Newman that all reliable scientists who are "engaged in the advancement of science . . . treat their own conclusions with a scepticism as profound and as corroding as that with which they treat Theology." He emphasized that the "scientific propositions which are regarded as most certain, are those the probability of which is being most continually tested and found to stand the test."[254] Froude felt that there was only one "tenable view, a priori" in defense of the certainty of faith; namely, to claim that men are intended to deal differently with their conclusions in matters of "religious belief" than they are in "the ordinary affairs of life—as if instinct were to guide them in the one case, logic in the other."[255] But this solution would involve "intractable difficulties." It would have to be assumed "that men are gifted with an instinctive faculty which enables them to perceive with certainty the fact of a super-natural occurrence and to recognize it as super-natural at once and by a conscious act of unerring recognition."[256]

Perhaps it was because this remark introduced the further question of supernatural faith that Newman hesitated to reply. He simply told Froude that the whole matter "requires great and careful investigation" and that he would "like to write on the subject in question."[257] In fact Newman held that there is a common pattern of concrete reasoning which we use in everyday inferences and in those leading to religious belief. He would later deliberately take his examples of this reasoning from a broad field to avoid suggesting that we need a special esoteric faculty in order to attain truths about God and religion in preparation for the gift of supernatural faith.

A number of conclusions can be drawn at this point. Newman began with a "law" of certain development which he found in his study of the history of revealed doctrine in the Church. He then applied this law to the "advance" of scientific knowledge. Froude began with a law of uncertainty which he found in the method of empirical science. He wrote that he had learned to discredit a "dogmatic habit of thought, first in its relation to . . . scientific inquiry" before directing his attention to religious dogmatism. The merit of faith rests in acting "confidently on the best . . . conclusion it can form," not in claiming a certainty "out of proportion to the evidence."[258] Both approaches are open to criticism.

On the one hand, Newman was often over-confident about the certain advance of science. There is no divine guarantee that truth is preserved in a community of scientists (or philosophers), as there is in the community of believers entrusted with revelation. Again, the method of inquiry in progressively understanding what is revealed is not the same as the methods science employs. There are no laboratory experiments under controlled conditions to test "theories." Again, Newman too quickly assumed that science achieves an *"advance* in real absolute knowledge." The fact that we can sometimes be sure we were mistaken, or certain that one theory is closer to the truth than another, is perhaps an argument that we do sometimes know (are sure). But often science is not sure it is progressing. It is often uncertain and can only say that one theory is probably closer to the truth than another one. Again, sometimes the celebrated "advance" of science is not simply, or even at all, an advance in "real absolute knowledge" about the nature of things. Sometimes it is a *certain* advance but only in better accounting for empirical data of a restricted sort, or only in answering the particular sort of questions the scientist asks himself, or only in providing useful information for technological solutions to concrete problems in domestic or industrial situations. Newman failed to appreciate these possibilities.

On the other hand, Froude too quickly assumed that the scientific method is the paradigm of all knowing. He argued that either reasoning in religious matters and in science are the same, and then they are fallible for science's methods are uncertain, or else they are different; but then religious belief, humanly considered, would rest on an "instinctive faculty" beyond the reach of reason.

Newman's response was ambiguous. On the one hand he wrote that "Christianity is proved by the same rigorous scientific processes" which science employs.[259] But then he seemed to have attributed to the methods of empirical science a "completeness of conviction" which, as Froude pointed out, is not justified.[260] On the other hand, he sought to illustrate "the popular, practical, personal evidence of Christianity . . . as contrasted to the scientific."[261]

Then he seemed to have assumed that all knowing is fallible and suggested that in religion we must resort to a decision or a sensation or an esoteric faculty which, as Froude noted, would place it beyond reason and logic.[262] A great deal of Newman's ambiguity seems to have resulted from a failure to appreciate fully the methods of experimental science.

In 1843 Newman wrote that science adopts "various methods and *calculi*," but "none of them carries out the lines of truth to their limits." We use them until they issue "in some great impossibility or contradiction." This "failure" shows that they were not a "true analysis or adequate image of those recondite laws which are investigated by means of [them] . . . our instrument of discovery . . . has never fathomed their depth, because it now fails to measure their course."[263] Science sets up constructs or theories which are useful for a time, until they are upset by new experimentation. It is constructural and demands an open mind on the part of the investigator. Its statements are not "simple representations or informants of things as they are"[264] but "all along" expedients "for practical purposes."[265]

Newman tended to understand the methods of science as identical with our ways of knowing generally. If scientific knowledge is mediated through uncertain constructs, perhaps all our knowledge is also mediate and uncertain. The result would be a "dreary and hopeless scepticism" unless one trusted in "the Being and Providence of God."[266]

Yet he had already criticized the view that religious faith is an "opinion" on which it is safe to act "for practical purposes." He had defended faith as an assent to "objective truth."[267] He was later to defend ordinary knowledge as an objective (certain) grasp "that certain things are and *in confuso* what they are."[268] Further, his study of the revealed object of faith as it developed through sustained reflection in the Church led him to speak of our knowledge generally as a real grasp of what is open to further understanding. It is not mediated through constructs more or less justified but never certified by experience. It is an immediate although often imperfect grasp of what is the case, which gives us an opening to the being of things.

When he turned to discuss the methods of science, he tended to understand the methods of science as identical with our ways of knowing in faith and in direct experience. Hence he tended to speak of the sciences themselves, not so much as attempts to verify constructs and theories, but as attempts to make explicit an immediate but implicit grasp of an aspect of reality. In 1852 he wrote that the conclusions of science are "aspects of things . . . incomplete in their relation to the things themselves," but when viewed together "they approximate to a representation or subjective reflexion of the objective truth, as nearly as is possible to the human mind, which advances towards the accurate apprehension of that object, in proportion to the number of sciences which it has mastered."[269] He seems to have treated the various conclusions of science in the very same way in which he had discussed the statements of Fathers and Councils which progressively illuminate what is revealed "as if fashioning it into shape by opposite strokes."[270] He also seems to have treated the "momentary collisions" of scientific theories in the same way in which he had discussed difficulties in revealed doctrine. A divine guarantee of the preservation of revelation in the Church would guide reflection in the latter case. Similarly "the sovereignty of Truth" would render the former collisions "ultimately consistent."[271]

His invective against "fanciful speculation,"[272] his defense of patient reflection on the implications of what we know to be the case (or grasp in faith to be so), seems to have led him to overlook that in many matters we do not know and here science *must* proceed by way of "speculation"—uncertain conjectures more or less confirmed by experiment. In 1855 he told the science faculty at Dublin: "It is the very law of the human mind in its inquiry after and acquisition of truth to make its advances by a process which . . . is circuitous. There are no short cuts to knowledge; nor does the road to it always lie in the direction in which it terminates, nor are we able to see the end on starting."[273] But he spoke confidently of the way of science. He felt that, despite temporary detours, it would eventually run again towards its goal "without effort." In scientific researches, as in ethics, we "gain the mean merely by receding from both extremes . . . No one can go straight up a mountain; no sailing vessel makes for its port without tacking."[274]

Newman's strong sense of the "sovereignty of Truth" influenced his attitude toward the role of error in inquiry. At first he allowed that sometimes error could provide a way toward truth. Later he affirmed that ultimately its "only effect" is to promote truth.

> Theories, speculations, hypotheses, are started; perhaps they are to die, still not before they have suggested ideas better than themselves. These better ideas are taken up in turn by other men, and, if they do not lead to truth, nevertheless they lead to what is still nearer to truth than themselves; and thus knowledge on the whole makes progress . . . A Science seems making no progress . . . yet imperceptibly all the time it is advancing, and it is of course a gain to truth even to have learned what is not true, if nothing more.[275]

The sometimes exaggerated rhetoric, the over-confidence in the certain advance of science, should not make us overlook his legitimate defense of objective (immediate) knowledge. On occasion we must resort to the uncertain method of theory and experiment, but not all coming to know is a matter of justifying a belief or testing a conjecture.

Karl Popper rejected the empiricist assumption that the truth of scientific theories "could be logically derived from the truth of certain observation-statements."[276] The empiricist sometimes assumes that, besides theories and conjectures, we have another and immediate grasp of "absolutely 'given' . . . data" on which the scientist can build "as if on rock." Instead, Popper wrote, "I pointed out that the apparent 'data' of experience were always interpretations in the light of theories and therefore affected by the hypothetical and conjectural character of all theories."[277] For Popper, all knowledge is a matter of conjecture. But he was forced to allow some objective (immediate) contact with experience. Consequently he spoke of "singular existential statements . . . testable, intersubjectively, by observation" which can serve as premises "in an empirical falsification" of a conjecture.[278] These statements are the points at which our theories "can clash with reality; and when they do" we are reminded "that our ideas may be mistaken . . . The very idea of error—and of fallibility—involves the idea of an objective truth as a standard of which we may fall short . . . It is only the idea of truth . . . which makes rational discussion possible."[279] Yet Popper wanted to avoid the "mistaken dogma that a satisfactory theory of truth would have to be a theory of true belief—of well-founded or rational belief" because of the regress of justifications that mistake seemed to entail.[280] Consequently he insisted that even basic observation statements are problematic. "Experiences can *motivate a decision,* and hence an acceptance or rejection of a statement, but a basic statement cannot be *justified by* them."[281]

In the end Popper seems to have accepted the dogma that all knowledge is mediated through theories and constructs, but added that even basic statements are corrigible. Consequently "every scientific statement must remain *tentative for ever.* It may indeed be corroborated, but every corroboration is relative to other statements which again are tentative. Only in our subjective experiences of conviction, in our subjective faith, can we be 'absolutely certain.' " Science "can attain neither truth nor probability . . . *We do not know: we can only guess.*"[282] He added that "Though there are no general criteria by which we can recognize truth . . . there are criteria of progress towards the truth." But again we can only guess we are progressing from one theory to another. "It always remains possible . . . that we shall make mistakes in our relative appraisal of two theories."[283]

Popper's account may be a correct description of much of science. But it is difficult to understand the notion of progress of any sort if not only science but all knowledge is a matter of guessing on the basis of further guesses that falsification has been avoided.

Newman attacked the view that "there is no truth" or objective grasp of what is the case so "that our merit lies in seeking, not in possessing."[284] If all knowledge is seeking, if it is always mediated through conjectures which may be mistaken, skepticism seems unavoidable. Cartesian rationalism sought a solution by appealing to *a priori* intuitions. This position eliminates the need or even the intelligibility of an intellectual activity by which we come to grasp what is the case. The empiricist sometimes seems to merely relocate clear-cut intuitions at the level of basic sensation statements, rather than at the level of full-fledged ideas. This maneuver also eliminates any intellectual activity other than a crude juggling of basic data or an imaginative theory-construction which avoids falsification by such data. The two positions disagree only as to where a Cartesian clear and distinct idea should be located. But Newman rejected the Cartesian assumption that certain (objective) knowledge is equivalent to clear and distinct intuition, whether of full-fledged ideas or basic sensations. He would not reduce neutral (objective) recalcitrant experience to "basics" which are juggled into shape or which confirm or fail to falsify a conjectured shape. Knowing cannot be adequately described as juggling or guessing because experience cannot be adequately described as static (particular) "basic" data. For Newman, knowledge is both certain (objective) and open to development; and experience is both neutral (objective) and general.[285]

Thomas S. Kuhn complained that Popper "consistently sought evaluation procedures which can be applied to theories with the apodictic assurance characteristic of the techniques by which one identifies mistakes in arithmetic, logic, or measurement."[286] But Kuhn seems to have carried the program of construing all knowledge as mediated through theory-construction to its skeptical conclusion. He eliminated Popper's "basic statements" but seems to have eliminated all contact with (objective) experience in the process. We are left with nothing but theories where, he wrote, "neither proof nor error is at issue."[287] One can speak of "mistakes" or "truth" only within a theory, not about a theory.[288] Since every "fact" is determined by one's theoretical interpretation there is no neutral (objective) reality which could justify our claims or in any sense immediately specify our grasp of the way things are. We can only appeal to the internal structure of the theory in question and point out its simplicity, utility or invulnerability.[289] Further, there is no sense in which a later theory can be said to be a "better approximation to the truth."[290] Kuhn allowed that there might be "a set of criteria" for distinguishing an older theory from its "descendent," so that "scientific development is, like biological evolution, unilateral and irreversible."[291] But an evolution of thought can be in one direction while being, in fact, in the wrong direction. Kuhn seems to have ruled out any ability to distinguish genuine progress toward the truth from mere change of opinion.

His remarks may, at times, correctly describe much of science. But if all knowledge is mediated through theories and constructs, now self-supported in terms of internal coherence and simplicity, again skepticism seems unavoidable. We can know nothing or grasp simply that it is the case.[292]

Newman admitted that beliefs often hang closely together in a system. In the case of religion, "the same doctrines . . . often are held differently, as belonging to distinct wholes or *forms.*" They are "exposed to the influence and the bias of the teaching, perhaps false, with which they are associated." Yet the truth or certainty of a proposition is not determined by the internal support it might receive from other beliefs in the system. They will bear on its "significance and effect" but "in spite of this . . . assent and certitude have reference to propositions one by one." Each proposition "stands . . . on its own basis." An individual's development of his knowledge, then, is not an "obliteration" of one system and "reception" of another. Instead he reflects on individual propositions which, when their truth is certified, are "carried into a new system of belief."[293]

In the case of scientific knowledge, where theory-construction is dominant, Newman noted that we would "waste our time, and make no advances" if we did not "deliberately . . . take things for granted which our forefathers had a duty to doubt about."[294] Yet he did not advocate an uncritical submission to indoctrination. "Truth is too sacred . . . a thing to be sacrificed to . . . party spirit, or the prejudices of education, or attachment (however amiable) to the opinions of human teachers."[295] "Circumstances . . . may arise when a question may legitimately be revived, which has already been definitely determined, but," he added, "a re-consideration . . . need not abruptly" throw us into "a scepticism about things in general."[296]

In the case of religion, Newman discussed the development of knowledge in two areas—in the Church and in the individual. Reflection in the Church on what has been revealed leads to the evolution of systematic theology "ascertaining and making clear for us the truths on which the religious imagination has to rest." But the truth of revelation is grasped and preserved in the faith of the Church. It precedes systematic expression. Religious faith accepts revealed truths "one by one . . . while theology . . . forms and protects them by virtue of its function of regarding them, not merely one by one, but as a system of truth." Religious faith and devotion can afford to be "careless about intellectual consistency." But it is "the nature and the duty of the intellect" to be "ever active, inquisitive, penetrating; it examines doctrine and doctrine; it compares, contrasts, and forms them into a science; that science is theology." Scripture and tradition, creeds and ritual present the objects of

faith's devotion and the data for theology's reflection. In the latter
case they are "intended as a check upon our reasonings, lest they
rush on in one direction beyond the limits of the truth."[297]

The conversion of an individual, again, begins with reflection on
propositions "one by one." But the situation is complex. "A religion
is not a proposition, but a system." The acceptance of a religion is
not one kind of assent to a single proposition. It includes a simple
and a complex, a natural and a real assent. It combines an act of
profession, credence, opinion and speculation. "It is a collection of
all of these various kinds of assents, all at once and together."[298]

Various systems, for example "Protestantism, Romanism, Socin-
ianism, and Theism," involve "elements" which are held in common. These elements, "whether true or false, when embraced with
an absolute conviction, are the pivots on which changes take place."
If someone has converted, he "started with just one certitude . . .
and he carried it out and carried it with him into a new system of
belief . . . He has indeed made serious additions to his initial ruling
principle, but he has lost no conviction of which he was originally
possessed."[299] Conversion is not a matter of replacing one hypothesis with another, but of reflecting and clarifying what one knows to
be the case. In this way, by "the light of those particular truths,"
often crouched in error, "we pick our way, slowly perhaps, but
surely . . . taking our certitudes with us, not to lose, but to keep
them more securely." There is "a continual accumulation of truths"
which claim from us and elicit in our intellects "fresh and fresh
certitudes."[300]

Of course, Newman admitted, the pivots on which conversions
turn, the elements shared by two systems, might be "but errors
held in common." Yet, he added, "when the common points . . .
are truths," the pull toward conversion is stronger because truth is
congenial to the mind. But this remark once again raises the question discussed in the last section. If "certitude does not admit of an
interior, immediate test," and yet if "a specific sense of satisfaction
and repose" is not sufficient to distinguish knowledge from mere
prejudice, if there must be "investigation and proof,"[301] how is this
to be understood? Is it a matter of a cumulation of evidence followed by a decision to be certain; or an insight on the occasion of a
convergence? Do we decide or in some sense grasp that this is the
right direction in which to move? In other words, Newman some-

times tended to take religious conversion as the paradigm of scientific advance. He tended to describe both as a deeper understanding of what we know. In so doing, he tended to overlook that much of scientific advance is a matter of theory-construction and experimentation to account for empirical data of a rather restricted sort. Nevertheless, he was pointing toward a kind of "coming to know" which is not a matter of "justifying conjectures." And it is here that the question arises: is this decision or insight?

Newman seems to have suggested that because "the human mind . . . embraces more than it can master,"[302] what we grasp in (objective/certain) knowledge opens us to the being of things. It is this, and not merely a decision to accept a theory's confirmation as definitive, which at times enables us to *know* we are advancing. But, again, he was ambiguous on this point. In 1870 he asked himself whether any account could be given of the "ratiocinative method" of informal proof which marks the certain advance of knowledge. The steps of this reasoning can, to some extent, be expressed in syllogistic form, and, throughout, the "personality . . . of the parties reasoning is an important element." But can more be said? He replied affirmatively, providing an illustration from geometry.

> We know that a regular polygon, inscribed in a circle, its sides being continually diminished, tends to become that circle . . . so that its tendency to be the circle, though ever nearer fulfilment, never in fact gets beyond a tendency. In like manner, the conclusion in a real or concrete question is foreseen and predicted rather than actually attained; foreseen in the number and direction of accumulated premises, which all converge to it, and as the result of their combination, approach it more nearly than any assignable difference, yet do not touch it logically . . . on account of the nature of its subject-matter, and the delicate and implicit character of at least part of the reasonings on which it depends.[303]

Newman seems to have been saying not that a gap remains and we must decide, but that sometimes we do grasp the "direction" in which our reflection should move. His point was, not that we are unable to grasp the way things are, but that what we do grasp in knowledge is rich and complex. In practical questions we often "advance to the truth by experience of error." We call virtue a mean because it lies between things that are wrong. "We know what is right, not positively, but negatively . . . we fall upon and try error, and find that it is *not* the truth. We grope about . . . and . . . exhaust the possible modes of acting till nought is left, but truth, remaining."[304] The same applies to speculative questions. "Veracity, like other virtues, lies in a mean."[305] It is the work of an "imperial intellect" to determine "in what direction inquiry is hopeless, or on the other hand full of promise."[306]

Although we often lack a clear grasp of the nature of things, although "we do not see the truth at once and make toward it,"[307] there is an inexhaustible wealth of objective truth available to us. But it is often acquired indirectly by the combined strength of various arguments—"by objections overcome, by adverse theories neutralized, by difficulties gradually clearing up, by exceptions proving the rule, by unlooked-for correlations found with received truths, by suspense and delay in the process issuing in triumphant reactions." Although such reasoning does not actually put one "in possession" of its object, it gradually leads the "experienced mind" to "make a sure divination that a conclusion is inevitable."[308] Newman could be interpreted as having meant that these various factors give us reasons for holding that a theory is probably true or that we are probably advancing. This could be a description of much of science, but he spoke of a "sure divination that a conclusion is inevitable." By an "indirect" mode of reflection, we can sometimes come to grasp that something "cannot be otherwise" for what we know to be the case "could not in reason be supposed to have happened, unless it were true."[309] In this case, our assent "is not the passive admission of a conclusion as necessary, but the recognition of it as true."[310] It is not an assent to a conclusion as "more probable," but a grasp of what is the case. "For myself," he wrote, "I never . . . took this ground of 'the *more* probable' but of a certitude which lay in an assemblage and accumulation of probabilities, which *rationally* demanded to be considered sufficient for certitude."[311]

Both in perception and in intellection Newman stressed, far more than Locke, the interpretative and yet objective role of the mind. In the former case through the complex activity of internal and external senses we perceive, not just a set of sensations, but something else—this object or that person.[312] In the latter case through these and other complex intellectual operations we come to know, not just a set of reasons and arguments, but that this is the way things are. As the data of sense combine in perception, so various known aspects of reality "complete, correct, balance each other . . . as regards the attainment of truth."[313] Newman described the process, not as an "accumulation" of facts "without forming judgments,"[314] but as an "illumination" which secures "to the intellect, the sight of things as they are."[315] The intellect undertakes an informal inference in order to discern a pattern of evidence within a set of independent but converging arguments. But it does not merely accumulate and add up the probabilities, in the scientific sense of probability. Rather it searches, in informal ways, after a speculatively certain truth which may or may not be contained in the set of arguments at hand. If it does discover a speculative certainty in the united impact of evidence which may not be independently convincing, then it is led to make an absolute assent to this complex truth. It recognizes "the sight of things as they are."[316]

Again, Newman seems to have pointed toward a realistic epistemology which Locke's empiricism could not sustain, though his own empiricist and nominalist tendencies made him drift occasionally into a voluntarist way of speaking, as if we decided we had certainly made an advance in "real absolute knowledge." The debate between himself and William Froude was, indeed, over "first principles,"[317] perhaps more so than Newman himself realized. It was a debate whether truth lies in a well but is sometimes attainable because knowledge is a direct grasp of experienced reality; or whether all knowledge is mediated through theory-construction such that the best we can achieve is a claim to know which is more or less justified but never certified by experience.

On this, Newman's realism seems to have emerged first from his recognition that faith is an assent to what God has revealed which is both objective and open to development. This was then applied to knowledge generally of what is the case, objectively grasped but open to development as philosophical reflection exposes real implications of what we know to be so. But he then on occasion tended to apply this same approach mistakenly to empirical science where often there is no grasp of the structure of reality and its implications. At times, however, he distinguished more clearly the methods of science from other direct ways of knowing.

In the first case, "ascertained truths are scanty, and courses of thought abound."[318] Here theory-construction and experimentation play their part. "From scanty data" reason develops "one main idea . . . into its consequences" and "draws out a whole system . . . And should means be found of ascertaining directly some of the facts which it has been deducing by this abstract process, then their coincidence with its *a priori* judgments will serve to prove the accuracy of its deductions."[319] He called this the "method of a strict science . . . founded on one idea or reducible to certain formulae."[320] He called it "inductive"[321] because it rests its judgments on an accumulation of experiments which increasingly confirm or falsify its hypotheses. Thus science advances from hypothesis to hypothesis. "Physical science . . . may be dissatisfied with its own combinations, hypotheses, systems; and leave Ptolemy for Newton . . . that is, it may decide that it has not yet touched the bottom of its own subject."[322] But, he added, "its aim will be to get to the bottom and nothing more."[323] In other words, the scientist asks one sort of question which his mode of investigation aims at answering. He "has nothing whatever to do with final causes." He does not ask why the "phenomena and laws of the material world" are as they are. He simply seeks to determine what they are. He begins with "phenomena" and reaches conclusions within the limits of the evidence they provide. He does not, in any proper sense, approach questions about the nature of matter and its laws. He does not ask "what causation is, what time is, what the relations of time to cause and effect, and a hundred other questions of a similar character."[324] Because he does not grasp why things are as they are, but generalizes from observation how they behave, because he must leap to an hypothesis ("if gases were of such and such a nature, then they would act thus and thus") verified by experimentation, the correct attitude is to keep an open mind. We have often had to abandon endlessly-verified theories. Our reasoning "outstrips" what we know absolutely to be so. Newman warned: "In such cases, there is much need for wariness, jealousy of self, and habitual dread of presumption, paradox and unreality, to preserve our deductions within the bounds of sobriety, and our guesses from assuming the character of discoveries."[325]

But there is a second way of coming to know. Here "the facts . . . are all known from the first" and "instead of advancing from idea to idea, Reason does but connect fact with fact . . . and what was, in the former case, the tracing of inferences, becomes a laying down of relations."[326] Newman called this method "deductive," but not in the sense of "mere logical inferences."[327] It is deductive in the sense that, through reflection on what is known to be the case, other things are recognized to be so. There is no experimental "research into facts." Here knowledge does not progress in the way science progresses.[328] He discussed this mode of argument especially in the case of theology where knowledge advances "simply by appealing to the authoritative keepers of revelation, dwelling upon and drawing out into detail, the doctrines which are delivered."[329] Theology comes to know "just what has been revealed and nothing more."[330] But he came to apply this method also to the philosopher "of the present day" who has "before him just the same evidences . . . in the Universe which the early Greeks had."[331] As the theologian is limited by "the doctrines which are delivered," so the philosopher is limited by common experience "where the facts are given."[332] He does not merely construct possible explanations of observed things. He contemplates what he knows to be the case and seeks there a full understanding of the structure of reality. He might begin with a constructural explanation, but if it becomes an observed reality then his "open mind" would close on a secure truth. For example, in studying the free human act, he would attempt to discover what precisely such an act is, what its structure is. An insight would be needed into our experience of free acts. From what they are and from what man is, there would have to be an intellectual grasp of what is seen to be the necessary cause of such an act and the purpose of such a trait in human activity. Where one cannot directly grasp in reality the necessary relations involved, then this mode of reflection is impossible and we must resort to the various scientific techniques of descriptive analysis.[333]

At times Newman exaggerated the range of this sort of understanding and suggested that empirical science regularly proceeds in this way.[334] But he did defend the fact that sometimes we do know and do not merely claim to know what is the case, so that we are capable in some instances of progressing, not by way of conjecture and experiment, but by way of reflecting directly on what is given in common experience (philosophy) or in revelation (theology). In such cases we must "take things as we find them; not . . . be wise above what is written whether in nature or in grace; not . . .

attempt a theory where we must reason without data; much less, even if we could frame one . . . mistake it for a fact instead of what it is, an arbitrary arrangement of our knowledge, whatever that may be, and nothing more."[335]

The "Grammar of Assent"

In the *Grammar of Assent* Newman attempted to distinguish some of the intellectual activities which combine in our objective (certain) knowledge in such a way that we are given an opening to reality. First, he wanted to stress that knowledge is a complex activity in which a variety of operations are synthesized. Secondly, he wanted to emphasize that the result of this activity is not a clear and distinct intuition. It is often an imperfect but objective grasp that certain things are so. Finally, he wanted to emphasize that this opening to the being of things allows for a development of knowledge which is not always or necessarily a matter of conjecture and experiment.

He began by surveying the field of knowledge keeping the proposition at the center of his discussion. He was interested in the mental act by which we grasp and affirm the significance of a judgment expressed in a proposition. When he wanted to stress the interpretation which we place on the *terms* constituting a proposition, especially the predicate, he called the act "apprehension."[336] When he wanted to describe the mental act of grasping the significance of a *proposition* taken as a whole, as an assertion of the entire judgmental meaning, he called it an act of "assent."[337] Apprehension and assent are features of one complex act of knowing what is the case. They differ only in the way that a restricted interpretation of terms differs from an inclusive interpretation and acceptance of the whole proposition containing those terms.[338]

Assent is not merely an assertion that a proposition is true. It "presupposes . . . some concomitant apprehension of its terms." "We cannot assent to a proposition without some intelligent apprehension of it." For "mental acts of whatever kind presuppose their objects." But apprehension is not equivalent to clear understanding of the full implications of its object. It "is simply an intelligent acceptance of the idea, or of the fact which a proposition enunciates." For example, we can apprehend what is meant by the statement that "John is Richard's wife's father's aunt's husband" without understanding at once that the successive relationships imply that "John is great-uncle-in-law to Richard." We can apprehend a man's conduct without understanding the principles on which he acts or the consequences which will result. A child can apprehend what it means to say that a proposition is true (for example, "that the quality of mercy is not strained, is true,") although he does not understand the full significance of what his mother tells him.[339]

Newman drew another fundamental distinction between notional and real *apprehension* depending on whether the mind interprets the terms of a proposition as signifying some abstract generality or some individual reality. Apprehension is "notional in the grammarian, it is real in the experimentalist."[340] But again he presented real and notional apprehension as two features of one complex act of knowing. "Without the apprehension of notions, we should ever pace round one small circle of knowledge; without a firm hold upon things, we shall waste ourselves in vague speculations. However, real apprehension has the precedence, as being the scope and end and the test of notional."[341]

Because assent presupposes apprehension, he also spoke of notional and real *assent*. Notional assent is the absolute acceptance of a proposition as such,[342] whereas real assent is the absolute acceptance of the real fact, individual existent or state of affairs intended by the proposition. For example, when schoolboys accept theories in textbooks, their assent is notional. But when "they come into the action of life," and acquire "an eye for their work," it becomes real. They "not only know the received rules of their profession, but enter into them."[343] When people admit in theory that slavery is unjust, their assent is notional. But when they are faced with "organized agitation" against the abuse, it becomes real.[344] An assent is not real simply because it is "intense,"[345] or because it is "carried out in conduct,"[346] but because it accepts the real state of affairs intended by the proposition in its existential fulness.[347]

Newman distinguished real and notional assent in order to synthesize them for obtaining maximum knowledge of the world.[348] Przywara has pointed out that, for Newman, real assent "as *real* does not exclude the *notional*, but rather precedes and includes it; so that the *notional* stands both at the beginning, as that which 'is to be realized,' and at the end, as that which breaks the *real* down into a notion."[349] Inference and notional assent are indispensable for sifting and controlling our real assents; yet we cannot be brought to real assent merely on the basis of logical demonstrations and notional assents. Human inquiry follows a sort of circular route, which James Collins described as a process "which begins with initial real assents about particular facts, generalizes the notional principles for inference, and eventually refers back to the existential order through our terminal real assents."[350] Throughout this process, Newman held that it is our real assents which provide "intellectual moorings" without which we would be left "at the mercy of impulses, fancies and wandering lights."[351]

It was Newman's understanding that *inference* is concerned with the particular grounds and steps which lead to the "conditional acceptance" of some proposition about an object. But *assent* is the direct and "unconditional" acceptance of that propositionally-stated object. Inference is always conditional and is expressed in a conclusion.[352] "Even if demonstrative, it is still conditional; it establishes an incontrovertible conclusion on the condition of incontrovertible premisses. To the conclusion thus drawn assent gives its absolute recognition."[353] Assent is always unconditional and is expressed in an assertion.[354] We may assent simply to the "connexion" or *"inferentia* in a complex conditional proposition," or to "the premiss, *inferentia,* and thing inferred, all at once," or to the "probability" of a proposition, or even to an "uncertainty." But in every case assent itself is an unconditional acceptance of its object.[355]

Although Newman was sometimes ambiguous, his inference/assent distinction should not be taken merely as a distinction between "thinking about an inference" and "actually inferring,"[356] or between an "inclination" to accept the conclusion of an inference and actually accepting it,[357] or between accepting an "if-then" implication and accepting a genuine "because-therefore" inference.[358] Properly qualified, these interpretations might express Newman's intentions, but by themselves they seem to suggest that all coming to know is inferential, that assent in concrete matters is either "an idle repetition" of inference—perhaps omitting "the thought of the premisses"[359] but still proportioned to their degree of probability—or else a decision to hold that a conclusion is certain because one "feels" confident about it. Newman rejected both these alternatives.

148Faith and Doubt

He noted that for Locke assent does become "a sort of reproduction and double of an act of inference."[360] "Absolute assent has no legitimate exercise, except as ratifying acts of intuition or demonstration," or concrete inferences which are more or less probable.[361] He also appealed to common experience and linguistic usage to defend a distinctive act of assent. Assent can endure when inference is forgotten, weakened or disproved. Inference can remain while assent is withheld or abandoned.[362] Again, in concrete matters, assent is not always strictly proportioned to the degree of evidence. "The facts of human nature" sometimes forced Locke himself to ignore his "pretentious axiom that probable reasoning can never lead to certitude."[363] If assent were merely "an idle repetition" of probable inference, then there would be "infinite" degrees of assent because there are infinite degrees of probability. But sometimes we know (are sure) that something is the case although "there is no proof . . . in mode and figure, equal to the proof of a proposition in Euclid."[364] Our grasp of the richness of reality may be more or less complete. Our ability to express ourselves or draw out the implications of what we know may be more or less precise. But something cannot be more or less true, and if assent is the recognition (knowledge) that something is the case (true), then there can be no degrees of assent.[365]

So for Newman inference is the acceptance of a conclusion as "somewhat, or not a little, or a good deal, or very like truth." But "assent is the acceptance of truth . . . the proper object of the intellect."[366] This is ambiguous. One can *decide to hold* (accept) a proposition *as* true, or he can *grasp* (accept) what *is* true. Newman was at times unclear on this point, but the drift of his argument shows that he meant to defend, not merely a decision, but, as Klubertanz put it, "an obscure, experimental grasp or touch of real being which can never be lifted to the clarity of conceptual abstraction."[367] The inference/assent distinction, then, is best expressed as a distinction between merely concluding and knowing. For example, an astronomer *concludes* from many calculations that there should be an unobserved planet. But he *assents* (knows) through a complex intellectual activity that he is sitting on a chair or that he was born of parents. His assent in knowledge is not merely a decision because he "feels" confident. It "cannot be given except under certain conditions," some obvious, some elusive, but which enable him to grasp that this is the case.[368] In this sense Newman combined inference and assent in the complex act of human knowledge. "Assent must be preceded by inferential acts" in a large sense,[369] but the complex of reasons does not lead to assent in the way that premises lead to a conclusion. The assents of objective knowledge will "dispense with, discard, ignore, antecedents of any kind, though antecedents may have been a *sine qua non* condition of their being elicited."[370] For we come to know, not just particular reasons and premises which lead us to draw a conclusion, but through a complex operation we come to know that something is simply true. This complex of intellectual activities and reasons has "by a law of our nature the same command over our assent, or rather the truth which it has reached has the same command, as our senses have . . . and the correlative of ascertained truth is unreserved assent."[371]

Newman sought to describe the complex act of knowledge by means of two further distinctions—one between simple and reflex assent; another between formal and informal inference.

Simple assents are made spontaneously or mechanically. Sometimes they "virtually" express an objective *grasp* that something is the case. Sometimes they merely express the fact that we *hold* something as true. In this latter case they express "our personal likings, tastes, principles, motives, and opinions." These "may and do change," but "certitudes endure." *Reflex assent* follows and includes inferential acts "which, when reduced to the shape of formal propositions, fail to satisfy the severe requisitions of science." It "is an assent, not only to a given proposition, but to the claim of that proposition on our assent as true; it is an assent to an assent, or what is commonly called a conviction."[372] I may "assent without a recognition of my assent or of its grounds, and then perhaps something occurs which leads to my reviewing and completing these grounds, analyzing and arranging them, yet without on that account implying of necessity any suspense . . . of assent."[373] Again, this could be ambiguous. I can decide to hold something as true while searching for reasons to overcome a challenge; or I can know (be sure) that something is the case while seeking to answer an objection. But Newman was interested in the latter situation. There is no "positive resolution" to continue to hold something as true. "The very force and absoluteness" of our knowledge "precludes any such resolution . . . for, since we have the truth . . . how can we possibly change?"[374] While occasionally Newman seems to have suggested that reflex assent deliberately decides to be certain, the drift of his argument was that reflex assent testifies to the presence of evidence which immediately shapes our (objective/certain) knowledge. To make a reflex assent, in this sense, is merely to fulfill a law of our intellectual nature.[375]

Yet it would be "paradoxical" to limit (certain) knowledge to those who have deliberately defended themselves. Consequently he emphasized that, while some simple assents are rightly "lost in the attempt" to defend them, others amount to *"material," "interpretative,"* or "virtual certitude" before they are deliberately defended.[376] Such simple assents are "convertible into [reflex] certitude on demand,"[377] for evidence is already present and operative. When men make a reflex assent, it will be "proportionate to their several capacities"[378] to draw out and express the vast and elusive evidence which shapes their knowledge. One might say: I know that so and so is not an automaton, for I spoke with him, had dinner with him and so on. I know I know.

Earlier he had said that real assent and notional inference combine in knowledge. Now he emphasized that "the simple and the reflex assent . . . together make up the complex act of certitude." This act can "be called a *perception,* the conviction a *certitude,* the proposition or truth a *certainty,* or thing known, or a matter of *knowledge,* and to assent to it is to *know."*[379] His discussion of "virtual" certitude was an effort to avoid oversimplifying—construing reflexivity in knowledge as a deliberate decision and the evidence which shapes our knowledge as premises in an inference.

Finally, Newman distinguished formal and informal inference.[380] *Formal inference* is the conceptually clear and explicit passage from one assertion to another. Because A is B and B is C, A is C.[381] It is "verbal reasoning, of whatever kind, as opposed to mental."[382] It is "ratiocination . . . restricted and put into grooves."[383] By itself it can bring about only a notional assent which remains hypothetical as far as real existence is concerned. *Informal inference* is the passage from one real assent to another real assent resting on the native power of the mind "by which we are enabled to become certain of what is concrete."[384] Because of various reasons, I am certain that I shall die.[385]

Again he could be taken to have assumed that all knowledge is inferential and hypothetical—although sometimes our inferences have the precise structure of logical deductions (formal), sometimes the loose structure of enumerative inductions (informal). In this case he would have been in agreement with Locke who spoke of the clear perception of relations between ideas (formal), and the probable conjectures of judgment resting on what is "observed to be *frequent* and *usual*" (informal).[386] But this was not Newman's meaning. "Syllogistic exhibitions" come "short of proof in concrete matters" for they merely assume their premises;[387] but generalizations from constant conjunction, by themselves, do "not lead to a necessary conclusion" in concrete matters. They can only provide "indications for judging of the particular" without "absolutely touching and determining facts."[388] Similarly, analogy from parallel cases[389] has "not force enough to warrant more than a probable conclusion."[390] Deduction "reaches truth in the abstract;" induction and analogy reach "probability in the concrete; but what we aim at" in informal inference "is truth in the concrete."[391]

Newman's distinction should be considered, not merely in terms of structure, but in terms of the type of assent which is generated. Formal inference is hypothetical with regard to real existence, not because it is formal in structure, but because it is used abstractly. It reaches conclusions from "general notions." And informal inference leads to real assent, not because it is rudimentary in structure, but because when it occurs it is a content-determined inference immediately shaped by experience. It is not merely a long, implicit and imperfect formal inference; it cannot be reduced to formal inference.[392]

But again, as notional and real combine in the complex act of knowledge, so formal and informal inference can combine in an intellectual activity which is both formally structured and in contact with real being. In this case, the formalized process expresses a "ratiocinative instinct" or simply states "a fact . . . in the form of an argument." Although by itself "it is neither the test of truth, nor the adequate basis of assent," when it is built upon an informal inference, it provides a "means of holding facts together" and teaches us "the direction in which truth lies."[393] Its arguments amount to "specimens and symbols of the real grounds . . . hints towards, and samples of, the true reasoning."[394] Its "systematizing" is employed "not in conjecturing unknown truths, but in comparing, adjusting, connecting, explaining facts . . . ascertained."[395] He wrote that "the real method of reasoning in concrete matters . . . does not supersede the logical form of inference, but is one and the same with it; only it is no longer an abstraction, but carried out into the realities of life;" for "its premises . . . carry it home definitely to the individual case, which is its original scope."[396] It familiarizes us with "those conditions" of our assent in knowledge which are, in fact, "the interpretation of it."[397] Again, Newman was interested in destroying the rationalistic illusion that all knowledge can be construed as a series of formal reasonings more or less justified by basic intuitions or impressions. He wanted to stress the complexity of experience which directly shapes our objective (certain) knowledge.

Newman introduced the expression, *illative sense,* to summarize and denote "the perfection" of our complex intellectual activity when it combines real assent and notional inference, formal exhibitions and informal reflection—in coming to know what is the case.[398] He called the illative sense "a transcendent logic,"[399] a "living *organon.*"[400]

> [It] is not mere common sense, but the true healthy action of our ratiocinative powers, an action more subtle and more comprehensive than the mere appreciation of a syllogistic argument. It is . . . a standard of certitude which holds good in all concrete matter . . . not indeed to the exclusion, but as the supplement of logic.[401]

It is not a distinct faculty, but the mind itself, which is "more versatile and vigorous than any of its works, of which language is one."[402] As such, it functions "in the beginning,[403] middle, and end of all verbal discussions and inquiry, and in every step of the process."[404] But also, as such, it is merely "a grand word for a common thing."[405]

He often referred to an *argumentum ad absurdum* when explaining the operation of our complex intellectual activity.[406] He compared the action of the illative sense with legal and scientific arguments where "the principle of circumstantial evidence is the *reductio ad absurdum.*"[407] He wrote that he knew (was sure) that "Great Britain is an island" and added "There is a manifest *reductio ad absurdum* attached to the notion that we can be deceived on such a point as this."[408] He wrote that he was certain of his "inevitable mortality" and added that "the strongest proof" he had of this "is the *reductio ad absurdum.*"[409] But there are no formal inconsistencies or self-contradictions involved in denying these facts. There are no semantic problems which would render a denial meaningless. Is Newman, then, merely saying that such facts are "beyond reasonable doubt," that while one could be (logically) mistaken, it is (psychologically) absurd to doubt? Or is he saying that sometimes we can know what is the case such that it is (really) absurd to doubt? The over-all thrust of his writing favors the latter interpretation:

> Am I to doubt of the truth of the laws of the human mind? . . .
> Am I to go on till I am sceptical of my own scepticism, and . . .
> may *rationally* have speculative doubts whether I live or feel?
> This, however, you will say, is a mere *reductio ad absurdum,* and
> not a positive answer . . . I am aware of it. And I must leave
> it so.[410]

He recognized that it is hopeless to attempt to prove skepticism false. It is hopeless to attempt a critical epistemology which would prove positively our ability to *know* and not merely claim to know the way things are. "If I may not assume that I exist, and in a particular way, that is, with a particular mental constitution, I have nothing to speculate about, and had better let speculation alone."[411]

He was careful to emphasize that the complex intellectual activity by which we come to know, is often or always surrounded by personal factors, moral dispositions and antecedent assumptions. In his early work he sometimes seems to have suggested that since personal factors dispose people to see things differently, experience is radically ambiguous—there is no objective truth.[412] But later, while continuing to *"stand by* . . . the *importance of antecedent probability,"*[413] he defended the objectivity of knowledge. He had meant to attack the adequacy of "cut and dried arguments," not our ability to grasp experienced reality. "Directly a mind takes in what is meant, a true view elicits from the mind proofs of itself by its own vigour."[414] The role of moral dispositions and will is not to replace reasons or make us act on insufficient evidence, but to aid the mind in recognizing a speculative or practical truth in a complex of evidence—by enabling us "to put down with a high hand as irrational" lingering doubts.[415] Dispositions and prejudices may raise "interminable difficulties" which cause disagreement among men, but "it does not prove that there is no objective truth, because not all men are in possession of it."[416] Sometimes in religious questions, "grace" is required to subdue an "irrational imagination—which, since the imagination *is* irrational, reason cannot do."[417]

But Newman sometimes failed to stress adequately the reciprocal influence between moral dispositions and imagination on the one hand, and intellectual reflection and insight on the other. This led critics to complain that, if reasoning convinces one man but not another only because the one is disposed to accept a conclusion while the other is not, then there is no point in arguing with an opponent. The only value of reasoning is to strengthen a conviction which is already a prejudice.[418] However he did recognize that dispositions "may be false or true . . . they are not necessarily true." And he added: "there *are* ways of unlearning them when they are false."[419]

In the end, his intention was to defend a complex intellectual activity in direct touch with experience, too rich and far-reaching to be captured in a syllogism.[420] The illative sense, the perfection of this intellectual activity, not only enables us to "bring together ALL the arguments, however subtle," but "to determine their place, and worth," and to place ourselves "in the *true centre of the* landscape."[421] The "conclusion" of our illative reflection on experience is (as it were) out of sight,"[422] not in the sense that we can come to know (be sure) of nothing, but in the sense that our mind "embraces more than it can master."[423]

Rationalistic empiricism sometimes takes a view of the mind which is both too narrow—for it restricts the operation of the intellect to the manipulation of concepts or basic impressions—and too pretentious—for it attempts to deduce or construct real existence from these concepts or impressions.[424] Newman was calling for a different view of the intellectual activity by which we come to know. The view he suggested is, in some ways, similar to that suggested by David Braine. Instead of defining knowledge as "justified true belief," Braine called it *"an intellectually satisfactory intellectual position"* in regard to what is the case.[425] It is "the satisfactory end-position" sought after in a question of truth or falsity, the "goal attained when we hit the target of truth, not accidentally, but reliably, as the result of exercising our faculties properly."[426] The grounds of our (objective) knowledge do not function like premises in an inference yet they are "of such a kind as *naturally* bring men reliably and securely to the truth."[427] They cannot be assessed as adequate "in advance of having relied upon" them.[428]

Newman would not accept the question: how can we be confident about our claims to know since we are always uncertain because evidence is incomplete? Instead he asked: how can we know (be sure) and not merely claim to know, which in fact is often the case, since evidence is incomplete in terms of Locke's account? If the answer is to be more than a choice between skepticism and voluntarism, if there is a *grasp* of what is the case and not merely a decision to be certain about an hypothesis, then one must reflect further to explain the unique and immediate relation with experience which is human knowledge.[429] Newman's own empiricist and nominalist tendencies, his lack of interest or ability in "metaphysics," and the "practical character" of his work—prevented him from developing his own thought in this direction.[430]

References

1. See *Essay* IV:14.4 (2:362).
2. *GA* 197.
3. *Ibid.* 204, 258.
4. *Diff* 1:79.
5. *GA* 256.
6. *Ibid.* 197–198.
7. *Apo* 180.
8. *GA* 222.
9. See *Ibid.* 252.
10. See below 97–100, 108.
11. *Apo* 31.
12. Anthony Quinton's description of certainty as "psychologically indubitable" (*The Nature of Things* (London, 1973) 144) and as "beyond reasonable doubt" (148) falls into the first sense of certainty above because in both cases a real possibility of being completely mistaken remains. His description of certainty as "logical necessity" (144) and perhaps as "self-authentication" (145) falls into the second sense above because there is no possibility of being mistaken on logical grounds. His description of "incorrigibility" at first sight appears to be a third sense where "a statement . . . is wholly verified by the experience that prompts its assertion," (146) but Quinton identified this with "infallibility" and added that "no contingent statements are incorrigible" (149). Incorrigibility seems to be another case of logical necessity. He will speak of "direct awareness as certain knowledge" (185) but only in the sense

that a claim which could conceivably be mistaken is "beyond reasonable doubt."

13. See *US* 348 ("Theory of Developments in Religious Doctrine" 2 February 1843).

14. *Diff* 2:248 (Letter to the Duke of Norfolk: 27 December 1874).

15. *GA* 61; see also 347.

16. Newman owned the two-volume third edition of 1851. He left the pages of the second volume uncut. On his reading of Mill see *PN* 1:224–227. On psychologism in the logicians with whom Newman was familiar see Wicker, "Logic" 66–111.

17. John Stuart Mill, *System of Logic* (1843) (London, 1879) I:1.6.4 note (1:129 note.)

18. *Ibid.* II:3.21.3 (2:103–104).

19. See Frederick Copleston, *History of Philosophy* (New York, 1962-1967) 8, pt. 1:93.

20. *MS* A.30.11 ("On Mill's Logic" 4 May 1857); see Locke's remark on something being possible although inconceivable. *Essay* IV:10.19 (2:322).

21. *MS* A.30.11 ("On Mill's Logic" 4 May 1857).

22. *Ibid.* Mill had written that "there *are* such certain and universal inductions." Newman added the emphasis and wrote in the margin: "N.B. here is the point to . . . insist upon." Newman wanted to stress the fact of general objective knowledge without appealing to the imagination in its defense. (Mill (1851 ed. in Newman's room at Birmingham) 1:359).

23. *MS* A.18.11 (Reason and Imagination: 23 July 1857); see *Mix* 265–267; *Idea* 400–401 ("Form of Infidelity of the Day" 1854) arguing that "truth lies in a well" so that sometimes we are inclined to reject what reason grasps "not because it really shocks our reason as improbable, but because it startles our imagination as strange." Newman applied this reason/imagination distinction to his treatment of miracles (*MS* A.30.11 "On Mill's Logic" 4 May 1857); his description of truths above but not contrary to reason (*PN* 2:101–107 "Beyond Reason" December 1859); and his defense of our ability to believe what we do not understand (*PN* 2:153 7 September 1861).

24. *MS* A.18.11 (Notes on Logic and Philosophy: January-February 1859).

25. *Ibid.*

26. *GA* 343.

27. Walgrave, 337–338.

28. John Hick, *Faith and Knowledge* (1957) (London, 1967) 208–209.

29. *Ibid.* 205–206.

30. Quinton, 173; see John L. Austin, *Sense and Sensibilia* (ed.) Geoffrey J. Warnock (1962) (Oxford, 1964) 104–131.

31. Quinton 162, 166, 191, 160, 191–192, 230.

32. *Ibid.* 150. See Henry Habberly Price, *Truth and Corrigibility, an Inaugural Lecture Delivered before the Oxford University on 5 March*

1836 (Oxford, 1936) 28. Price argued that perceptual judgments, intro-spective judgments and memory judgments, although corrigible, are "cor-rigent"—that is, they can correct other judgments. He admitted that we must say that the "intrinsic probability" of these judgments "is something which is just *evident* or *obvious*. We shall just have to *know directly* that *p* is intrinsically probable (when *p* is a judgment of one of these three kinds). Or, if we care to put it so, the judgment that *p* is intrinsically probable is an *incorrigible* judgment."

33. Quinton, 230. See Alfred J. Ayer, "Basic Propositions" in his *Philosophical Essays* (London, 1954) 105–124.

34. Quinton, 160. See Karl Popper, *The Logic of Scientific Discovery* (1934–1935) (London, 1968) 111.

35. Quinton, 230–231, 227.

36. Hick and Price seem to have said that basic sense impressions are incorrigible; Quinton wanted to say that while basic material object perceptions are corrigible they provide some foundation for our beliefs.

37. Hick, 203, 208. Also Quinton, 227.

38. *GA* 223–224, 228. See Illtyd Thethowan, *Certainty: Philosophical and Theological* (London, 1948) 7–8.

39. *GA* 224; also *Dev* 82; *VM* 1:85–86; *Ess* 1:172 ("Fall of De la Mennais" October 1837); see also Perrone, 2 (b) pars. 3: 409 distinguish-ing certitude from infallibility.

40. *GA* 224.

41. Norman Malcolm, *Knowledge and Certainty* (London, 1963) 40, in reply to Ayer's remark that "there can be doubt so long as there is the possibility of error." (Alfred J. Ayer, *Problem of Knowledge* (London, 1956) 43). Malcolm distinguished logical and real possibility of error; see also C. A. Campbell, "Self-Evidence" *Philosophical Quarterly* 10 (1960) 138–155.

42. *GA* 232; see *LD* 11:170–171 (1 June 1846).

43. *GA* 230; see 228–232.

44. See Hick, 205; *GA* 255.

45. *GA* 346.

46. *US* 249 note 5 (added 1871).

47. *GA* 239. Newman was sometimes over-confident of the certain ad- vance of science; see below 132.

48. *GA* 237.

49. See Trethowan, 6. However it seems odd to say "I am sure this is probable" for to say "it is probable" is to say "I am not sure; I do not know."

50. Clarence I. Lewis, *Analysis of Knowledge and Valuation* (La Salle, Ind., 1946) 186–187.

51. Price, 23.

52. Quinton, 156–157.

53. *Ibid.*

54. Quinton takes incorrigibility and infallibility as synonymous. *Ibid.* 146.

55. *GA* 239.

56. Hick, 204. He is quoting M. C. D'Arcy, 43; see *Prepos* 279; *HS* 1.264–271 ("Marcus Tullius Cicero" Spring 1824).

57. Hick, 205; also Quinton, 150–151.

58. A further variation on this theme is sometimes drawn from the work of Ludwig Wittgenstein. See his *On Certainty* (1950–1951) (trans.) Gertrude E. M. Anscombe and D. Paul (Oxford, 1969). The "basics" or foundations of knowledge are not "known" in the traditional sense. They are assumed as indubitable for the time being and used as criteria for judging other claims. These other claims are "known" to the extent that they are justified, but the "basics" are not "known" for the only candidates for knowledge are *claims to know* which are dubitable and so justifiable by further claims until we reach "basics" which are justified by nothing beyond themselves. We simply *decide* not to call these basics in question, but to use them to settle other questions.

59. *GA* 177–178.

60. Hick, 203.

61. *GA* 343–344.

62. *Ibid.* 227.

63. *MS* A.18.11 ("A-Introduction 1860?") 5. Newman spoke of "contuition" or an "insight into a thing through and by means of the things which lie about it," but added that it is difficult to distinguish this from "intuition" in practice.

64. *Ari* 109–110.

65. See Quinton, 123 on "vernacular" intuition.

66. *PN* 2:75 ("Proof of Theism" 7 November 1859).

67. *GA* 333–335, 337–338. See Ian T. Ramsey, *Religious Language,* 11–48.

68. See Quinton's defense of "empirical intuition" of basic statements in this sense (126, 135) where a long unarticulated convergence amounts to an inference which justifies considering these basics as "beyond reasonable doubt" for the time being (189, 185).

69. See George P. Klubertanz, "Where is the Evidence for Thomistic Metaphysics?" *Revue Philosophique de Louvain* 56 (1968) 298, on Newman's informal inference.

70. *MS* A.18.11 ("A-Introduction 1860?") 4–5. Newman wrote that "it is very difficult to separate what is called reasoning from intuition." (*PN* 2:75: "Proof of Theism" 7 November 1859). At this time he was reading Dugald Stewart who criticized Locke's "somewhat arbitrary" distinction between "intuition and reasoning." (Stewart 332). Stewart sought to join them in the act of reasoning (317). He wanted to extend the term "intuition" to the recognition of "the fundamental laws of belief" (314). A. Karl has argued that for Newman "weder reine Intuition noch rein diskursives Denken ist, sondern sich zwischen deisen beiden Polen spannt, von beiden etwas in sich hat, in der Vermischung je nach dem Individuum welchselnd." A. Karl, *Die Glaubensphilosophie Newmans* (Bonn, 1941)

60. Johannes Artz agreed that for Newman intuition and syllogism "beide erheischen einander." (Johannes Artz, "Newman und die Intuition," *Theologische Quartelschrift* 136 (1956) 180).

71. *LD* 24:309 (17 August 1869).

72. *Ibid.* 313 (18 August 1869).

73. *Ibid.* 312.

74. *Ibid.* 314 (20 August 1869).

75. See Artz, 180–183: in practice Newman did not divide instinct of particulars from intuition of general knowledge.

76. *MS* A.18.11 ("A-Introduction 1860?") 5.

77. *Ibid.* By "condition" Newman meant, not a logical premise, but simply a "supporting reason" in a large sense; just as by "conditional" assent he did not mean a "hypothetical" one, but one "resting on reasons" in a large sense. (*GA* 172).

78. *MS* A.18.11 ("A-Introduction 1860?") 4–5.

79. See *PN* 2:78 ("On H. M. Chalybäus' *Historical Development*" 8 February 1860); also *PN* 1:227–234. Chalybäus gave a subjectivist reading of Kant. Thus Newman (who did not read Kant directly) viewed him primarily as a subjectivist confined to representations in consciousness. Newman's empiricist tendencies made him critical of German Idealism and skeptical of Kant's "transcendental" methods. His copy of Kant's *Critique of Pure Reason* (1781) (trans.) John M. D. Meiklejohn (London, 1855) was left in his room at Birmingham with half its pages uncut.

80. *MS* A.18.11 ("A-Introduction 1860?") 4.

81. *Ibid.* 13; see *GA* 269–270.

82. *GA* 236, 258.

83. Richard I. Aaron, "Intuitive Knowledge" *Mind* 51 (1942) 317–318. Dr. Ewing replied to Aaron in "Professor Aaron on Intuition" *Mind* 52 (1943) 51–53, defending "fallible intuitions" on the grounds that certain knowledge must be restricted to infallible deductions of logical entailment from necessary truths.

84. *GA* 258.

85. *LD* 24:375 (17 November 1869).

86. *Idea* 401 (1854).

87. David Braine, "The Nature of Knowledge" *Proceedings of the Aristotelian Society* n.s. 72 (1971–1972) 54, 51.

88. *GA* 202. See Braine 50–54 on "the mistake of making justification depend on inference."

89. *GA* 227. Newman is quoting William Chillingworth, *Religion of Protestants: A Safe Way to Salvation,* Chapter 2, para. 154 (1637) (London, 1845) 179–182.

90. *GA* 269, 255; see also 195.

91. *Ibid.* 345; 350.

92. *Ibid.* 252.

93. See Braine, 51.

94. *GA* 196.

95. See Braine, 44–45, 47–50.

96. *GA* 195.

97. *Ibid.* 196, 350.

98. *LD* 14:46 (20 August 1850).

99. He read this text in Wiseman's article, "The Anglican Claim of Apostolical Succession" *Dublin Review* 7 (1839) 139–180; see Augustine, *Contra Epistolam Parmeniani* Liber iii. Ch. 3. (400) in *PL* 43:95–97. See *Apo* 117.

100. *PN* 2:167–169 (28 January 1867); see *Diff* 2:303 (Letter to the Duke of Norfolk: 27 December 1874).

101. *Prepos* 46–47. He added that the truth of tradition depends on its source (51–52). He read and underlined Locke's remark that "the general consent of all men" gives only the "highest degree of probability." (*Essay* IV:16.6 (2:375), Newman's copy at Birmingham).

102. *MS* A.18.11 ("A-Introduction 1860?"). See *GA* 227, and 375: "it does not prove that there is no objective truth, because not all men are in possession of it."

103. *LD* 14:46 (20 August 1850).

104. *Dev* 203.

105. *LD* 11:60 (11 December 1845); and *ibid.* 16:106 (10 April 1854) quoting George Crabbe, *Tales of the Hall* 9: "The Preceptor Husband" ll. 200–204 (1819) in *Tales, 1812 and Other Selected Poems* (ed.) Howard Mills (Cambridge, 1967) 400.

106. *Idea* 461, 467; see 475 ("Christianity and Scientific Investigation" 1855).

107. *Ess* 1:284–285 ("Prospects of the Anglican Church" April 1839).

108. *Dev* 186.

109. *Prepos* 294.

110. *Idea* 94 (1852).

111. See *GA* 373–375.

112. *Idea* 462–463 ("Christianity and Scientific Investigation" 1855).

113. *Ibid.* 401 ("A Form of Infidelity" 1854).

114. *Ibid.* 461 ("Christianity and Scientific Investigation" 1855).

115. *VM* 1:87, notes 8 and 9 (added 1877).

116. *Ibid.* 123; also 68–69; Trethowan, 5–6.

117. *VM* 1:xxii (Preface 1877), also xxv–xxvii; *HS* 1:402, 420–421 ("Primitive Christianity" 1833–1836).

118. *GA* 271, 287; see *Idea* 58–59 (1852); also W. V. O. Quine, "Two Dogmas of Empiricism" in his *From a Logical Point of View* (New York, 1953) 20–46; and Jonathan Bennett's criticism of Quine's coherence theory of truth in "Analytic-Synthetic" *Proceedings of the Aristotelian Society* n.s. 59 (1958–1959) 163–188.

119. *MS* A.30.11 ("The Conceivable" December 1863).

120. *GA* 81.

121. *MS* A.30.11 ("The Conceivable" December 1863).

122. *Ibid.* See *MS* A.30.11 ("On Conception" 3 December 1863).

123. *MS* A.30.11 ("The Conceivable" December 1863).

124. *GA* 323.

125. *VM* 1:118, note 6 (added 1877).

126. *GA* 323. He also mentioned that "the consequences of *denying* its certainty" might provide a test of the truth of an idea. (*LD* 14:46, 20 August 1850). But the question remains whether these "consequences" are logical, practical, or in some sense "real." See below 152–153.

127. *MS* A.30.11 ("A-Introduction 1860?").

128. *MS* B.7.4 ("Certainty of Faith" 16 December 1853).

129. *MS* B.3.2 ("no truth is more certain" 1856?).

130. *GA* 345.

131. *Ibid.* 348–350; see *MS* A.30.11 ("Evidences of Religion" 12 January 1860) where he distinguished supernatural faith from human reasoning about the being of God and the fact of revelation. His investigation of the latter led to this line of thought in the *GA*.

132. *GA* 354; see *PN* 2:163 (3 September 1865); *DA* 249–250 (Tract 85: 21 September 1838); Collins, *Readings* 156 (29 April 1879). On Newman's relation to Aristotle see *PN* 1:150–163; Franz Michel Willam *Aristotelische Erkenntnislehre bei Whately und Newman* (Freiburg, 1960); B. J. Mahoney, "Newman and Aristotle: the Concept of Conscience" (Ph.D. dissertation, University of Birmingham, 1967); Johannes Artz, "Die Eigenständigkeit der Erkenntnistheorie John Henry Newmans" *Theologische Quartelschrift* 139 (1959) 194–222.

133. *Idea* 463-464 ("Christianity and Scientific Investigation" 1855); *Mix* 88.

134. *MS* A.30.11 ("A-Introduction 1860?").

135. *GA* 233; also see 319.

136. Pailin interpreted Newman's inference/assent distinction in this way (Pailin 161–185); also, in places, Wicker ("Logic" 150, but see 151).

137. *LD* 13:267 (1 October 1849).

138. *MS* A.23.1 (On opinion, belief, etc. 30 April 1853).

139. *GA* 174.

140. *MS* B.7.4 dated 20 August 1866 but with the comment, "From Fr. Edward Caswell's notes on Lectures with the Father 1853." The lectures were given 17 May—18 June 1851 from a paper written over Easter 1848 found in B.9.11.

141. *MS* A.23.1 (On opinion, belief, etc. 30 April 1853).

142. *MS* B.7.4 ("Caswell's notes" Easter 1848).

143. *MS* A.23.1 (On opinion, belief, etc. 30 April 1853).

144. *MS* A.18.11/B.9.11 ("Analysis of religious inquiry" 11–18 May 1853).

145. *MS* B.7.4 ("Caswell's notes" Easter 1848).

146. *LD* 18:334 (24 April 1858).

147. *MS* A.30.11 (Certainty and Probable Evidence: 26 June 1865).

148. *MS* A.23.1 ("Essay on Certitude" 20 July 1865).

149. *Ibid.*

150. *MS* A.30.11 (titled "p. 17 A Comparison of the Moral Sense and Certitude 1865." Perhaps written on 11 August 1865); see *AW* 270

(Journal: 30 October 1870) mentioning a paper with that date on "Certitude-Intuition-Instinct."

151. *MS* A.23.1 (On opinion, belief, etc. 30 April 1853) and A.18.11/ B.9.11 ("Analysis of religious inquiry" 11–18 May 1853).

152. *MS* A.18.11/B.9.11 ("Analysis of religious inquiry" 11–18 May 1853). Besides "Certainty" Newman listed "Belief, Surmise, Disbelief, Suspicion and Suspense." He called "Persuasion, Doubt, Prejudice and Ignoring" simple "creations" of will. Compare with Braine's definition of knowledge as an "intellectually satisfactory intellectual position." (Braine, 54).

153. *MS* A.18.11/B.9.11 ("Analysis of religious inquiry" 11–18 May 1853).

154. *Ibid.*

155. *Ibid.*

156. *Ibid.*

157. *MS* A.23.1 ("Essay on Certitude" 20 July 1865).

158. *MS* A.30.11 ("Comparison of the Moral Sense and Certitude 1865").

159. See the early mention of reflexivity in *AW* 150 (1820–1821).

160. *MS* B.7.4 ("Certainty of Faith" 16 December 1853).

161. *Ibid.* This sentence is a marginal note which may have been added later.

162. *Ibid.*

163. *Ibid.*

164. Newman gave the example of Newton and his disciples who could be equally certain of some of Newton's conclusions although Newton himself might have had greater "evidentia" available in support of them (*Ibid.*). See *LD* 15:498 (11 December 1853); *MS* A.18.11 (Reason and Imagination: 23 July 1857); *GA* 372–373 where Newman described the use of reason in coming to know as "true originality of mind" in contrast with "mere exhibitions of ingenuity" in an effort to avoid voluntarism.

165. *MS* A.23.1 ("Essay on Certitude" 20 July 1865).

166. *MS* B.7.4 ("Certainty of Faith" 16 December 1853).

167. *MS* A.23.1 ("Essay on Certitude" 20 July 1865).

168. *MS* B.7.4 ("Certainty of Faith" 16 December 1853).

169. *MS* A.23.1 ("Essay on Certitude" 20 July 1865).

170. *Ibid.*

171. *MS* A.23.1 ("Meaning of Certitude" 25 September 1865).

172. *Ibid.*

173. *Ibid.*

174. *AW* 270 (30 October 1870); see *LD* 22:274 (12 August 1866); *PN* 2:167 note 2; and Wilfrid Ward 2:245 for a letter of 31 August 1870.

175. *AW* 270 (30 October 1870). Certitude is a *complex, reflex* assent.

176. *MS* A.30.11 (Apprehension and Assent: 26 April, 5 May, 7 September 1868).

177. *MS* A.30.11 ("On Conception" and "The Conceivable" December 1863).

178. Josef Pieper, *Leisure the Basis of Culture* (London, 1952) 31–34. See Eric Mascall, "Two Ideals of Knowledge" in his *Words and Images* (1957) (London, 1968) 63–70, where he argued that this description applies to our knowledge of the everyday world of material things.

179. See, for example, Louis M. Regis, *Epistemology* (New York, 1959); also Aquinas, *Summae* I. 77–78, 84–85 in *Leon.* 5:236–249, 250–257, 313–329, 330–346; *De Veritate* 18 in *Leon.* 22:529–559; also Francis Cunningham, "Certitudo in St. Thomas" *Modern Schoolman* 30 (1953) 297–324; and James F. Anderson, "The Notion of Certitude" *Thomist* 18 (1955) 522–539.

180. *GA* 293, 292.

181. *Ibid.* 268.

182. *Dev* 357.

183. *US* 8 ("The Philosophical Temper, first enjoined by the Gospel" 2 July 1826).

184. *US* 90 ("Personal Influence, the Means of Propagating the Truth" 22 January 1832).

185. *Letters* 2:311 (1840).

186. *VM* 1:129, see *US* 100–101 ("On Justice" 8 April 1832).

187. *VM* 1:16 note 5 (added 1877); see *Diff* 1:395–396.

188. *VM* 1:xxii (1877 preface).

189. *Apo* 70.

190. *VM* 1:129.

191. See *Dev* 3.

192. *US* 331 ("Theory of Developments in Religious Doctrine" 2 February 1843).

193. *Ibid.* 317.

194. *Ath* 2: 144–145; see 146.

195. *Ibid.* 447; see *HS* 3:193–194 ("Strength and Weakness of Universities" 1854); *GA* 249.

196. *Ath* 2:446. The terms in his example are "Son" and "Word." See *Idea* 453 ("Christianity and Physical Science" November 1855); *US* 337, 340 ("Theory of Developments" 2 February 1843).

197. *Dev* 439; see *US* 201 ("Faith and Reason Contrasted" 6 January 1839) describing our situation as a "night battle." The same image occurs in Matthew Arnold, "Dover Beach" ll. 35–37 (1867) in *The Poetical Works of Matthew Arnold* (ed.) Chauncey B. Tinker and H. F. Lowry (Oxford, 1950) 210–212.

198. *Dev* 55; see 64, 74–75.

199. *Ibid.* 94. *See Mix* 261.

200. *LD* 11:86 (8 January 1846). See *ibid.* 12:227 (27 June 1848); and *ibid.* 14:38 (12 August 1850).

201. *Diff* 1:396.

202. *Ibid.* 213; see 377.

203. *GA* 498 (added 1880).

204. *Ibid.*

164   Faith and Doubt

205. *MS* A.30.11 (Human Reason and Objects of Faith: September 1863); see *VM* 1:215.
206. *Apo* 179–180; see 185.
207. *Ibid.*
208. *GA* 499. He was speaking of "religious truth" but in the *GA* and *Idea* he applied this same "law" to scientific and historical truth as well.
209. See *LD* 16:105 (1855?).
210. *MS* A.18.11 ("A-Introduction 1860?") 33.
211. *Ibid.* 36; see *GA* 348; *MS* A.30.11 ("On Conception" 3 December 1863) on the mind's ability to reach "beyond experience for the ultimate benefit of experience itself."
212. *MS* A.18.11 ("A-Introduction 1860?") 36–37.
213. *Ibid.* 45. He referred to Aristotle, *Nicomachean Ethics* 6:11 (322–309 B.C.) (*Ethica Nicomachia* (ed.) Ingram Bywater 1894 (Oxford, 1942) 125–126). MS A.18.11 ("A-Introduction 1860?") 54–59.
214. *GA* 367; see Michael Polanyi's discussion of "the *structure of tacit knowing.*" (*Personal Knowledge* (1958) (London, 1962) x); and the criticism by Alan R. White that his "personalism" drifts into "subjectivism." *Philosophical Quarterly* 10(1960) 377–378; also Avery Dulles' effort to link Polanyi and Newman ("Faith, Reason and the Logic of Discovery" *Thought* 45 (1970) 485–502).
215. *US* 316 ("Theory of Developments" 2 February 1843).
216. Jerry H. Gill seems to have spoken of latent ideas merely as psychologically unconscious, in his application of Polanyi's work to religious belief. ("The Tacit Structure of Religious Knowing" *International Philosophical Quarterly* 9(1969) 533–559, esp. 542). Timothy C. Potts' objections to latent ideas weigh against Gill but not Newman. ("What Then Does Dr. Newman Mean?" *Newman-Studien* 6 (1964) 55–81).
217. *US* 267 ("Implicit and Explicit Reason" 29 June 1840).
218. *US* 324; see 326 ("Theory of Developments" 2 February 1843).
219. *Ibid.* 329. Locke would not allow any idea in the mind which is not clearly and distinctly perceived; see *Essay* IV:3.8 (2:199); I:1.5 (1:41). Ideas, then, are incapable of development as well as of confusion; see Gibson, 25. Austin Farrer attacked "the ideal of clarity and distinctness . . . The ideal . . . of philosophical knowledge . . . is objective, the fullest apprehension of what really exists, whether we can get our thinking about it perfectly clear or not." (1947) *Reflective Faith* (ed.) Charles C. Conti (London, 1972) 70.
220. *US* 331 ("Theory of Developments" 2 February 1843).
221. *Ibid.* 334, 339.
222. *Ibid.* 340–343.
223. *Ibid.* 327.
224. *Dev* 36.
225. *PPS* 6:98 ("Difficulty of realizing Sacred Priveleges" 31 March 1839).
226. *US* 328 ("Theory of Developments" 2 February 1843).

227. Newman, "Unpublished Paper by Newman on Development of Doctrine" 15 February 1868 (ed.) Charles Stephen Dessain, *Journal of Theological Studies* n.s. 9 (1958) 331–332.

228. *Dev* 38.

229. *Ibid.* 40; see *PN* 2:157 (15 September 1861).

230. See *Dictionary of National Biography* (Oxford, 1937–1938) 7:731–732; also the biography of Froude's friend and associate, Brunel: L. T. C. Rolt, *Isambard Kingdom Brunel* (London, 1957) 324.

231. *LD* 14:178 (28 December 1850).

232. *Ibid.* 179.

233. *Ibid.*

234. *Ibid.* 181.

235. *Ibid.* 16:104 (10 April 1854).

236. *Ibid.* 106–108 (1855?).

237. *Ibid.* 19:270 (29 December 1859).

238. *Ibid.*

239. *Ibid.* 271; 2 *Timothy* 3:7.

240. *LD* 19:270 (29 December 1859).

241. *Ibid.*

242. *Ibid.* 172–173 (2 January 1860).

243. *Ibid.* 284 (15 January 1860).

244. *Ibid.* 284–285 (16 January 1860).

245. *Ibid.* Newman distinguished "the scientific proof of Christianity" from the "popular . . . personal evidence on which a given individual believes it."

246. *Ibid.* 297 (25 January 1860).

247. *Ibid.* 296, 297.

248. *Ibid.* 299 (26 January 1860).

249. *Ibid.* 298–299.

250. *Ibid.* 440 (Memorandum: 14 December 1860).

251. That is, a suspension of judgment.

252. *LD* 19:441 (Memorandum: 14 December 1860).

253. *Ibid.* See *ibid.* 20:430 (9 April 1863).

254. Gordon Huntington Harper (ed.), *Cardinal Newman and William Froude* (Baltimore, 1933) 177–178. Partly printed in *LD* 21:245 note 1 (29 September 1864). Froude enclosed a copy of *Frazer's Magazine* and drew Newman's attention to Fitzjames Stephen's review of the *Apologia* (*Frazer's Magazine* 80 (1864) 265–303); see *LD* 22:73 note 1.

255. Harper, *Cardinal* 181 (8 October 1864).

256. *Ibid.*

257. *LD* 21:245 (30 September 1864).

258. *Ibid.* 19:270, 271 (29 December 1859).

259. *Ibid.* 284 (15 January 1860).

260. *Ibid.* 297 (25 January 1860).

261. *Ibid.* 294 (23 January 1860).

262. *Ibid.* 297 (25 January 1860); Harper, *Cardinal* 181 (8 October 1864).

263. *US* 345 ("Theory of Developments" 2 February 1843); see *Essay* IV:12.10–14 (2:350–354).

264. *Idea* 48 (1852).

265. *US* 345 ("Theory of Developments" 2 February 1843).

266. *Ibid.* 348.

267. *Ess* 1:34 (Tract 73: 2 February 1835).

268. *US* 349 note 5 (added 1871).

269. *Idea* 51, 47 (1852).

270. *Dev* 439.

271. *Idea* 465 ("Christianity and Scientific Investigation" 1855).

272. *US* 8 ("Philosophical Temper" 2 July 1826).

273. *Idea* 474 ("Christianity and Scientific Investigation" 1855).

274. *Ibid.* 474–475; see *US* 257 ("Implicit and Explicit Reason" 1840).

275. *Idea* 478–479; see Gilbert Harman, "Inference to the Best Explanation" *Philosophical Review* 74 (1965) 88–95; and "Enumerative Induction as Inference to the Best Explanation" *Journal of Philosophy* 65 (1968) 529–533, who spoke of new scientific theories explaining the success of older ones.

276. Karl Popper, *The Open Society and Its Enemies* (1945) (London, 1966) 2:185. See above 95–103.

277. Karl Popper, *Conjectures and Refutations* (1963) (London, 1969) 387.

278. Popper, *Logic* 102–103, 43.

279. Popper, *Conjectures* 117, 229.

280. *Ibid.* 225.

281. Popper, *Logic* 105.

282. *Ibid.* 280, 278.

283. Popper, *Conjectures* 226, 235.

284. *Dev* 357–358; see *GA* 208.

285. See Mortimer Adler, *Conditions of Philosophy* (New York, 1965) 113–114, 33–36, esp. 35, who distinguished common experience and particular experience and accused Popper of ignoring the former.

286. Thomas S. Kuhn, "Logic of Discovery or Psychology of Research" in *Criticism and the Growth of Knowledge* (1969) (ed.) I. Lakatos and A. Musgrave (Cambridge, 1972) 13.

287. Thomas S. Kuhn, *Structure of Scientific Revolutions* (Chicago, 1962) 150.

288. *Ibid.* Also Kuhn, "Logic" 264.

289. See above 111; also Karl R. Kordig, "The Theory-ladenness of Observation" *Review of Metaphysics* 24 (1971) 448–484 criticizing Paul K. Feyerabend, Norwood R. Hanson, T. S. Kuhn and Stephen Toulmin on observation; and his "Objectivity, Scientific Change and Self-Reference" *Boston Studies in the Philosophy of Science* (eds.) Roger C. Buck and Robert S. Cohen (Dordrecht, 1971) 8:519–523; and I. Scheffler, *Science and Subjectivity* (New York, 1965) 21.

290. Kuhn, "Reflections on My Critics" in *Criticism* 265; see Kuhn, *Structure,* 196.

291. Kuhn, "Reflections" 264.
292. See *ibid.* where he allowed men involved in inter-theory discussion to "resort to their shared everyday vocabulary." This seems inconsistent with the claim that there is no objective (neutral) recourse.
293. *GA* 251, 243, 232, 245, 247.
294. *Ibid.* 229.
295. *US* 8 ("Philosophical Temper" 2 July 1826).
296. *GA* 229–230. Kuhn distinguished the puzzle-solving of "normal" science where one accepts theories "on the authority of teaching and text, not because of evidence," (*Structure* 80) and tries "to force nature into . . . the paradigm," (*ibid.* 23–24)—and the problem-solving of "extraordinary" science where theories are revolutionized. Newman would join Kuhn's critics in rejecting this distinction. See Popper, "Normal Science and its Dangers" in *Criticism* 52.
297. *GA* 120, 140, 147, 133.
298. *Ibid.* 243.
299. *Ibid.* 245, 248, 247. See *DA* 200 (Tract 85: 21 September 1838); *Dev* 200; *Apo* 49–52.
300. *GA* 249, 251.
301. *Ibid.* 249, 255, 258.
302. *Letters* 2:311 (1840); see *GA* 46–47.
303. *GA* 320–321.
304. *PPS* 5:107–108 ("State of Innocence" 11 February 1838).
305. *VM* 1:lix (added 1877).
306. *Idea* 461 ("Christianity and Scientific Investigation" 1855).
307. *PPS* 5:107 ("State of Innocence" 11 February 1838).
308. *GA* 321.
309. *Ibid.* 321–322; and see *Apo* 31.
310. *MS* A.23.1 ("Essay on Certitude" 20 July 1865).
311. *LD* 21:146 (6 July 1864). He gave the illustration of a cable of separate threads, each one feeble in itself, but sufficient together, in contrast with the iron rod of mathematical demonstration. Whately had spoken of "the *more* probable." (Whately, *Rhetoric* 1828 ed. 102–103; 1846 ed. 100–101).
312. See *PN* 2:95–96 ("Formation of Thought" 3 December 1859).
313. *Idea* 99 (1852).
314. *US* 288–289 ("Wisdom" 1 June 1841).
315. *Idea* 180 (1852).
316. *Ibid;* and Collins, *God* 368.
317. *LD* 14:178 (28 December 1850).
318. *US* 295 ("Wisdom" 1 June 1841).
319. *Ibid.* 290.
320. *Idea* 460 ("Christianity and Scientific Investigation" 1855).
321. *Ibid.* 436. See *GA* 69–70; *Diff* 2:253 (Letter to Duke of Norfolk: 27 December 1875).
322. *Ibid.* 432.
323. *Ibid.*

324. *Ibid.* 433–434.

325. *US* 295 ("Wisdom" 1 June 1841).

326. *Ibid.* 290.

327. *Idea* 466 ("Christianity and Physical Science" November 1855); *US* 334, 339 ("Theory of Developments" 2 February 1843); see above 106, 125–127.

328. *Idea* 436–437 ("Christianity and Physical Science" November 1855).

329. *Ibid.* 446.

330. *Ibid.* 441.

331. *Ibid.* 436.

332. *US* 290 ("Wisdom" 1 June 1841).

333. See *PN* 2:173–179 (Free Will: 8 February 1874); *PPS* 6:98 ("Difficulties of Realizing Sacred Priveleges" 31 March 1839). On constructural and ontological ways of knowing see Gavin Ardley, *Aquinas and Kant* (London, 1950).

334. Newman spoke of some interplay between theology, philosophy and science. See *Idea* 49, 72–73 (1852).

335. *US* 110 ("Justice" 8 April 1832).

336. *GA* 9.

337. *Ibid.* 13–14, 16.

338. See Collins, *Readings* 40; Zeno, 41–45.

339. *GA* 13, 18, 8, 5, 19–20, 16, 52. On the logic of testimony see below 190–192. In *GA* 45–52 Newman discussed assent to mysteries or propositions conveying "incompatible notions." In science and philosophy informal inference can bring one to assent to what must be the case although he does not understand how it can be so. (*GA* 46–47, 328). He recognizes that the proposition in question is a mystery—not mere nonsense, and that the apparently incompatible notions are only "economical" expressions of "aspects of things." (*GA* 49–52; also *MS* A.30.11 "Chapter II" September 1863). Newman admitted that one might be mistaken *"ab initio"* (*GA* 49), but tended to ignore this possibility. In faith, one's God-given ability to assent to a divine testimony, enables him to accept what he cannot understand. (*GA* 52). He recognizes in faith that certain notions, such as God's mercy and justice, do not belong to the object of his faith "in that fulness which would involve" an incompatibility. (*GA* 51). But Newman sometimes too quickly appealed to "our ignorance" as the "token of the supra, sed non contra rationem." (*PN* 2:103 "Beyond Reason" December 1859). One who knows in faith that what appears to be an "objection" which "cannot be *repelled*" is in fact only a *"question"* which "cannot be *solved,"* (*ibid.* 101) can use rational argument to defend himself. See below 187–190; also *LD* 12:548–550 ("Letter on Mysteries" May 1859); *Theses* 258; and John Courtney Murray, *The Problem of God* (Yale, 1969) 31–76 criticizing "a negative theology that begins too soon."

340. *GA* 20. He often fell into nominalist ways of speaking in these

pages; see above 77–78; Zeno, 125–129; Boekraad, *Personal Conquest* 201–210.

341. *GA* 34.

342. On kinds of notional assent see *GA* 42–74; Zeno, 129. To assent to "the truth" or "the probability" of a proposition is notional.

343. *GA* 76.

344. *Ibid.* 77.

345. *Ibid.* 47. Henry H. Price in his *Belief* (London, 1969) 333 took Newman's distinction as one of degree of vivacity of the images accompanying assent; but see *GA* 81.

346. *GA* 82–83.

347. See Klubertanz, 296–297. Real assent is "the categorical assertion of real existence;" notional, the mere "affirmation of a proposition."

348. *GA* 10–11.

349. Erich Przywara, *J. H. Kardinal Newman. Christentum. Ein Aufbau,* vol. 4: *Einführung in Newmans Wesen und Werk* (Freiburg, 1922) 46. Quoted material translated from German.

350. Collins, *Readings* 43.

351. *GA* 88. On real assent to revealed mysteries and the role of conscience see *ibid.* 102–121, 127–141.

352. *Ibid.* 259, 5.

353. *Ibid.* 172; see Price, *Belief* 146–148 who took Newman as saying all inference is conditional, that is, doubtful.

354. *GA* 5, 183, 175. Price seems to have overlooked these remarks when he wrote that when evidence is inconclusive Newman allowed only two possibilities—the suspension of all judgment or an unreasonable assent to a proposition as certainly true. (*Belief* 146–148).

355. On the affinity of assent to real apprehension and inference to notional apprehension, and the consequences for action in the first case and syllogism in the second, see *GA* 36–41, 266–267; Boekraad, *Personal Conquest* 173–177.

356. See Price, *Belief* 145; *GA* 165–166.

357. See Price, *Belief* 149, 154; see *GA* 182–185 for Newman's interpretation of "conversational expressions" such as "half-assent," "conditional" or "deliberate" or "hesitating" assent, "firm or weak assent."

358. See Price, *Belief* 149, 154; Wicker, "Logic" 134; Pailin, 125–160.

359. *GA* 166, 165.

360. *Ibid.* 165; see above 81.

361. *GA* 159. Newman felt that *GA* 159–187 was his fullest reply to Locke; see *Dev* 328 note 1 (added 1878).

362. *GA* 165–169.

363. *Ibid.* 160, 161–164.

364. *Ibid.* 81.

365. *Ibid.* 174. Newman quoted J. E. Gambier, *An Introduction to the Study of Moral Evidence or of That Species of Reasoning Which Relates to Matters of Fact and Practice* (1806) (London, 1824). Newman

respected his insistence that there is a determinate evidence which enables us to reason properly in concrete matter; but rejected his claim that there are degrees of assent.

366. *GA* 165, 172; see also 259.

367. Klubertanz, 301; see above 114–122.

368. *GA* 157, and see 292.

369. *Ibid.* 171. In fact where "nothing better" can be found, "obstinate men" will give their decision as their reason. See *ibid.* 6; Collins, *Readings* 41.

370. *GA* 4, 180.

371. *Ibid.* 170.

372. *Ibid.* 188, 220, 412, 195; see also 197, 221; Zeno, 131–132; Cronin, 62–71. See above 117. Newman noted that because "the reflex or confirmatory assent" is given "to the truth . . . of our assent to the simple assent" it is notional and does not motivate action as forcefully as simple real assents; see *GA* 214.

373. *GA* 189–190.

374. *Ibid.* 193.

375. See *Ibid.* 412.

376. *Ibid.* 211, 213; see Zeno, 156–158.

377. *GA* 220; see 211–212. He was speaking of the certain faith of the unlearned and of martyrs, but found this analysis applicable "in secular subjects as well as religious."

378. *Ibid.* 212.

379. *Ibid.* 216, 196.

380. See Zeno, 172–190; Boekraad, *Personal Conquest* 140–172; Cronin, 45–51.

381. *GA* 266.

382. *Ibid.* 263.

383. *Ibid.* He sometimes used "logic," "inference," and "formal inference" as synonymous.

384. *Ibid.* 288.

385. *Ibid.* 198.

386. *Essay* IV:14.4 (2:362); see above 79–81.

387. *GA* 269.

388. *Ibid.* 279.

389. See *Essay* IV:16.12 (2:380).

390. *GA* 284.

391. *Ibid.* 279.

392. *Ibid.* 283, see 178. See also Klubertanz 298–300. Both *"propter quid"* and *"quia"* demonstration in the scholastic sense would be "informal" for they variously recognize real causal dependence; see Aquinas *Summae* I.2.2, *Leon.* 4:30.

393. *GA* 287 note 1, 287, 285–286.

394. *US* 275, see 258–259 ("Implicit and Explicit Reason" 29 June 1840).

395. *Ibid.* 294, see 290 ("Wisdom" 1 June 1841).

396. *GA* 292, see 293–294; see above 121–122.

397. *US* 101 ("Justice" 8 April 1832).

398. *GA* 345, 353; see Zeno, 17–31; Cronin, 52–53.

399. *GA* 216, see 303, 207; and Collins, *Readings* 156 (29 April 1870) calling it "the inductive sense;" see above 107–108.

400. *GA* 316.

401. *Ibid.* 317. It is a "supra-logical judgment" or "the 'judicium prudentis viri' " but applying to speculative as well as practical questions.

402. *GA* 362; see *LD* 16:103–104 (26 August 1851).

403. Before inquiry it determines "the aspects in which a question is to be viewed," "the principles on which it is to be considered," and "the arguments by which it is to be decided." *GA* 381; see 371–383.

404. *GA* 361.

405. *LD* 24:375 (17 November 1869).

406. See *LD* 13:364 (5 January 1860); *LD* 14:46 (20 August 1850).

407. *GA* 321–322; see 319–320.

408. *Ibid.* 295.

409. *Ibid.* 300.

410. *LD* 17:334 (24 April 1858); see *GA* 230, 234; also Joseph M. Boyle, "Self-Referential Inconsistency, Inevitable Falsity, and Metaphysical Argumentation" *Metaphilosophy* 3 (1972) 26–44, and Joseph Boyle, G. Grisez, O. Tollefsen, "Determinism, Freedom and Self-Referential Arguments" *Review of Metaphysics* 26 (September 1972) 18–20 on a "performative" absurdity; also Adler, 115, 120 on "common experience" rendering denial absurd. But purely negative argument can suggest that we only achieve knowledge of what *possibly* could be the case. Newman, however, seems to have rested his *reductio ad absurdum* on a positive (objective) grasp of what *actually* is so. Thus progress is not always the development of better possible interpretations of what is never known; but sometimes the development of a more comprehensive statement of what we know to be the case.

411. *GA* 347.

412. See *PPS* 8:121–122 ("Inward Witness to the Truth of the Gospel" 18 December 1825); *Ess* 1:223–233 ("Theology of St. Ignatius" January 1839); *US* 187–199 ("Faith and Reason Contrasted" 6 January 1839); *Ess* 2:222 ("Milman's View of Christianity" January 1841); *DA* 293 (Tamworth Reading Room: February 1841); *AW* 170 (Journal: 26 January 1823).

413. *LD* 15:381 (12 June 1853).

414. *Ibid.;* see *Dev* 178–181; *LD* 12:233, 290 (3 July, 12 October 1848).

415. *GA* 219; see 217, 302.

416 *Ibid.* 374–375; see *Idea* 400–402 ("Form of Infidelity" 1854).

417. *PN* 2:195 (7 November 1877); see 169 (19 May 1867); 171 (23 July 1868); *LD* 18:335–336 (24 April 1858).

418. Harold L. Weatherby, *Cardinal Newman in His Age* (Nashville, 1973) 188–189; see his "Newman and Victorian Liberalism: a Study

in the Failure of Influence" *Critical Quarterly* 13 (1971) 205–213; also Francis L. Patton, "The Grammar of Assent" *Princeton Review* 43 (1871) 252; Thomas Harper, "Dr. Newman's Essay in Aid of a Grammar of Assent" *Month* 12–13 (1870) 57; Leslie Stephen, "Dr. Newman's Scepticism" *Nineteenth Century* 29 (1891) 198; Cronin, 75–82.

419. *Prepos* 279.
420. See *GA* 343, 291.
421. *PN* 2:163 (3 September 1865); see *GA* 321.
422. *GA* 328.
423. *Letters* 2:311 (1840).
424. See Klubertanz, 301.
425. Braine, 54.
426. *Ibid.* 57–58.
427. *Ibid.* 61.
428. *Ibid.* 62. Braine and Newman both refer to Aristotle's *Nicomachean Ethics* as an important source for their reflections. *Ibid.* 55; *GA* 353–358.
429. See Regis, 183–192, 210. Newman apparently did not appreciate as fully as would have been desirable the inability of a hard empiricism to sustain the objective (certain) knowledge he sought to defend.
430. *GA* 343–344. Five years before his death, he wrote: "My turn of mind has never led me toward metaphysics." (*SE* 94 "Revelation in its relation to Faith" probably written January 1886 in reply to Principal Fairbairn's article: "Reason and Religion" *Contemporary Review* 48 (December 1885) 842–850. Newman considered publishing this reply in the March issue of the *Review* but decided to withhold it. See Wilfrid Ward 2:509.) He sought to avoid "scepticism" by defending "a faculty in the mind" which has "truth for its object" (*SE* 97); or "the exercise of a power of the mind itself. . . . For convenience we speak of the mind as possessing faculties instead of saying that it acts in a certain way and on a definite subject-matter; but we must not turn a figure of speech into a fact." (*Ibid.* 102–103).

CHAPTER VI

NEWMAN'S FINAL POSITION

The certainty of faith

On December 16, 1853, Newman wrote a long paper "On the Certainty of Faith."[1] First he distinguished

> two modes of apprehending or holding truth, the Evidentia Veritatis, and the Evidentia Credibilitatis. We may 1. *see* that a proposition is true, or 2. *feel* that it is true . . . to see a proposition true, is to have its truth actually before us; to feel it to be true is to have a presentiment or anticipation of its truth. In the first case, we say the thing *is;* in the latter, it *must be.*[2]

He then attempted to give "literal" meaning to the "metaphors"— "seeing" and "feeling." To apprehend that a proposition is true "as having evidentia or being clear," is to recognize that "previous truths and their separate and joint relations to the proposition in question" amount to "proofs." "Evidentia is the lumen rationis."[3] In proof the truth of a proposition is grasped "by means of the things which lie about it."[4] "In *intuition* the light is the proposition itself."[5] To apprehend that a proposition is credible is to "have reason for anticipating that did we know . . . existing truths more fully, we should see that they did presuppose or require it."[6] In this case the truth of propositions "is not evident, yet the grounds for thinking their truth, that is, for believing them, are evident."[7]

It is not always clear exactly what Newman was distinguishing. While he sometimes seems to have been distinguishing assent (knowing) and inference (concluding), more often he seems to have been distinguishing formal and informal inference.[8] It is in this sense of the evidence of credibility as the source of informal inference that he wrote that it supplies a proof "as complete and sufficient" as that provided by the evidence of truth, although the former is "more

173

elaborate, circuitous, and trying to the patience" than the latter. It is in this sense that he spoke of "Prudentia or Judgment," or "the mental faculty which sees, furnishes, uses and applies the premisses of the evidentia credibilitatis." Again it is in this sense that he spoke of a "reflex assent" or "speculative certainty" resting on the evidence or credibility as well as of truth. In both cases "certainty is its own criterion, for it is mere ascertainment and testimony to a fact."[9]

After this introductory discussion he turned to "revealed (religious) truth" where there is evidence of credibility, not truth, for the being of God or the fact of revelation. He defined motive as "the reasons constituting or producing the evidentia," and then concluded "that there is no faith without sufficient motivum . . . next, that prudentia forms and shapes the motivum."[10]

There are many ambiguities in Newman's discussion. Sometimes he seems to have limited the range of objective (certain) knowledge to the conclusions of formal demonstration from the evidence of truth. He added that a truth "apprehended on the evidentia credibilitatis" ought to be believed. The question arises: did he mean we ought to accept what we *grasp* to be the case although it is not capable of being formally demonstrated; or did he mean we ought to *decide* we are certain about what remains a probability? He seems to have wanted to say the former but he hesitated.

Part of the difficulty was that he wanted to distinguish an objective (certain) judgment that revelation is credible from both the certainty (necessity) of logical demonstration, and the unique certainty of divine faith. In the first case the formal/informal distinction is relevant. The judgment of credibility is an objective (certain) assent resulting from an informal reflection on experience, not a formal demonstration from premises. In the second case, however, the inference/assent distinction would be relevant—although it would be used to mark a unique distinction. The judgment of credibility is contrasted with the grace-created state of divine faith. It is not the objective (certain) grasp (in faith) of the object of faith which only grace can supply. In contrast with that supernatural "assent" (*knowing* in faith), it remains a natural "inference" (*concluding* from reasons).[11]

In October 1853 Newman had tried to avoid speaking "of divine grace, where it comes in, or what it does."[12] But in the December paper he seems to have recognized that a treatment of the certainty of faith demands a discussion of "the process of supernatural faith, and the portion of it which is supernatural."[13] He began by noting that "every step of the process . . . up to the assent to the credibilitatis of the supernatural revelation *inclusive,* is natural" and "may be mastered by a mind destitute of the grace of Christ . . . A mind which gets as far as this does not yet believe. It only sees that Revelation is credible."[14] He continued: "The steps which follow are rational . . . but supernatural also, or require grace:" first, "a practical judgment . . . that it is right and fitting . . . to believe what is credible;"[15] secondly, a "pia affectio or voluntas credendi" or "wish to believe;"[16] and finally, "Fides divina" itself or "the act of faith, in the intellect . . . the object being at once Revelatio and Res Revelata, viz. that God has spoken and that He has spoken thus."[17]

But the operation of grace in this last case is quite different from its operation in the first two cases. The will, aided by grace, might command the intellect to believe (the second case) but the object of this human faith remains the credibility of revelation; while divine faith in the intellect (the third case) has as its object revelation and the revealed content—that is, it follows the logic of testimony.

Newman seems to have been uncertain of himself on this point in his December paper. He hesitated to speak of a "fides humana . . . aided by grace" preceding the act of "fides divina." Yet he wrote, "fides divina, I suppose, has this difference from fides humana . . . that fides in the latter phrase has something of a vague sense, and does not necessarily suppose a speaker—and hence is applicable to belief in our experimental conclusions in science."[18] It is this notion of "a speaker" which distinguishes the grace-created act of divine faith from every grace-supported act of human faith. As he developed this essential feature of divine faith, he clarified these two distinct operations of grace. In divine faith grace enables one to believe, not arguments and evidence, but "the Divine Speaker."[19]

On January 17, 1854, he wrote a further paper on the object of divine faith. "I may believe things from reason etc. and then the form of belief is demonstration. But faith is belief in God telling me —i.e. in God, as God Revealing." He summarized his meaning in a long sentence interrupted by comments. "The Formal Object of Faith

is God . . . God, as God Revealing . . . or, as it is commonly said,
Divine Revelation . . . that is, the Divine Authority in revealing
. . . or (if we would consider the matter more accurately), the
truth of God in speaking . . . or even the truth of God, all-know-
ing and all-wise, in speaking . . . or the wisdom and veracity of
God."*[20] It is because divine faith follows the logic of testimony that
the operation of grace, reason and will *before faith* must be distinguished from their operation *in faith.*

Of particular interest is Newman's last letter to William Froude
in which he summarized the situation *before faith.* Froude had remained unconvinced by the *Grammar of Assent,* and when Newman
offered to dedicate an 1871 edition of essays to him, William accepted with much reluctance.[21]

> I am always in fear lest I should be somehow sailing under false
> colours in your sight . . . by allowing you somehow through affec-
> tion for me to think more of me and better of me as if somehow
> you were supposing that were you to probe me to the bottom you
> would find . . . a more real root of what you would regard as
> 'Faith' than a thorough search would in fact disclose . . . For
> myself I ought to say that . . . the entire absence of certitude
> has long ceased to be painful to me.[22]

In July 1878 Froude's wife died, and William, his health shaken,
accepted an invitation from the government to cruise to South
Africa. From there he sent Newman what were to be his final
thoughts on the topic of their long correspondence. He wrote that
while he might not deny the existence of a creator with "Infinite
power," nevertheless "the idea of a divine Person does not, to me,
seem rightly to grow out of the perception of the existence of laws
by which the course of nature is governed."[23] He could not accept
the attempt to infer "a personal Lawgiver" from "the Law of right
and wrong," nor the attempt to "infer God . . . from phenomena
not yet explained" by science.[24] Further, he claimed to find "the
very foundations" of the "traditionary idea" that God "is to be ap-
peased by propitiatory sacrifice . . . in the present beliefs of savage
nations."[25] In the end, so it seemed to Froude, "Man made God in
his own image."[26]

This letter was received by Newman before leaving England for
Rome in the spring of 1879. While waiting in Rome for his formal

elevation to the cardinalate, he composed a long reply on April 29th, but before it was sent, news arrived that Froude had died of dysentery on May 4th in Simonstown.[27]

Newman wrote that the "fundamental difference" between himself and Froude was their sense "of the word 'certain.' I use it of minds, you of propositions." He compared the exercise of reason in religion and in science. Men of science seemed to "observe" what they professed to "ignore," namely, "a law of human intellect to accept with an inward assent as absolutely true, what is not yet demonstrated."[28] Froude himself seemed to admit "that there is a mental faculty which reasons in a far higher way than that of merely measuring the force of conclusions by the force of premisses."[29] He seemed to admit in science "the gradual process by which great conclusions are forced upon the mind, and the confidence of their correctness which the mind feels from the fact of that gradualness."[30] In addition he seemed to admit the need for "preparation and exercise of long thought" and "study . . . for understanding" scientific ideas.[31] In short, Froude seemed to admit in science what Newman merely applied to religion.

Newman had often written that "Faith cannot exist without grounds or without an object."[32] Yet "no analysis is subtle and delicate enough to represent adequately the state of mind under which we believe."[33] Without denying that divine faith itself is a grace-created assent to the "Divine Speaker," he allowed that "an act of Faith may be said (improperly) to include in it the reasoning process which is its antecedent, and to be in a certain aspect, an exercise of Reason."[34] But this use of reason before faith is informal. As in other disciplines it involves a "subtlety of evidence" and an "intricacy of reasoning"[35] which set it apart from demonstrations that are logically and universally compelling. However this does not set religious reasoning apart as esoteric, "special and recondite." After all, "Faith is not the only exercise of Reason, which approves itself to some and not to others."[36]

Granting the fact of an informal mode of knowing, what is the positive evidence which might lead men who are perhaps incapable of complicated argument to conclude that revelation is credible? Newman insisted that "in every case of man, woman, and child" the credibility of revelation rests on "right reason . . . exercising itself in legitimate proof."[37] This "body of proof . . . consists of all

the facts and truths of the case, each in its right place, as the prudentia sees and arranges them, conspiring to the conclusion of the
credibilitas of Revelation" and carrying "the mind to a distinct
judgment, or assent to that credibilitas."[38] But he emphasized that
this judgment is "variously gained" by appealing to "a variety of
grounds" according to the inclination and ability of persons of all
ages and learning.[39] "From the things which are seen, from the
voice of tradition, from the existence of the soul, and from the
necessity of the case, the natural reason can infer the existence of
God . . . [and so effect] a certain sort of belief, however different
from that faith which is imparted to us by grace."[40]

Newman had often criticized "the popular argument" for a
Creator from "design in the physical world."[41] He felt that this
argument involved philosophical difficulties.[42] Moreover it seemed
to lead to an impersonal and perhaps finite power, not a transcendent and personal Creator. It seemed to lead to a "naturalistic,
pantheistic" religion,[43] but he did not mean to deny that there could
be "proofs of the being of a God gained from the existence of physical nature."[44] When "Final Causes" are understood in the sense of
"order" there could be "a proof of an intelligent mind."[45]

> The being of a God . . . [is] handed down by history, inferred
> by an inductive process, brought home to us by metaphysical
> necessity, urged on us by the suggestions of conscience. It is a
> truth in the natural order, as well as in the supernatural.[46]

Newman himself preferred an argument from conscience leading to
"the being and presence of a Moral Governor of mankind,"[47]
though he wrote "I am far from denying the real force of the
arguments in proof of a God, drawn from the general facts of
human society and the course of history."[48] A variety of evidence,
then, can bring individuals "before conversion" to a speculative
"certainty."[49]

In his last letter to Froude, he also discussed "the relation of the
will to assent, in theological matters."[50] Because the reasoning is
informal "it is always . . . possible . . . to resist a conclusion,
even tho' it be one which all sensible men consider beyond question." In this case one must set aside unreasonable doubts "by a
vigorous act of the will."[51] Informal reasoning "legitimately leads"
to certainty of the credibility of revelation "unless an act of the

will" directly "interferes to hinder it" or indirectly fails to set aside irrational doubts.[52]

Finally, in 1855 he explained the role of grace before faith: "Perhaps . . . what divines call grace, the supernatural assistance of the Father of Lights, may be the necessary preparation for our understanding the force of the arguments in the subject matter of religion; and perhaps prayer may be the human means . . . of gaining that supernatural assistance."[53] In other words, grace may be necessary to aid the will in putting down "a wild unhealthy state of mind" comparable to the state of mind which unreasonably suggests, "perhaps there is poison in my breakfast."[54] In this way it indirectly brings about "that moral condition of which the recognition of certain intellectual truths" is "the natural result."[55] The process of informal reasoning remains *"natural"* although in the concrete it is (perhaps always) aided by grace.[56]

As a general rule in his letters to unbelievers, Newman discussed the operation of reason, will and grace *before faith*. When he spoke of an ability to know (be certain) that revelation is credible, he was not speaking of the certainty of faith itself which is the direct creation of grace. At the end of his last letter to Froude, he compared the situation of a believer with that of someone who is certain of his friend's loyalty despite irrational doubts. He added: "And if it be said that his friend is visibly present, and the object of faith invisible, there the action of grace comes in, which I cannot enter upon here."[57]

But when writing to believers, Newman did not hesitate to enter upon the unique role of grace *in faith* itself. In 1862 he wrote to William George Ward: "Human faith lies *in* the intellect as well as Divine faith; but the former is created there by previous acts of mere human reason, the latter is the creation of supernatural grace."[58] Before faith grace indirectly lends assistance to what human reason achieves. In divine faith, however, the roles are reversed. Reason lends assistance, but grace directly creates. But this must not be misunderstood. Reason and evidence are "essential to Christianity, as it comes to us."[59] Grace does not "contradict or . . . dispense with nature" whose "evidences in favour of a revelation" remain an important part of divine faith,[60] and a legitimate way to faith. But reason's role is "critical" not "creative."[61] "A judge does not make men honest, but acquits and vindicates them: in like manner, Reason need not be the origin of Faith . . . though it does test and verify it."[62] Reason might provide arguments which "will be a stay, a refuge, an encouragement, a rallying point for faith."[63] It might lead us to faith. Nevertheless "The two things are quite distinct from each other, seeing you ought to believe, and believing; reason, if left to itself, will bring you to the conclusion that you have sufficient grounds for believing, but belief is the gift of grace."[64] In 1860 he called reason, in relation to divine faith, "an antecedent condition in the order of nature . . . The real source and cause of religious faith is beyond nature and actual reason, still reason is its antecedent, and cause *sine qua non*."[65]

Newman was interested, not in theoretical questions about nature and grace, but in the individual coming to faith. This led him to remark that "grace and nature might clearly be contrasted with each other but it is not the fact . . . Many . . . are under the influence partly of reason and partly of faith."[66] In stressing the concrete situation he did not mean to imply an informal rationalism in religion, that is, the position that faith is merely the result of an informal argument aided by grace.[67] He did not mean to imply that grace merely lends supernatural value to a natural act. Divine faith is completely reasonable, but it is also completely the free gift of grace which enables one not only to appreciate the force of arguments but to grasp in faith God testifying to Himself.[68] This is why he called divine faith "spiritual sight,"[69] or "an original means of knowledge."[70] And this is why he compared the unbeliever to a blind man who has access only to notions and inferences but lacks a real familiarity with the object of his discourse.[71]

Men coming to faith will recognize the truth "dimly, though certainly, as the sun through mists and clouds," but "it is the office of grace to clear up gloom and haziness, to steady that fitful vision, to perfect reason by faith, and to convert a logical conclusion into an object of intellectual sight."[72] Divine faith is not the acceptance of the conclusion of an argument, nor the acceptance of a particular way of looking at the world; it is an acceptance of God revealing a definite message.

Locke had emphasized the place of revelation, but he had insisted that belief in revelation rests entirely on human reasons which show that a revelation has occurred.[73] There is an unavoidable element of self-evidence in the fact that we cannot believe

God's word with certainty unless we are sure it is His word. But it is a mistake to pretend that nothing more was being said when Locke added that this certainty must be reached as the conclusion of an argument by means of natural knowing resources. To make this addition is, in fact, to beg the question against divine faith. It is to pretend that it is *a priori* evident that there can be no way of grasping that God reveals, which could be different from our ordinary ways of grasping philosophical or historical conclusions. It is assumed that God could not have any other way of making Himself known as revealed and revealer, and that we could not know that an alleged revelation is God's word unless it were shown to be such by formal or informal arguments.

Such an account, however, seems to totally bypass supernatural faith in the traditional sense. Its logical pattern is straightforward: we prove that God is, that He has revealed Himself in history, that these are His words, that He cannot lie—and then conclude that these words are true. But the logic of faith is that of hearing and accepting the word of the "Divine Speaker" who enables us to grasp in faith Himself testifying to His own revelation. The mystery of God's self-revelation is approached in reflection, but also in prayer and awe.

So Newman rejected Locke's view that faith must necessarily be resolved into sight and reason, that it could not be "a new mode of arriving at truth . . . that, though Faith rests on testimony, not on reasonings, yet that testimony in its turn, depends on Reason for the proof of its pretensions."[74] It was his understanding that:

> the more Scriptural representation seems to be this, which is more agreeable to the facts also, that, instead of there being any such united process of reasoning first, and then believing, the act of Faith is sole and elementary, and complete in itself, and depends on no process of mind previous to it.[75]

> Now faith . . . is a certainty of things not seen but revealed; a certainty preceded indeed in many cases by particular exercises of the intellect, as conditions, by reflection, prayer, study, argument . . . but caused directly by a supernatural influence on the mind from above.[76]

It is *"sui generis,"* not merely "a believing upon evidence, or a sort of conclusion upon a process of reasoning, a resolve formed upon a calculation," or the holding of "divine truths merely as an opin-

ion."[77] It is "the gift of God,"[78] for "nature cannot see God . . .
grace is the sole means of seeing Him."[79]

His discussion of objective (certain) knowledge is relevant at
this point. He had distinguished inference (concluding) from assent
(knowing).[80] Objective knowledge is not an opinion or conclusion
more or less justified by a vast set of premises. It is sometimes an immediate grasp, through a complex activity, that something is the
case. Now he would call divine faith "in a special manner, knowledge"[81] because, like knowledge, it cannot be explained as a conjecture supported by reasons that function like premises in a demonstration. Scripture tells us that in faith we do "not conjecture, or
suppose, or opine, but 'know,' see, 'all things.' "[82] The history of
martyrs assures us that "it was the spiritual sight of God which
made them what they were." He went on to insist, "No one is a
Martyr for a conclusion, no one is a Martyr for an opinion; it is
faith that makes Martyrs . . . The Martyrs saw, and how could
they but speak what they had seen?[83] A man without faith might
conjecture that the resurrection of the body is consistent with the
doctrine that God took mortal flesh upon Himself; he might reason
that evidence could support particular doctrines and in this way
serve faith, but, he wrote,

> still it is not faith; it does not rise above an intellectual view or
> notion; it affirms, not as grasping the truth, not as seeing, but as
> 'being of opinion,' as 'judging,' as 'coming to a conclusion.' . . .
> [Without the light of grace] I do not say you will have no thought
> at all about God . . . but you will not be able to do more than
> reason about Him . . . to infer a thing is not to see it in respect
> to the physical world, nor is it in the spiritual.[84]

Knowledge is an objective (certain) grasp that something is the
case. Similarly divine faith is an objective (certain) grasp although
by the borrowed light of faith that God is both revealed and revealer.

John Hick described faith as a kind of knowledge or awareness of God, not "a reasoned conclusion or an unreasoned hunch
that there is a God," but his phenomenalist/coherence account of
knowledge determines the meaning of these remarks.[85] He gave little
emphasis to revelation or an authoritative testimony. To have faith

is not to believe for various reasons, signs, complex experiences and inner graces, that a faith-community bears within it God's word. Rather, men believe because they "experience" God, although this is not a simple, neat and direct encounter.[86] The world is "experienced-as" mediating a divine presence.[87] Believers see the world or discern significance in such a way that they find they have no alternative but to believe that God is, and this "mediated" religious knowledge is perfectly consistent with our ordinary "cognitive experience." There is an unavoidable "ambiguity in the given" of our experience such that all significance is relative to interpretation.[88] Just as one cannot help seeing the world as made up of physical objects and other minds, so the believer cannot help seeing the world as he does. The realist and solipsist interpret the same facts differently. There are no rigorous empirical proofs to validate the realist's expectations; nevertheless his stance makes reality vivid and productive. Likewise the religious believer cannot prove the truth of his claims; yet his stance provides a new depth and intelligibility to reality.[89]

Hick himself recognized that this could lead to agnostic positions. Christian faith could be taken "as merely a *blik*,"[90] as having nothing to do with factual claims about God's existence. Yet believers do claim that God exists, although this cannot be justified simply by referring to the fact that they experience the world in a certain way. Still, it must be verified if it is to be intelligible. Consequently Hick developed what he called "eschatological verification,"[91] that is, when transferred into resurrected bodies, if faith is right, we will be in a kingdom of God where the evidence in favor of what Christ has said will be overwhelming.[92] But even then there would be room for doubt: "Survival after death would not in the least constitute a final verification of theistic faith." There is no "Beatific Vision" in its traditional sense, no "direct vision of God."[93] The situation remains logically ambiguous although to a reasonable man the evidence points "unambiguously to the existence of a loving God."[94] The situation is so unchanged that if a believer on earth already interprets experience as mediating God's presence, then "the life of heaven will not fundamentally change his cognitive relation to his Maker."[95] His existential religious claim remains unverified, although his interpretation is placed "beyond reasonable doubt"— not as "true," but as viable, consistent and, to him, unavoidable.

Hick seems to have forgotten the very reason why he introduced the notion of "eschatological verification" in the first place.[96]

For Hick faith is knowledge but it is forever unverified. For Newman faith is not knowledge in an unqualified sense. It is not a grasp of the truths of revelation by their own evidence. It relies on the borrowed light of God's testimony, but it is certain.

Again the personalism of faith seems to be limited in Hick's account. For Newman faith is a gift personally granted by God as the result of a quest. Our human calculations, our "experiencing-as," our hopes are changed into something else. A loved Person is made most accessible, bearing an authoritative testimony different from all other testimony. For Hick there seems to be a wall which keeps one from literally meeting God or being sure that He is. On our side of the wall we can decide or happen to experience the world as if He is; on God's side, He can bring about events that we feel to be mediating Him. He may even cause in us an ambiguous stimulus or tendency to interpret events this way, but there is no living contact. There is no gift to break the epistemological barrier of a hard empiricism; there are no real grounds for saying, objectively and truly—"God exists," and there is no God who obscurely but really touches us under the force of His own calling and who enables us to reach Him so that we can be certain, although *in via*, of His truth.

Newman held that on earth, even without the gift of divine faith, one can be in the position which Hick allowed only in the heavenly kingdom. Newman seems to have allowed three broad levels of "revelation": first, the evidence of creation which can bring men to some objective knowledge of the Creator; secondly, the direct communication of a divine relevation in history culminating in the Person of Christ which gives man in faith the correct interpretation of his experience; and thirdly, the Beatific Vision through which creatures grasp the truth by a unique share in God's own knowledge. Hick seems to have suggested that all three levels follow the pattern of the first level, where, for Hick, we do not (objectively) grasp what is the case, but adopt a coherent interpretation of ambiguous data. Scripture merely provides further data, and the afterlife still further data to be variously, but never definitively, interpreted. We cannot be sure, but we might decide our interpretation is correct.

Newman's own empiricist tendency led him to speak sometimes in voluntarist terms about knowledge, as if we do not know or grasp what is the case but decide to act as if we know.[97] The same tendency can be found in his discussion of faith, though he seems to have been much less inclined to drift into this way of speaking about objective (certain) faith. Divine faith is an "acceptance of things as real, which the senses do not convey . . . it is an instrument of indirect knowledge concerning things external to us."[98] It is to accept and reflect upon revealed propositions "as if we were contemplating what is real and independent of human judgment." It is "kept in the narrow path of truth by . . . the Light of heaven which animates and guides it."[99]

To have faith is not to believe what is revealed because it has been revealed that a revelation has occurred. This would become circular. Rather in faith grace enables one to grasp God revealing Himself. In this sense it is *like* (objective) knowledge. To know that there is a chair here is not to know that it is so because I know that an infallible act of knowledge has occurred. Knowledge is not circular because it is objective; and faith need not be circular for the same reason.

Again to have faith is not to say: "If there is a God, He could give this gift by which I could be certain that He is." This would be hypothetical. Rather in faith one is certain and God does grant this gift. Again in this sense it is *like* (objective) knowledge. To know that there is a chair here is not to say: "If there were a chair, it could cause me to perceive that it is so." Rather there is a chair and I perceive it. Knowledge and perception are not hypothetical because they are objective; and faith need not be hypothetical for the same reason.[100]

For Newman then the certainty of faith is like the certainty of knowledge—namely, another word for its objectivity. When he said that "grace gives certainty"[101] he was not saying that it gives us confidence about an opinion or an interpretation, but that it enables us to (objectively) recognize by the borrowed light of faith that God is revealed and revealer. The certainty of divine faith is distinctive. It is not "a mere conviction in reason," but "a clear certainty greater than any other certainty; and this is wrought in the mind by the grace of God, and by it alone."[102] It should not be confused with the (objective) certainty of informal knowledge. Informal reflection might "create legitimately a human certainty . . .

but . . . the human certainty . . . [is] swallowed up by the faith from God's grace, which is its reward."[103] But while the certainty of faith transcends every human certainty, the word "certainty" has the same *meaning* when applied to (objective) faith as it has when applied to (objective) knowledge. The fact that faith relies on the borrowed light of God's testimony does not alter the meaning of its certainty.

To know or grasp that something is the case does not allow of more or less. Likewise in the early Church "To believe a little, to believe more or less, was impossible; it contradicted the very notion of believing."[104] Therefore, "faith is incompatible with doubt" because, as objective, it "implies . . . that the thing believed is really true; but, if it is once true, it never can be false." For this reason, to say, "I believe as far as I can tell, but there may be arguments in the background which will change my view," is not yet to have divine faith.[105]

For this same reason, to "love our Lord" but with the feeling that "After all, perhaps there is no such person," would be to love "a mere vision, or picture, and is so unreal as to be degrading."[106] If someone claimed to have "devotion without certainty" he would be "worshipping his own mind . . . and not God . . . his idea of God was a mere accidental form which his thoughts took at this time or that."[107]

Again for this reason, "it is no difficult thing for" someone with faith "to believe . . . the difficult thing is for him to doubt. He has received a gift which makes faith easy."[108] He is sure that revelation is true "on the ground of its being divine, not as true on intrinsic grounds, not as probably true, or partially true, but as absolutely certain knowledge."[109]

Of course Locke had also written that the certainty of faith is distinctive. "The assurance of faith . . . is quite distinct from . . . [and] neither stands nor falls with knowledge." Yet, because for him (certain) knowledge is restricted to intuition and demonstration, because every other knowledge-claim is a matter of "judgment" or "opinion," Locke was compelled to add that "to talk of the certainty of faith seems . . . a way of speaking not easy to me to understand." His presuppositions could allow it to be understood only as an assurance about what must remain tentative—an assurance that "has nothing to do with the certainty of knowledge."[110]

Newman held that divine faith, like knowledge, is objective—but it relies entirely on the borrowed light of God's word. For this reason sometimes it is possible to know what faith grasps but not in the way in which faith grasps it.

A philosopher, taught by his accurate reasonings that there is but one God believes a truth, but he does not believe on the authority of God revealing. Therefore neither does he believe by the grace of God operating Fides Divina in his mind.[111]

He argued that religion has always been understood as "synonymous with Revelation."[112] It is not a matter of deducing something from what we know. It is a matter of hearing what we are to believe. Christian revelation "is not a mere collection of truths, not a philosophical view, not a religious sentiment or spirit, not a special morality . . . but an authoritative teaching, which bears witness to itself." It is a "definite message from God to man" which is therefore to be "embraced, and maintained as true."[113]

Someone might conclude that faith is credible, but, in faith itself, this would become an assent to the "Divine Speaker." The act of mind and the operation of grace in each case are distinct.

The assent of the mind as given to the *Conclusion* of the motiva which lead to faith . . . is an assent to its credibility and on this the mind . . . acting upon this conclusion thus recognized, goes on to view the conclusion in a new aspect and makes a direct assent to . . . the revelation with its content. Perhaps it is not a subtlety to say . . . that the conclusion drawn from the motiva or reasonings is . . . revelation as the *subject* of the proposition, 'there is a revelation' but the object of the assent [of faith] is . . . the revelation itself with its contents.[114]

Newman's position on faith as an (objective) certain assent to the "Divine Speaker" shaped his remarks on the role of reason in faith: "the mind may be allowably, nay, religiously engaged, in reflecting upon its own Faith; investigating the grounds and the Object of it, bringing it out into words, whether to defend, or recommend, or teach it to others."[115] On the one hand before faith one is in the position of a blind man reasoning about what he cannot see. Here reason can correct its own mistakes in religious matters just as "The blind man who reasoned himself into errors in Optics might possibly reason himself out of them."[116] On the other hand

one with the "spiritual sight" of faith can use his reason to correct
heresies in self-defense of the revelation which has been given,[117]
"to investigate the meaning of its declarations . . . and to bring
them into dependence on each other, to trace their mutual relations,
and to pursue them to their legitimate issues."[118]

However it would be a mistake "to make our reason the standard
and measure of the doctrine revealed," to speak of Revelation "as
the word of God, and to treat it as the word of man; to refuse to
let it speak for itself . . . to put aside what is obscure, as if it had
not been said at all . . . to frame some gratuitous hypothesis"
about the mysteries God has revealed "and then to garble, gloss,
and colour them, to trim, clip, pare away, and twist them, in order
to bring them into conformity with the idea to which we have subjected them." Reason has a place in faith, but its place is set by the
fact that "Faith is, in its very nature, the acceptance of what our
reason cannot reach, simply and absolutely upon testimony."[119]

Consequently, theology is the work of reason; it is not merely "a
series of pious or polemical remarks upon the physical world viewed
religiously."[120] Nor is it merely "a mode of looking at Physical Nature, a certain view taken of Nature, private and personal, which
one man has . . . and which all would be the better for adopting"
—this would be nothing more than a "Theology of Nature," although "Nature with a divine glow upon it."[121] Belief in God would
be "no more than an acknowledgement of existing, sensible powers
and phenomena, which none but an idiot can deny," and reflection
about God would be "nothing more than a poetry of thought or an
ornament of language."[122] Knowledge of God would be "nothing
distinct from" knowledge of the visible world, but only "a mode of
viewing it."[123] God Himself would be nothing more than a "subjective reflection and mental impression," and it would be only "a
question of words whether or not we go on to the hypothesis of a
second Being, not visible but immaterial, parallel and coincident
with Nature, to whom we give the name of God."[124]

Instead, for Newman, theology is "the Science of God, or the
truths we know about God put into a system."[125] He could speak
this way because, for him, faith is "an intellectual act, its object
truth, and its result knowledge."[126] Its subject-matter lacks the
"luminous evidence" of sight and touch but it is nonetheless
given in Revelation.[127] So he reasoned that the idea of revelation in-

cludes a direct intervention or divine communication of truths. This, in turn, implies "recipients" and "an authoritative depository of the things revealed." As a result knowledge of these truths "is gained, not by any research into facts, but simply by appealing to the authoritative keepers of them . . . dwelling upon, and drawing out into detail, the doctrines which are delivered."[128] In other words theology does not deal with Scripture or tradition in the Church in the way in which science sometimes deals with nature, that is, "as a large collection of phenomena, from which, by an inductive process" one can arrive at and accept "certain probable conclusions till better are found."[129] Rather the object of faith's assent and theology's reflection is simply what God has revealed; this "we can but explain, we cannot increase . . . without it we should have known nothing of its contents, with it we know just as much as its contents, and nothing more."[130]

A man might be certain that he is able to make free and responsible choices despite the objections of determinists; he might be certain that he is not the only person alive despite the arguments of solipsists. Likewise the believer will be certain in faith such that "nothing shall make him doubt, that, if anything seems to be proved . . . in contradiction to the dogmas of faith, that point will eventually turn out, first, *not* to be proved, or, secondly, not *contradictory*, or thirdly, not contradictory to any thing *really revealed,* but to something which has been confused with revelation."[131] But in each case it is not enough to argue that error "is like other delinquents; give it rope enough, and it will be found to have a strong suicidal propensity."[132] Both the realist and the theologian must take active part "in encouraging, in helping forward the prospective suicide;" they must "not only give the error rope enough, but show it how to handle and adjust the rope;" they must "commit the matter to reason, reflection, sober judgment, common sense."[133] The theologian in particular should not attempt to avoid difficulties by appealing to his own way of seeing things. He must enter "into the philosophical arena" and meet objections "by argument,"[134] remembering that his arguments will always be "subservient to faith, as handling, examining, explaining, recording, cataloguing, defending, the truths which faith, not reason, has gained for us, as providing an intellectual expression of supernatural facts."[135]

Newman was aware that many would insist that there can be no science of theology in this sense because we cannot "get hold of facts and truths." We are "not in a position to determine what is true or false" in religious matters. We might have "opinions," "theories," and "probabilities," but "such persuasions are not knowledge . . . they are consistent with your allowing your friend to entertain the opposite opinion."[136] He added, however, that this position rests on the "mere assumption" that faith and revelation in the traditional sense are impossible. It would be a mistake to seek knowledge of the truth in religious matters if it could not, in principle, be reached. But it has not been shown "to be self-evident that religious truth *is* really incapable of attainment," while "it has at least been powerfully argued by a number of profound minds that it *can* be attained." The burden of proof lies with those who deny the very possibility of what "the whole world" recognizes as actually the case.[137]

His final position on the place of reason in theology and the distinctive nature of (objective) certain faith rests on the conviction that God can make Himself heard in such a way that one has available to himself in faith an independent source of information. This revelation is determined from Scripture, from the tradition and practice of the faith-community to which it has been entrusted, and from the authoritative statements of those promised supernatural aid to preserve it. It provides a unique restraint on reason's tendency to explain away revealed "truths, faintly apprehended and not understood."[138] One's (objective) conscience provides a restraint on action. Moral experience is recalcitrant: You could do such-and-such, but you should not. It is not right. One's (objective) knowledge provides a restraint on our factual claims. Cognitive experience is recalcitrant: You could say such-and-such, but you should not. It is not true. Likewise, for Newman, one's (objective) faith provides a unique restraint on theology. Revelation is recalcitrant: You could profess such-and-such, but you should not. It is not what has been heard and accepted as God's word to His people.

The justification of faith

The way in which one attempts to justify faith is determined by the way in which he defines it. For Newman faith is not a conclusion that comes from argument, rather, faith comes by hearing.[139]

It simply "accepts testimony. As then testimony is distinct from experience, so is Faith from Reason,"[140] but it is not like other cases of accepting something which we cannot see or prove on the word of another. In human faith we take someone's word "for what it is worth." We accept and act on it, more or less, depending on "our necessity, or its probability." We retain the right of questioning its validity at any time. In divine faith, however, the situation is quite different: "he who believes that God is true, and that this is His word, which He has committed to man, has no doubt at all . . . he is certain, *because* God is true, *because* God has spoken, not because he sees its truth or can prove its truth."[141] In the case of human faith in the testimony of another there is no doubt that the other exists and is speaking, but reason must more or less determine whether the witness is trustworthy.[142] In the case of divine faith the existence, the words and the trustworthiness of God run together and become the one object of faith's "trust" in and certain "assent . . . to the Divine Speaker."[143]

Because faith follows the logic of testimony something of its nature can be learned from human faith. Divine faith includes several notions at once: believing God is, believing in God, believing God. The *reason* for believing something is because one believes Someone. This occurs in human faith as well. Suppose a veteran returns from the war and tells me that my brother, who I thought was dead, is alive. He tells me that he has just left him in prison. He tells me much about my brother and my brother was like that. To the extent that I can, I check his credentials to verify his credibility. But sooner or later I must decide if I will believe him. He came freely and has pledged his word and now he wants a response. He wants me to share his joy, to say "yes" to his word, to believe things really are as he says they are. If I say "your account reassures me and gives me hope. If only I could check it further," he would rightly answer, "in other words, you do not believe me." For belief in a context where one bears witness to what he knows, is simply to assent because of his word, to say "yes" and not "perhaps" or juggle probabilities or proclaim hopes.[144]

There are two points of similarity between human and divine faith. First, faith is inferior to knowledge. It is to assent, to say "yes" and not "perhaps" but without seeing that things are so. It shares in and essentially leans upon the knowledge of another.[145] Secondly,

faith is personal and interpersonal. It is first directed to a person.
It is to believe someone. To believe what a man says and to believe
him are two very different things. A judge may believe what a
scoundrel says is true, not because he believes him, but because
things are such that it is likely that what he says is true. Likewise
someone can believe things to be true which God allegedly said,
but for other reasons than because he believes Him. This would be
to hold what faith holds but in a way which is different from the
way in which faith holds it.[146]

But there are important points of difference between human and
divine faith as well. Christian faith is in a social context. A believing
community is surrounded by an unbelieving one. Within and by this
community a message is announced and declared to have a divine
origin and authority; there are signs and evidence given to defend
that this is accepted not as the word of men, but of God.[147] Yet the
faith called for has peculiar traits. One is asked to believe the word
socially present in this community but in an intensely personal way.
To mature in this community one must believe those who teach the
word, but not believe precisely *them*. If one believed just the apostle
or teacher or society, he would not have divine faith. Only one who
can say "I believe You, God, bearing witness to Yourself in this
community" has come to full Christian faith. Only then can he
enter into the spirit of this community which is created by the
personal faith of its members.

Of course, one may be in the situation of the man who wants to
believe the man returning from the war. He may want to believe.
He may recognize good credentials. He may judge that reasons
commend the authenticity of the divine testimony with which he
would like to be personally related. Yet he may be utterly unable
to believe. He may only be able to sustain a hoped-for faith. For
if the Christian community's message about what faith is, is real,
then faith is possible only when the personal God makes the individual able to grasp His testimony as His in the dynamic interchange of
faith and grace.

The difficulties are great. The potential believer is asked to accept
declarations which he cannot personally check; he is asked to accept
them on the word of a hidden Witness who he does not meet in the
straightforward way one meets a war veteran; he must believe in

the existence of the witness he believes, and he must give an assent of a quality which he gives to no other witness, an unquestionable and firm "yes."

No man could demand this of another. Its very possibility seems unlikely. But it would be a mistake to attempt to prove *a priori* that such a faith is possible, just as it would be a mistake to begin philosophy by attempting to prove that knowledge is possible or that perception is possible. Newman said that the unbeliever is like a blind man discoursing about colors.[148] For if one were the only seeing-man in a country of the blind, he could not prove to the blind that there *is* such a thing as sight, that is, an independent source of information not available to them. If they said that his talk about colored objects is an interesting interpretation of available data and his talk of sight, an interesting conjecture, he would answer that there are colored objects and he does see them. He would know that some of their arguments are simply wrong even if he could not enter into their complex calculations and show the error. But he could do that.[149] He could show that the information he has is not in conflict with theirs. He could point out that they would be unable to prove the possibility of hearing as an independent source of information to the deaf (provided that some means of communication were established). In such cases one is sure of the possibility of (objective) knowledge or of a mode of (objective) experience only when it is found to be actual.[150]

Likewise, faith is found possible only when it is found to be actual. Intelligent people with faith are astounded that it is a reality while certain that it is. It is no exhilarating mystical experience; it is not a super-knowledge. And the one with it cannot manage it in the way in which a philosopher or scientist can manage what he knows. Rather the man of faith holds revelation to be true by a borrowed light, and though he is certain, his certainty is surrounded with obscurity and admitted ignorance.[151]

He cannot directly prove the existence of this (objective) faith to the unbeliever just as he cannot prove the existence of (objective) knowledge or perception to the skeptic, without appealing to the very fact the other denies. But he can employ indirect arguments against its impossibility. As a blind man with cataracts from birth might be led by indirect argument to do the things he should do to gain sight, the unbeliever might be led by indirect argument to do what he should do to receive the gift of faith—namely, invoke the living God in prayer.

Further, the believer can directly point to some feature of experience which the agnostic admits and which seems to demand the existence of a Creator or Moral Governor. Still, this would remain, essentially, the justification of a truth about the world of our ordinary experience which requires the existence of a Supreme Being in some sense; it would not be a direct justification of the gift of faith itself.

Such a justification is impossible for the authority of God and the light of faith are not special new empirical phenomena which can be set up as prize exhibits in a proof for the validity of faith. These causal factors are rather "perceived in [their] effects"[152] by the nature of the certainty which the profession of faith enjoys. The believer does not *see* that the claims of faith are true. He has no visions of divine realities. He can best describe his own conviction in a plain historical way: first, reasons led him to be convinced in complex, informal and unsatisfying ways that God Himself is the source of the faith-community's word. But doubts remained. "I believe You" was uttered as a hope for a more direct contact with God. There was a desire for a "You" who could provide an utter conviction about Himself.

Faith then is not a conclusion from an argument. Many reasons show it to be desirable or reasonable, but because of its very structure it cannot simply be born of calculations. One may reason from, for example, the experience of conscience to a vague sense of the reasonableness of theism;[153] he may then reason to the credibility of Christian revelation;[154] but after reasoning there must come invocation—a calling out to a real Being who acts in history and in individual human lives, and who alone can be the Author of a different pattern of grasping divine things.[155]

Faith cannot be a question of concluding that "God must be and must have spoken, because I know these other things and calculate such." In that case our reasonings would generate faith. But faith is a gift. It must be a question of God causing the realization that it is He who has spoken. In this case God's own presence causes the believer to realize without clarity of vision that it is God's word which he had thought to be present in the witnessing community.

The believer does not *see* the causal factors which must be for faith to be real, but he invokes God and his "I want to" becomes "I believe You." It becomes something new. The result is permanent, although faith can be rejected or lost. Even so, believers can experience "dark nights of the soul." They can experience a deep sense of God's absence while remaining faithful to His word for no other reason than because it is His word. When the pain of anxiety makes them forget every extrinsic reason for believing that it is His word; when every proof, every sign is forgotten, faith can remain for its inner strength was never signs and arguments but God testifying obscurely but surely that it is He who calls us to faith in community.

John Henry Newman was aware of the possibility of unbelief; he was deeply aware of difficulties present in Christian belief, yet he spoke of divine faith as "a clear certainty greater than any other certainty" but added that "this is wrought in the mind by the grace of God, and by it alone."[156] The "pre-eminence of strength in divine faith," the certainty of faith, does not consist in its differing from human faith merely in degree of assent "but in its being superior in nature and kind." Human and divine faith do "not admit of a comparison" with one another. Yet the "intrinsic superiority" of divine faith

> is not a matter of experience, but is above experience. Assent is ever assent; but in the assent which follows on a divine announcement, and is vivified by a divine grace, there is, from the nature of the case, a transcendant adhesion of mind, intellectual and moral, and a special self-protection, beyond the operation of . . . ordinary laws of thought.[157]

He spent much time outlining the ordinary laws of thought, the arguments and evidence which can bring a man to faith, but he warned: "I hope no reader will misunderstand me, and think that I am forgetting its divine origin because I am investigating its human history."[158] Perhaps it was with this in mind that he placed on the title page of the *Grammar of Assent*, the words of St. Ambrose: "It was not by dialectical discussion that it pleased God to save His people."*[159]

References

1. *MS* B.7.4 ("Certainty of Faith" 16 December 1853); this paper contains all the key ideas of the *GA* but with much ambiguity. See above 53.
2. *Ibid.*
3. *Ibid.*
4. *MS* A.18.11 ("A-Introduction 1860?") 5. In *MS* B.7.4 ("Certainty of Faith" 16 December 1853) he gave the example of proof of an afterlife from reflection on conscience.
5. *MS* B.7.4 ("Certainty of Faith" 16 December 1853). In 1860 he wrote that it is difficult to distinguish "contuition" or an "insight into a thing" from what lies about it, and intuition. *MS* A.18.11 ("A-Introduction 1860?") 5.
6. *MS* B.7.4 ("Certainty of Faith" 16 December 1853).
7. *Ibid.*
8. See above 148–152.
9. *MS* B.7.4 ("Certainty of Faith" 16 December 1853).
10. *Ibid.*
11. This would be a novel use of the distinction which Newman did not explicitly employ. While the judgment of credibility is not supernatural *knowing* (objective certain faith), it is natural *knowing* (objective certain knowledge). Supernaturally considered it remains "inference;" but naturally considered it is "assent."
12. *LD* 15:467 (11 October 1853).
13. *MS* B.7.4 ("Certainty of Faith" 16 December 1853).
14. *Ibid.*
15. He added that this "does not immediately lead to faith." *Ibid.*
16. This also "is not sufficient ad credendum, except with human faith which has doubt or fear." *Ibid.*
17. *Ibid.*
18. *Ibid.*
19. *MS* B.7.4 ("Object of Faith" 17 January 1854).
20. *Ibid.*
21. See Harper, 185–192; *Ess* 1:v (1871).
22. Harper, 186–187 (July 1871).
23. *Ibid.* 197, 196 (1879).
24. *Ibid.* 196, 197.
25. *Ibid.* 197.
26. *Ibid.* 199. See Alfred J. Ayer's restatement of many of Froude's arguments in "The Claims of Theology" *The Listener* 90 (9 August 1973) 165–173.
27. See Wilfrid Ward 2:465–466.
28. Harper, 201–202 (29 April 1879).
29. *Ibid.* 204.

30. *Ibid.*
31. *Ibid.* 206.
32. *US* 254 ("Implicit and Explicit Reason" 29 June 1840).
33. *Ibid.* 267.
34. *Ibid.* xvi (1871 preface).
35. *Ibid.* 215 ("Nature of Faith" 13 January 1839).
36. *Ibid.* 210.
37. *MS* B.7.4 ("Certainty of Faith" 16 December 1853).
38. *Ibid.*
39. *Ibid.*
40. *Mix* 152 ("Nature and Grace"). He wrote that informal reason can give "absolute certitude" "as to the truths of natural theology" and "as to the fact of revelation." *Apo* 31.
41. *SE* 105 (January 1886); see *Idea* 449–455 ("Christianity and Physical Science" November 1855); Wilfrid Ward 2:269 (13 April 1870).
42. See *SE* 107 (January 1886); *LD* 12:34 (14 February 1847).
43. *Idea* 455 ("Christianity and Physical Science" 1855); see *US* 114–115 ("Justice" 8 April 1832).
44. *SE* 106 (January 1886).
45. *Ibid.* 107; see *GA* 72; *Mix* 285–295, 314.
46. *Idea* 25 (1852).
47. *LD* 18:334 (24 April 1858); see above 26 note 37. Newman regarded the commanding act of conscience as one of the irreducible forms of personal self-awareness bound up with the certitude of one's own existence. (See *PN* 2:31–37 "Proof of Theism" 7 November 1859). It is one of the phenomena of consciousness from which we can make valid existential inferences. "From the nature of the case its very existence carries on our minds to a Being exterior to ourselves." (*OS* 64 ("Dispositions for Faith" 21 December 1856)). As sunshine implies the sun, as a knock at the door implies someone outside, (*ibid.*) as "an echo implies a voice," (*Call* 315) "so this Word within us . . . raises our minds to . . . an unseen Teacher." (*OS* 65 ("Dispositions for Faith" 21 December 1856)). See also *US* 206 ("Nature of Faith" 13 January 1839); *PPS* 2:13–25 ("Faith without Sight" 21 December 1834); Boekraad, *Argument* 53–87.
48. *Apo* 217.
49. *LG* 384; see *MS* B. 7. 4 ("Certainty of Faith" 16 December 1853) on how an educated man faces more objections than a child but has access to more evidence. His prudentia is "increased intellectually" as well as "stimulated by grace."
50. Harper, 207 (29 April 1879).
51. *Ibid.* 208, 209.
52. *LD* 18:334 (24 April 1858). He spoke of a "duty" to reject irrational doubt; a duty to obey the laws of our intellectual nature and *a fortiori* the law of our Creator who provides us with the means to achieve "objective truth" in this matter. *Ibid.* 335–336; see *ibid.* 464 (24 September 1858); *VM* 1:88–89 note 6 (added 1877).
53. *LD* 16:108 (1855?).

54. *PN* 2:195 (7 November 1877).

55. *Ibid.* 195–197 (7 November 1878); see *US* 208 ("Nature of Faith" 13 January 1839).

56. *US* 17 ("Influence of Natural and Revealed Religion" 13 April 1830).

57. Harper, 209 (29 April 1879).

58. *LD* 20:171 (15 March 1862); also in Wilfrid Ward 1:638. Vargish mistakenly dated this letter as 1859 (Vargish, 150). In 1852 Newman had spoken of the "intellectual excellence" engendered by a liberal education (*Idea* 121) which can "aid" divine faith insofar as it expels the "excitements of sense;" (*Ibid.* 186) but, by itself, tends to make a "Religion of Reason" (*Ibid.* 182) "making . . . our minds the measure of all things," (*Ibid.* 217) revelation included. He had suggested that divine faith effects "its own enlargement" of mind or "Wisdom" as its "reward." (*Ibid.* 133; *US* 284, 294 ("Wisdom" 1 June 1841)). In 1862 he asked Ward: "May there not be a 'Divine *philosophy*' or largeness . . . of mind on all objects . . . proceeding from grace and begotten of a spiritual . . . connaturality with their true worth and real place in God's sight, as well as a Divine faith?" It would be "parallel to intellectual philosophy, as Divine faith is parallel to human faith." (*LD* 20:171).

59. *GA* 387.

60. *Ibid.* 388. Perhaps the situation is similar to the way in which a complex of evidence (sensible and intellectual) remains a part of perception or knowledge that something is the case; see above 121–122.

61. *US* 183 ("Faith and Reason Contrasted" 6 January 1839).

62. *Ibid.*

63. *Ibid.* 199.

64. *Mix* 211 ("Faith and Private Judgment").

65. *MS* A.30.11 ("Evidences of Religion" 12 January 1860).

66. *Mix* 188 ("Illuminating Grace"); see *GA* 492.

67. See above 39–40.

68. Newman's discussion of infallibility parallels his treatment of reason and grace before and in faith. He argued that if a meaningful (objective) truth, not merely data to be variously interpreted, is revealed and ensured preservation, an infallible guide is implied; (*Apo* 220–240) otherwise we would have merely a circle of hypotheses which "could not support itself." (*Diff* 1:137). We should not posit unjustified intuitions in epistemology nor unjustified authority in theology. Rather we should locate the authority by locating the truth, by informal reasoning before faith and by the light of grace in faith; see *VM* 1:310 note 1 (added 1877); *Dev* 78–89.

69. *PPS* 2:151–152 ("Saving Knowledge" January or February 1835); see *ibid.* 6:327–342 ("Faith without Demonstration" 21 May 1837).

70. *Jfc* 267.

71. See *US* 61–62 ("Usurpations of Reason" 11 December 1831); *Mix* 172–173 ("Illuminating Grace"); *SN* 313 (10 January 1853).

72. *Mix* 187 ("Illuminating Grace").
73. See above 17–19.
74. *US* 181–182 ("Faith and Reason Contrasted" 6 January 1839).
75. *Ibid.* 202 ("Nature of Faith" 13 January 1839).
76. *Diff* 1:270.
77. *US* 179 ("Faith and Reason Contrasted" 6 January 1839), he referred to *Hebrews* 10:37–38; *Mix* 178 ("Illuminating Grace").
78. *Mix* 224 ("Faith and Doubt").
79. *Ibid.* 189 ("Illuminating Grace"). He found this account "the only rational, consistent account of faith," (*ibid.* 178; see 187–188) but he left the question of how grace imparts supernatural knowledge to theology. For a survey of some theological discussions of this matter see Trethowan, 55–144; Aubert, especially 720–745; Charles Journet, *The Dark Knowledge of God* (1943) (trans.) James F. Anderson (London, 1948).
80. See above 148–149.
81. *PPS* 2:151–152 ("Saving Knowledge" January or February 1835).
82. *Mix* 190 ("Illuminating Grace"); 1 *John* 2:20.
83. *Ibid.* 181.
84. *Ibid.* 176, 171.
85. Hick, 115; see his *Arguments for the Existence of God* (Glasgow, 1970) 101–120; also John Baillie, *Our Knowledge of God* (London, 1939) ch. 3. sec. 10. See above 90–103.
86. See Ronald W. Hepburn's criticism of encounter theology in his *Christianity and Paradox* (London, 1958) 29–59.
87. See Hick, *Faith* 115; also his "Religious Faith as Experiencing-As" in *Talk of God* (ed.) P. Vasey (London, 1968); also the similar analysis by John E. Smith, *Experience of God* (New York, 1968) 23 and 63; and John H. Randall Jr., *The Role of Knowledge in Western Religion* (Boston, 1958) 76–142.
88. Hick, *Faith* 96, 101.
89. See *ibid.* 108–111.
90. *Ibid.* 169; see Richard M. Hare in *New Essays in Philosophical Theology* (ed.) Antony Flew and Alasdair MacIntyre (London, 1969) 99–103.
91. Hick, *Faith* 169–199.
92. See his parable of the "Celestial City" where two men are travelling the same road with alternative interpretations. The correct one is verified only when they have gone round the last bend. *Ibid.* 177–178.
93. *Ibid.* 186, 187.
94. *Ibid.* See 191.
95. *Ibid.* 194.
96. *Ibid.* 197. Jerry H. Gill rejected both Hick's discussion of "eschatological verification" and, with it, the reason why it was introduced—in his "John Hick and Religious Knowledge" *International Journal for the Philosophy of Religion* 2 (1971) 129–147.
97. See above 120–122.

98. *US* 207 ("Nature of Faith" 13 January 1839).

99. *Ess* 1:34 (Tract 73: 2 February 1836); *US* 249 ("Love the Safeguard" 21 May 1839).

100. Someone could hold that knowledge is an objective grasp while faith can only be a decision. But Newman would argue that this is not the *fact.*

101. *Mix* 182 ("Illuminating Grace").

102. *Ibid.* 224 ("Faith and Doubt"), and see 195–197 ("Faith and Private Judgment").

103. *LD* 21:270 (24 October 1864); see *ibid.* 15:467 (13 October 1853); *LG* 385.

104. *Mix* 197 ("Faith and Private Judgment").

105. *Ibid.* 215–216 ("Faith and Doubt").

106. *LD* 18:472 (2 October 1858); *PN* 2:121 (28 February 1860); *PN* 2:129 (2 March 1861).

107. *Mix* 220 ("Faith and Doubt"). See *LG* 386.

108. *Mix* 222.

109. *GA* 387.

110. *Works* 4:146 ("First reply to the Bishop of Worcester" 1697); see above 19.

111. *MS* B.7.4 (On Divine Faith: 7 July 1867).

112. *DA* 296 (Tamworth Reading Room: February 1841).

113. *GA* 387; see *DA* 134 (Tract 85: 21 September 1838): "Religion cannot but be dogmatic." See the objection to faith "as propositional belief" in Hick, *Faith* 11–94; and Richard B. Braithwaite, "An Empiricist's View of the Nature of Religious Belief" (1955) in *Philosophy of Religion* (ed.) Basil Mitchell (Oxford, 1971) 72–91. Kai Nielsen used the verification principle to attack a cognitive (dogmatic) faith but admitted that many philosophers have found flaws in this principle. Kai Nielsen, *Contemporary Critiques of Religion* (Glasgow, 1971) 94. See the criticism of non-cognitive theories of faith in Mascall, 49–62.

114. *MS* B.9.11 (Assent of Faith: 20 April 1877).

115. *US* 253 ("Implicit and Explicit Reason" 29 June 1840).

116. *Ibid.* 63 ("Usurpations of Reason" 11 December 1831).

117. See *ibid.* 45 ("Evangelical Sanctity the Perfection of Natural Virtue" 6 March 1831).

118. *Ess* 1:32 (Tract 73: 2 February 1836).

119. *Ibid.* 31–32; see above 4–5, 122–125, 145–146.

120. *Idea* 61 (1852).

121. *Ibid.* 39.

122. *Ibid.* 38.

123. *Ibid.* 40.

124. *Ibid.* 39, 40.

125. *Ibid.* 61.

126. *Ibid.* 28.

127. *Ibid.* 514 ("Christianity and Medical Science" November 1858).

128. *Ibid.* 445–446 ("Christianity and Physical Science" November 1855).

129. *Ibid.* 224–225 (1852).

130. *Ibid.* 223–224.

131. *Ibid.* 446–467 ("Christianity and Scientific Investigation" 1855).

132. *Ibid.* 467.

133. *Ibid.*

134. *Ibid.* 470; see 474–475.

135. *Dev* 336.

136. *Idea* 387–388 ("Form of Infidelity" 1854).

137. *Ibid.* 390.

138. *Ess* 1:34 (Tract 73: 2 February 1836).

139. *Romans* 10:17.

140. *US* 180 ("Faith and Reason Contrasted" 6 January 1839).

141. *Mix* 195 ("Faith and Private Judgment").

142. See Price, *Belief* 426–454; and C. K. Grant, "Belief in and Belief that" *Proceedings of the XIIth International Congress of Philosophy* (Venice 12–18 September 1958) (Florence, 1960) 5:187–194, who argued that *trust* is not reducible to a factual belief "that" someone is trustworthy. Price said it is an affective state; and Grant, a positive action, a "doing something."

143. *MS* B.7.4 ("Object of Faith" 17 January 1854).

144. This analogy is given in Pieper, *Belief* 13–14.

145. This is why faith is, in fact, most commended when one accepts a worthy testimony when the situation is such that it makes what is said most unlikely, for example, Abraham in *Genesis* 22.

146. See above 187.

147. 1 *Thessalonians* 2:13.

148. *Mix* 172–177 ("Illuminating Grace"); *US* 61–62 ("Usurpations of Reason" 11 December 1831).

149. See *US* 63–65 ("Usurpations of Reason" 11 December 1831).

150. The blind man analogy is weak insofar as sense-perception is a possession, while faith is a source of truth without evidential possession. It relies entirely on the word of another for possession. But the analogy applies insofar as faith, like knowledge, is an independent source of information.

151. The believer can lose faith without losing reason and what it controls.

152. *PPS* 6:108 ("The Gospel Sign Addressed to Faith" 12 November 1837).

153. See *GA* 389–408 on the sense of sin and sacrifice in primitive culture.

154. See *GA* 409–492 on prophecy, the coincidence of the Old and New Testaments and the testimony given to the divine message in the Church by the witness of martyrs.

155. Newman wrote: "I should like an inquirer to say continually 'O

my God, I confess that *Thou canst* enlighten my darkness—I confess that Thou *only* canst. I *wish* my darkness to be enlightened. I do not know whether Thou wilt; but that Thou canst, and that I wish, are sufficient reasons for me to *ask,* what Thou at least has [sic] not forbidden my asking. I hereby promise Thee that, by Thy grace which I am seeking, I *will embrace* whatever I at length feel certain is the truth, if ever I come to be certain . . . ' If a man tells me he has thus heroically cast himself upon God, and persisted in such a prayer, and yet is in the dark, of course my argument with him is at an end. I retire from the discussion, and leave the matter to God." (*LD* 16:108–109 (10 April 1854)).

156. *Mix* 224. Teresa of Avila wrote: "How, you will ask, can we become so convinced of what we have not seen? That I do not know; it is the work of God." (*Interior Castle* (1577) *Works of Teresa of Avila* (trans.) Edgar A. Peers (London, 1946) 2: 252.) John of the Cross also spoke of a "secret wisdom . . . communicated and infused into the soul through love . . . hidden from the work of the understanding." (*Dark Night of the Soul* (1582–1588) (trans.) Edgar A. Peers, (New York, 1959) 159).

157. *GA* 186–187.

158. *MS* A.30.11 ("Evidences of Religion" 12 January 1860); see *LD* 21:270 (24 October 1864); *GA* 187.

159. *GA* iii; St. Ambrose, *De Fide ad Gratianum Augustum* 1.5. Section 42 (381), in *PL* 16:537: "*Non in dialectica complacuit Deo salvum facere populum suum.*"

SELECT BIBLIOGRAPHY

Where two dates are given, the date given in parentheses, before that of the edition used, is that of the original edition. For an explanation of the dating system followed in the list of abbreviations and in the notes, see page xvii.

1. SELECTED LIST OF NEWMAN'S WRITINGS

Unpublished

The unpublished manuscripts used in this study are listed chronologically. References are to the packet numbers at the Oratory, Hagley Road, Egbaston, Birmingham B168UE. Some of these manuscripts are partly printed in David A. Pailin, *The Way to Faith* (London, 1969), Appendix ii, 202–223. Many of them are available in the volume edited by Hugo M. De Achaval and J. Derek Holmes, *The Theological Papers of John Henry Newman: On Faith and Certainty*, Oxford, 1976.

17 June 1846. Assent of Faith. MS B.9.11.
1847. English Draft of Preface for the University Sermons. MS B.9.11.
Easter 1848. "Certainty of Faith." MS B.9.11.
Easter 1848. "From Fr. Edward Caswell's notes on Lectures with the Father 1853," dated 20 August 1866. The lectures were given 17 May-18 June 1851 from the paper written over Easter 1848 found in MS B.9.11. See MS B.7.4.
14 April 1853. "Certainty of Faith." MS A.30.11.
30 April 1853. On opinion, belief etc. MS A.23.1.
11–18 May 1853. "Analysis of religious inquiry." MS A.18.11/B.9.11.
16 December 1853. "Certainty of Faith." MS B.7.4.
17 January 1854. "Object of Faith." MS B.7.4.
1856. "no truth is more certain." MS B.3.2.
4 May 1857. "On Mill's Logic." MS A.30.11.
23 July 1857. Reason and Imagination. MS A.18.11.
11 January 1859. "Questions of greater consequence." MS A.18.11.
January-February 1859. Notes on Logic and Philosophy. MS A.18.11.
1860. "A-Introduction 1860?" MS A.18.11.
5 January 1860. "On the popular, practical, personal evidence for the truth of Revelation." MS A.30.11.
12 January 1860. "Evidences of Religion." MS A.30.11.

September 1863. Human Reason and Objects of Faith. MS A.30.11.
December 1863. "The Conceivable." MS A.30.11.
3 December 1863. "On Conception." MS A.30.11.
26 June 1865. Certainty and Probable Evidence. MS A.30.11.
20 July 1865. "Essay on Certitude." MS A.23.1.
11 August 1865. "p. 17 A Comparison of the Moral Sense and Certitude
1865." MS A.30.11.
25 September 1865. "Meaning of Certitude." MS A.23.1.
7 July 1867. On Divine Faith. MS B.7.4.
26 April, 5 May, 7 September 1868. Apprehension and Assent. MS
A.30.11.
20 April 1877. Assent of Faith. MS B.9.11.

Published
The standard edition of Newman's collected works, used in this study
with the exception of the *Apologia,* is that of Longmans, Green and Co.
(London, 1874–1921) in 40 volumes. A complete survey of his works is
given by A. Läpple in *Newman-Studien* (eds.) Heinrich Fries and Werner
Becker, 1 (1948) 287–294. There is a supplement to this survey by N.
Schiffer and Werner Becker in 2 (1954) 325; and by Werner Becker and
Günter Biemer in 3 (1957) 286–292. Material used in this study is listed
alphabetically by title.

Apologia Pro Vita Sua. (1865). Ed. Martin J. Svaglic. Oxford, 1967.
The Arians of the Fourth Century. (1833) London, 1901.
Callista: a Tale of the Third Century. (1855) London, 1904.
Cardinal Newman and William Froude, a Correspondence. Ed. Gordon
Huntington Harper. Baltimore, 1933.
"Cardinal Newman's Theses de Fide and His Proposed Introduction to
the French Translation of the University Sermons." Ed. Henry
Tristram, *Gregorianum* 18 (1937) 219–241.
Certain Difficulties Felt by Anglicans in Catholic Teaching. 2 vols. (1850)
London, 1907.
*Correspondence of John Henry Newman with John Keble and Others
1839–1845.* Eds. Fathers of the Birmingham Oratory. London, 1917.
Discourses Addressed to Mixed Congregations. (1849) London, 1906.
Discussions and Arguments on Various Subjects. (1872) London, 1907.
An Essay in Aid of a Grammar of Assent. (1870) London, 1906.
An Essay on the Development of Christian Doctrine. (1845) London,
1906.
Essays Critical and Historical. 2 vols. (1871) London, 1907.
Fifteen Sermons Preached before the University of Oxford. (1843)
London, 1906.
Historical Sketches. 3 vols. (1872–1873) London, 1903–1906.
The Idea of a University. (1852) London, 1907.

John Henry Newman, Autobiographical Writings. Ed. Henry Tristram. London, 1955.

Lectures on the Doctrine of Justification. (1838) London, 1900.

Lectures on the Present Position of Catholics in England. (1851) London, 1903.

Letters and Correspondence of John Henry Newman During His Life in the English Church. 2 vols. Ed. Anne Mozley. London, 1891.

The Letters and Diaries of John Henry Newman. Vols. 11–22. Ed. Charles Stephen Dessain (Dessain and Vincent F. Blehl: vols. 14–15; Dessain and Edward E. Kelly: vol. 21). London, 1961–1972. Vols. 23–30. Eds. Dessain and Thomas Gornall. Oxford, 1973–1975.

Loss and Gain: the Story of a Convert. (1848) London, 1906.

Parochial and Plain Sermons. 8 vols. (1834–1843) London, 1901–1907.

The Philosophical Notebook of John Henry Newman. Ed. Edward Sillem. 2 vols. 2: *The Text.* Revised, A. J. Boekraad. Louvain, 1970.

Philosophical Readings in Cardinal Newman. Ed. James Collins. Chicago, 1961.

Select Treatises of St. Athanasius in Controversy with the Arians. Trans. John Henry Newman. 2 vols. (1841–1844) London, 1903.

Sermon Notes of John Henry Cardinal Newman 1849–1878. Eds. Fathers of the Birmingham Oratory. London, 1913.

Sermons Preached on Various Occasions. (1857) London, 1904.

Stray Essays on Controversial Points Variously Illustrated. Privately printed, Birmingham, 1890.

"Unpublished Paper by Newman on Development of Doctrine." Ed. Charles Stephen Dessain. *Journal of Theological Studies* n.s. 9 (1958) 324–335.

The Via Media of the Anglican Church. Illustrated in Lectures, Letters, and Tracts Written Between 1830 and 1841. 2 vols. (1837, 1883) London, 1901.

2. SELECTED LIST OF WRITINGS ON NEWMAN

Werner Becker and Heinrich Fries give a full bibliography of works on Newman in *Newman-Studien* 1 (1948) 301–326. Supplements to this list appear in 2 (1954) 327–343; 3 (1957) 293–298; 4 (1960) 347–352; 5 (1962) 305–316; 6 (1964) 252–260; 7 (1967) 311–316; and 8 (1970) 243–252. Works used in this study are listed alphabetically by author.

Artz, Johannes. "Die Eigenständigkeit der Erkenntnistheorie John Henry Newmans." *Theologische Quartelschrift* 139 (1959) 194–222.

———. "Newman und die Intuition." *Theologische Quartelschrift* 136 (1956) 174–198.

Bacchus, Francis, and Tristram, Henry. "Newman (John-Henry)." *Dictionnaire de Theologie Catholique,* Paris, 1931, 11:351.

Bastable, James D. "Cardinal Newman's Philosophy of Belief." *Irish Ecclesiastical Record* 83 (1955) 241–252, 346–351, 436–444.

Beer, John. "Newman and the Romantic Sensibility." In *The English Mind: Studies in the English Moralists Presented to Basil Willey*, 193–218. Eds. Hugh S. Davies and George Watson. Cambridge, 1964.

Boekraad, Adrian J. *The Personal Conquest of Truth According to John Henry Newman.* Louvain, 1955.

Boekraad, Adrian J., and Tristram, Henry. *The Argument from Conscience to the Existence of God.* Louvain, 1961.

Bouyer, Louis. *Newman, His Life and Spirituality.* New York, 1958.

Cameron, James M. *The Night Battle.* London, 1962.

Chadwick, Owen. *From Bossuet to Newman: the Idea of Doctrinal Development.* Cambridge, 1957.

Collins, James. Introduction to *Philosophical Readings in Cardinal Newman.* Chicago, 1961.

Coulson, John, and Allchin, A. M., eds. *The Rediscovery of Newman: an Oxford Symposium.* London, 1967.

Coulson, John, Allchin, A. M., and Trevor, Meriol. *Newman: a Portrait Restored.* London, 1965.

Cronin, John F. *Cardinal Newman: His Theory of Knowledge.* Washington, 1935.

Culler, A. Dwight. *The Imperial Intellect: a Study of Newman's Educational Ideal.* New Haven, 1955.

D'Arcy, Martin Cyril. *The Nature of Belief.* (1931) London, 1945.

Dessain, Charles Stephen. *John Henry Newman.* London, 1966.

Duffy, Eamon. "Newman's Use of Butler's Maxim 'Probability is the Guide of Life.'" M.A. thesis, Hull University, 1968.

Flanagan, Philip. *Newman, Faith and the Believer.* London, 1946.

Gilson, Etienne. Introduction to *Grammar of Assent*, by John Henry Newman. New York, 1955.

Graef, Hilda. *God and Myself: the Spirituality of John Henry Newman.* (1967) Gateshead, 1968.

Hollis, Christopher. *Newman and the Modern World.* (1967) London, 1970.

Karl, A. *Die Glaubensphilosophie Newmans.* Bonn, 1941.

Keogh, Cornelius B. "Introduction to the Philosophy of Cardinal Newman." M.A. thesis, Université Catholique de Louvain, 1950.

Klubertanz, George P. "Where is the Evidence for Thomistic Metaphysics?" *Revue Philosophique de Louvain* 56 (1968) 294–315.

Lennan, John E. "Search for Absolute Holiness: A Study of Newman's Evangelical Period." *Ampleforth Journal* 73 (1968) 161–174.

Mahoney, B. J. "Newman and Aristotle: the Concept of Conscience." Ph.D. dissertation, University of Birmingham, 1967.

Middleton, Robert D. *Newman at Oxford: His Religious Development.* Oxford, 1950.

Nédoncelle, Maurice. *La Philosophie religieuse de John Henry Newman.* Paris, 1946.

Newsome, David. "Newman and the Oxford Movement." In *The Victorian Crisis of Faith*. Ed. Anthony Symondson. London, 1970.

———. *The Parting of Friends: a Study of the Wilberforces and Henry Manning*. London, 1966.

Pailin, David A. *The Way to Faith*. London, 1969.

Potts, Timothy C. "What Then Does Dr. Newman Mean?" *Newman-Studien* 6 (1964) 55–81.

Przywara, Erich. *John Henry Kardinal Newman, Christentum, Ein Aufbau*. Vol. 4: *Einführung in Newmans Wessen und Werk*. Freiburg, 1922.

Rickaby, Joseph. *Index to the Works of John Henry Newman*. London, 1914.

Robinson, J. "Newman's Use of Butler's Arguments." *Downside Review* 75(1958) 5–10.

Sillem, Edward. General Introduction to *The Philosophical Notebook of John Henry Newman*. Vol 1. Louvain, 1969.

Trevor, Meriol. *Newman: the Pillar of the Cloud*. London, 1962.

———. *Newman: Light in Winter*. London, 1962.

Vargish, Thomas. *Newman: the Contemplation of Mind*. Oxford, 1970.

Walgrave, Jan-H. *Newman the Theologian*. (1957) London, 1960.

Ward, Maisie. *Young Mr. Newman*. London, 1948.

Ward, Wilfrid. *Last Lectures*. London, 1918.

———. *The Life of John Henry Cardinal Newman, Based on His Private Journals and Correspondence*. 2 vols. London, 1912.

Weatherby, Harold L. *Cardinal Newman in His Age*. Nashville, 1973.

———. "Newman and Victorian Liberalism: a Study in the Failure of Influence." *Critical Quarterly* 13 (1971) 205–213.

Wicker, Brian J. "Logic and Certainty: Aspects of the Philosophy of John Henry Cardinal Newman." M.A. thesis, University of Birmingham, 1960.

———. "Newman and Logic." *Newman-Studien* 5 (1962) 251–268.

Willam, Franz Michel. *Aristotelische Erkenntnislehre bei Whately und Newman*. Freiburg, 1960.

Zeno, OFM Cap. *John Henry Newman: Our Way to Certitude*. Leiden, 1957.

3. SELECTED LIST OF LOCKE'S WRITINGS

An extended history of Locke's writings is available in Hans O. Christophersen's *Bibliographical Introduction to the Study of John Locke* (Oslo, 1930) 7–70. The edition of Locke's works used in this study, with the exception of the *Essay*, is the ten-volume edition, London, 1812. References to the *Journal* manuscripts are to the folio numbers of the Lovelace Collection in the Bodleian Library. Materials used in this study are listed alphabetically by title.

The Conduct of Understanding. (1706) in *Works* 7:1–158.

A Discourse of Miracles. (1706) in *Works* 9:256–265.

An Early Draft of Locke's Essay, Together with Excerpts from His Journals. Draft A. Eds. Richard I. Aaron and J. Gibb. Oxford, 1936.

An Essay Concerning Human Understanding. (1690) Ed. Alexander C. Fraser. 2 vols. New York, 1959.

First Letter Concerning Toleration. (1689) in *Works* 6:1–58.

First Letter to the Bishop of Worcester. (1697) in *Works* 4:1–96.

First Reply to the Bishop of Worcester. (1697) in *Works* 4:97–185.

First Vindication of the Reasonableness of Christianity. (1695) in *Works* 7:159–190.

Journal. 26 August 1676: MS f.1:420–424; 26 June 1681: MS f.5:77–83; 19 February 1682: MS f.6:20–22.

"Locke and Sydenham: a Fragment on Smallpox" (1670). Ed. Patrick Romanell. *Bulletin of the History of Medicine* 32 (1958) 293–321.

The Reasonableness of Christianity. (1695) in *Works* 7:1–158.

Second Reply to the Bishop of Worcester. (1699) in *Works* 4:191–498.

A Second Vindication of the Reasonableness of Christianity. (1697) in *Works* 7:191–424.

4. SELECTED LIST OF WRITINGS ON LOCKE

A full bibliography of works on Locke is given by Hans O. Christophersen in his *Bibliographical Introduction to the Study of John Locke.* This survey is supplemented by Roland Hall and Roger Woolhouse, "Forty Years of Work on John Locke (1929–1969) A Bibliography," *Philosophical Quarterly* 20 (1970) 258–268, 394–396. Works used in this study are listed alphabetically by author.

Aaron, Richard I. *John Locke.* (1937) Oxford, 1955.

Ashcroft, Richard. "Faith and Knowledge in Locke's Philosophy." In *John Locke: Problems and Perspectives,* 194–224. Ed. John W. Yolton. Cambridge, 1969.

Bennett, Jonathan F. *Locke, Berkeley, Hume: Central Themes.* Oxford, 1971.

Bourne, Henry Richard Fox. *Life of John Locke.* 2 vols. London, 1876.

Collins, James. *British Empiricists.* Milwaukee, 1967.

Copleston, Frederick C. *A History of Philosophy.* Vol. 5, pt. 1: *The British Philosophers.* (1957) New York, 1964.

Cranston, Maurice. *John Locke.* New York, 1957.

Gibson, James. *Locke's Theory of Knowledge and Its Historical Relations.* (1917) Cambridge, 1968.

Hefelbower, Samuel G. *The Relation of John Locke to English Deism.* Chicago, 1918.

Helm, Paul. "Locke on Faith and Knowledge." *Philosophical Quarterly* 23 (1973) 52–66.

King, Lord Peter. *The Life and Letters of John Locke.* London, 1864.

Mabbot, John D. *John Locke.* London, 1973.

O'Connor, Daniel J. *John Locke.* (1952) New York, 1967.

Ramsey, Ian T. Introduction to *"The Reasonableness of Christianity," with "A Discource of Miracles," and part of "A Third Letter Concerning Toleration."* Ed. I. T. Ramsey. Stanford, 1958.

Van Leeuwen, Henry G. *The Problem of Certainty in English Thought, 1630–1690.* Hague, 1963.

Ware, Charlotte S. "Influence of Descartes on John Locke." *Revue Internationale de Philosophie* 4 (1950) 210–230.

Woolhouse, Roger S. *Locke's Philosophy of Science and Knowledge.* Oxford, 1971.

Yolton, John W. *John Locke and the Way of Ideas.* Oxford, 1956.

5. SELECTED LIST OF OTHER WORKS CONSULTED

This list includes works with which Newman was familiar, studies of the history of the period, and material by classical and contemporary authors bearing on the subject of this study. Entries are listed alphabetically by author.

Aaron, Richard I. "Intuitive Knowledge." *Mind* 51 (1942) 315–320.

Adler, Mortimer. *The Conditions of Philosophy.* New York, 1965.

Aldrich, Henry. *Artis Logicae Rudimenta.* (1691) Ed. Henry L. Mansel. Oxford, 1856.

Alfaro, Juan. *Fides, Spes, Caritas.* Rome, 1968.

Ambrose, St. *De Fide ad Gratianum Augustum* (381). In *Patrologiae Cursus Completus, Series Latina,* 16:527–698. Ed. J. P. Migne. Paris, 1845.

Anderson, James F. "Notion of Certitude." *Thomist* 18 (1955) 522–539.

Aquinas, St. Thomas. *Quaestiones Disputatae de Veritate.* (1256–1259). In *Opera Omnia,* Leonis XIII edita. Vol. 22. Rome, 1972.

——. *Scriptum super Sententiis Magistri Petri Lombardi.* (c. 1256). Ed. R. P. Mandonnet. 4 vols. Paris, 1929–1947.

——. *Summa Contra Gentiles.* (1261–1263). In *Opera Omnia,* Leonis XIII edita. Vols. 13–15. Rome, 1918–1930.

——. *Summae Theologiae.* (1265–1273). In *Opera Omnia,* Leonis XIII edita. Vols. 4–12. Rome, 1888–1906.

Ardley, Gavin. *Aquinas and Kant.* London, 1950.

Aristotle. *Ethica Nicomachea.* (309–322 BC). Ed. Ingram Bywater. (1894) Oxford, 1942.

Aubert, Roger. *Le Probleme de l'acte de foi.* Louvain, 1950.

Augustine, St. *Confessiones.* (400). In *Patrologiae Cursus Completus, Series Latina,* 32:659–868. Ed. J. P. Migne, Paris, 1861.

———. *Contra Epistolam Parmeniani.* (400). In *Patrologiae Cursus Completus, Series Latina,* 43:33–108. Ed. J. P. Migne. Paris, 1861.

Austin, John L. *Sense and Sensibilia.* (1962) Ed. G. J. Warnock. Oxford, 1964.

Ayer, Alfred J. "Basic Propositions." In *Philosophical Essays,* 105–124. London, 1954.

———. "The Claims of Theology." *Listener* 90 (9 August 1973) 165–173.

———. *The Problem of Knowledge.* London, 1956.

Baillie, John. *Our Knowledge of God.* London. 1939.

Battiscombe, Georgina. *John Keble: a Study in Limitations.* London, 1963.

Bennett, Jonathan. "Analytic-Synthetic." *Proceedings of the Aristotelian Society* n.s. 59 (1958–1959) 163–188.

Berkeley, George. *The Principles, Dialogues and Philosophical Correspondence.* (1710, 1713). Ed. Colin M. Turbayne. New York, 1965.

Billuart, Charles R. *Tractatus de Fide et Regulis Fidei.* (1746–1751). In *Cursus Theologiae,* vol. 9. Paris, 1827.

Boyle, Joseph M. "Self-Referential Inconsistency, Inevitable Falsity and Metaphysical Argumentation." *Metaphilosophy* 3 (1972) 26–44.

Braine, David. "Nature of Knowledge." *Proceedings of the Aristotelian Society* n.s. 72 (1971–1972) 41–63.

Braithwaite, Richard B. "An Empiricist's View of the Nature of Religious Belief." In *The Philosophy of Religion,* 72–91. Ed. Basil Mitchell. Oxford, 1971.

Brilioth, Yngve T. *The Anglican Revival: Studies in the Oxford Movement.* London, 1934.

———. *Three Lectures on Evangelicalism and the Oxford Movement.* London, 1934.

Butler, Joseph. *The Analogy of Religion.* (1736) Glasgow, 1831.

Campbell, C. A. "Self-Evidence." *Philosophical Quarterly* 10 (1960) 138–155.

Chadwick, Owen. *The Mind of the Oxford Movement.* London, 1960.

———. *The Victorian Church.* 2 vols. London, 1966, 1970.

Chalybäus, Heinrich M. *Historical Development of Speculative Philosophy from Kant to Hegel.* Edinburgh, 1854.

Charlesworth, Max. "Linguistic Analysis and God." *International Philosophical Quarterly* 1 (1961) 139–167.

Chillingworth, William. *The Religion of Protestants: a Safe Way to Salvation.* (1638) London, 1845.

Church, Richard William. *The Oxford Movement.* (1891) Ed. Geoffrey Best. Chicago, 1970.

Cockshut, A. O. J. *The Unbelievers: English Agnostic Thought 1840–1890.* New York, 1966.

Collins, James. "Analytic Theism and Demonstrative Inference." *International Philosophical Quarterly* 1 (1961) 235–263.

——. *The Emergence of the Philosophy of Religion.* (1967) New Haven, 1969.

——. *God in Modern Philosophy.* (1959) London, 1960.

Copleston, Frederick C. *A History of Philosophy.* Vol. 8 pt. 1: *Modern Philosophy: British Empiricism and the Idealist Movement in Great Britain.* (1965) New York, 1967.

Crehan, Joseph H. "Conscience." In *A Catholic Dictionary of Theology,* 2:99–105. Eds. H. Francis Davis, Aidan Williams, Ivo Thomas and Joseph Crehan. London, 1966.

Cunningham, Francis. "Certitudo in St. Thomas." *Modern Schoolman* 30 (1953) 207–324.

Davies, Horton. *Worship and Theology in England.* Vol. 4: *From Newman to Martineau.* Princeton, 1962.

Dawson, Christopher. *The Spirit of the Oxford Movement.* London, 1933.

De Lugo, Juan. *De Virtute Fidei Divinae.* (1652). In *Opera Omnia Theologica,* 1:202–274. Paris, 1868.

Descartes, René. *Philosophical Writings.* (1629–1649) Ed. Norman K. Smith. New York, 1958.

Dulles, Avery. "Faith, Reason and the Logic of Discovery." *Thought* 45 (1970) 485–502.

Eliott-Binns, Leonard B. *Early Evangelicals: a Religious and Social Study.* London, 1953.

Farrer, Austin. *Reflective Faith.* Ed. Charles C. Conti. London, 1972.

Flew, Antony, and McIntyre, Alasdair, Eds. *New Essays in Philosophical Theology.* London, 1969.

Gambier, J. E. *Introduction to the Study of Moral Evidence or of That Species of Reasoning Which Relates to Matters of Fact and Practice.* (1806) London, 1824.

Gill, Jerry H. "John Hick and Religious Knowledge." *International Journal for the Philosophy of Religion* 2 (1971) 129–147.

——. "Tacit Structure of Religious Knowing." *International Philosophical Quarterly* 9 (1969) 533–559.

Gilson, Etienne. *God and Philosophy.* (1941) New Haven, 1967.

——. *Reason and Revelation in the Middle Ages.* New York, 1938.

Grant, C. K. "Belief and Belief that." *Proceedings of the XIIth International Congress of Philosophy,* Venice 12–18 September 1958, 187–194. Florence, 1960.

Griffiths, A. Phillips, ed. *Knowledge and Belief.* (1967) Oxford, 1968.

Harman, Gilbert. "Enumerative Induction as Inference to the Best Explanation." *Journal of Philosophy* 65 (1968) 529–533.

——. "Inference to the Best Explanation." *Philosophical Review* 74 (1965) 88–95.

Helm, Paul. *The Varieties of Belief.* London, 1973.

Hepburn, Ronald W. *Christianity and Paradox.* London, 1958.

Hick, John. *Arguments for the Existence of God.* Glasgow, 1970.

212   Faith and Doubt

——. *Faith and Knowledge.* (1957) London, 1967.
Holden, Henry. *The Analysis of Divine Faith: or Two Treatises of the Resolution of Christian Belief.* (1652) Trans. W. G. Paris, 1658.
Huet, Pierre Daniel. *An Essay Concerning the Weakness of Human Understanding.* (1723) Trans. Edward Combe. London, 1725.
Hume, David. *Enquiries Concerning Human Understanding and Concerning the Principles of Morals.* (1748, 1751) Ed. L. A. Selby-Bigge. Oxford, 1962.
——. *Natural History of Religion.* (1757); and *Dialogues Concerning Natural Religion.* (c. 1779) In *Hume on Religion,* 31–204. Ed. Richard Wollheim. London, 1963.
——. *Treatise of Human Nature.* (1739–1740) Ed. L. A. Selby-Bigge. Oxford, 1968.
Journet, Charles. *The Dark Knowledge of God.* (1943) Trans. James F. Anderson. London, 1948.
Kant, Immanuel. *Critique of Pure Reason.* (1781) Trans. John M. D. Meiklejohn. London, 1855.
Keeler, Leo. *Problem of Error from Plato to Kant.* Analecta Gregoriana, Vol. 6. Rome, 1934.
Keble, John. *The Christian Year.* (1827) London, 1906.
Kordig, Karl R. "Objectivity, Scientific Change and Self Reference." In *Boston Studies in the Philosophy of Science,* 8:519–523. Eds. Roger C. Buck and Robert S. Cohen. Dordrecht, 1971.
——. "Theory-Ladenness of Observation." *Review of Metaphysics* 24 (1971) 448–484.
Kuhn, Thomas S. *Structure of Scientific Revolutions.* Chicago, 1962.
Lakatos, I., and Musgrave, A., eds. *Criticism and the Growth of Knowledge.* (1969) Cambridge, 1972.
Lewis, Clarence I. *An Analysis of Knowledge and Valuation.* LaSalle, Ind., 1946.
Liddon, Henry Parry. *Life of Edward Bouverie Pusey.* 3 vols. London, 1893–1897.
Malcolm, Norman. *Knowledge and Certainty.* London, 1963.
Mansel, Henry L. *The Limits of Religious Thought.* London, 1858.
Maritain, Jacques. *Approaches to God.* (1954) New York, 1965.
Mascall, Eric. *The Openness of Being.* London, 1971.
——. *Words and Images.* (1957) London, 1968.
Mill, John Stuart. *System of Logic.* (1843) London, 1879.
Mitchell, Basil, ed. *Faith and Logic.* London, 1957.
——. "Justification of Religious Belief." *Philosophical Quarterly* 24 (1961) 213–226.
Murray, John Courtney. *The Problem of God.* New Haven, 1968.
Nielsen, Kai. *Contemporary Critiques of Religion.* Glasgow, 1971.
Noort, Gerardus Van. *Dogmatic Theology.* Vol 3: *The Sources of Revelation. Divine Faith.* Trans. J. J. Castelot and W. R. Murphy. Westminster, Md., 1961.
Pattison, Mark. *Memoirs.* London, 1885.

——. "Tendencies of Religious Thought in England, 1688–1750." In *Essays and Reviews*, 254–329. London, 1861.

Penelhum, Terrence. *Problems of Religious Knowledge*. London, 1971.

Perrone, Giovanni. *Praelectiones Theologicae*. 8 vols. Rome, 1840–1844.

Pieper, Josef. *Belief and Faith*. London, 1963.

——. *Leisure, the Basis of Culture*. London, 1952.

——. "The Meaning of God Speaks." *New Scholasticism* 43 (1969) 203–211.

Polanyi, Michael. *Personal Knowledge*. (1958) London, 1962.

Popkin, Richard H. *The History of Scepticism from Erasmus to Descartes*. New York, 1961.

Popper, Karl. *Conjectures and Refutations*. (1962) London, 1969.

——. *The Logic of Scientific Discovery*. (1935) London, 1968.

——. *The Open Society and Its Enemies*. (1945) London, 1966.

Price, Henry H. *Belief*. London, 1969.

——. *Truth and Corrigibility*. Oxford, 1936.

Quine, Willard Van Orman. "Two Dogmas of Empiricism." In *From a Logical Point of View*, 20–46. New York, 1953.

Quinton, Anthony. *The Nature of Things*. London, 1973.

Ramsey, Ian T. *Religious Language*. (1957) London, 1969.

Randall, John H. Jr. *The Role of Knowledge in Western Religion*. Boston, 1958.

Regis, Louis M. *Epistemology*. New York, 1959.

Scheffler, Israel. *Science and Subjectivity*. New York, 1965.

Smith, John Edwin. *Experience of God*. New York, 1968.

Stewart, Dugald. *Elements of the Philosophy of the Human Mind*. (1792–1827). Ed. G. R. Wright. 3 vols. London, 1854.

Suarez, Francis. *De Fide Theologica*. (1621) In *Opera Omnia* 12:1–596. Paris, 1856.

Sumner, L. W., and Woods, John, eds. *Necessary Truth: a Book of Readings*. New York, 1969.

Tillotson, John. *The Rule of Faith*. London, 1666.

Trethowan, Illtyd. *Certainty: Philosophical and Theological*. London, 1948.

Tullock, John. *Movements of Religious Thought in Britain During the Nineteenth Century*. London, 1885.

Vasey, P., ed. *Talk of God*. London, 1968.

Vidler, Alec R. *The Church in an Age of Revolution*. London, 1971.

Ward, W. R. *Victorian Oxford*. London, 1965.

Whately, Elizabeth Jane. *Life and Correspondence of Richard Whately*. 2 vols. London, 1866.

Whately, Richard. *Elements of Logic*. (1826) London, 1872.

——. *Elements of Rhetoric*. (1828) London, 1846.

——. *Historic Doubts Relative to Napoleon Bonaparte*. London, 1819.

Willey, Basil. *Nineteenth-Century Studies*. (1949) London, 1969.

Wittgenstein, Ludwig. *On Certainty*. Trans. Gertrude E. M. Anscombe and Denis Paul. Oxford, 1969.

Index

virtual, 150; distinct from and related to certainty, 83, 150; distinct from infallibility, 98-99, 101, 157 n. 39.

Chalybäus, H. M., 159 n. 79; Newman's reading of, 6-7, 14 n. 41.

Chillingworth, William, 85 n. 18; his view of regressing justification, criticized by Newman, 108, 159 n. 89; on certainty in religion, 70.

Christian Year, The (Keble), 13 n. 18.

Cockshut, A. O. J., 26 n. 37.

Coleridge, Samuel Taylor, 13 n. 22.

Collins, James, 14 n. 38 and n. 46, 85-86 n. 26, 87 n. 46, 147.

Conceptualism, 76.

Conduct of the Understanding (Locke), 10, 81.

Conjectures and Refutations (Popper), 135-136.

Convergence of probabilities, see *Evidence, cumulative.*

Coulson, John, 13 n. 22.

Crabbe, George, his poem "The Preceptor Husband," quoted by Newman, 110, 160 n. 105.

Cranston, Maurice, 23 n. 1.

Critique of Pure Reason, The (Kant), Newman's copy of, 159 n. 79.

Cronin, John F., 88 n. 65, 171-172 n. 418.

Dalgairns, John Bernard, 42-44, 46; his supervision of a French translation of Newman's *Oxford University Sermons* and *Essay on Development*, 22, 42.

D'Arcy, Martin C., 14 n. 43, 158 n. 56.

Davies, Horton, 13 n. 23.

Deism, xi, 25 n. 30; its relation to Locke, 24 n. 14.

De Lemennais, Felicite, 66 n. 143.

De Lugo, Juan, 60 n. 82, 62 n. 108.

Descartes, Rene, 5; his influence on Locke, 10, 15 n. 63, 68-69, 84 n. 5 and n. 10 and n. 14 and n. 16; on the intuition of clear and distinct ideas, 2, 69.

Dessain, Charles S., 66 n. 146.

Development of doctrine, see *Dogma; Knowledge.*

Discourse of Miracles (Locke), 19.

Discourses to Mixed Congregations (Newman), 28, 94, 178, 180-182, 185-186, 193.

Discussions and Arguments (Newman), 32; "Internal Argument for Christianity," 34; "Tamworth Reading Room," 21, 23, 33, 36, 88 n. 69, 187; "Tract 85," 3, 31, 200 n. 113.

Divinae Fidei Analysis (Holden), 61 n. 87; Newman's evaluation of, 43.

Dogma, 123-127; and apologetics, 43; and objective truth in religion, 3-5, 200 n. 113; as creed, inseparable from religious faith, 31; as revealed, the object of faith, 36, 52; attacked in principle by the skeptic, 3; development of revealed, 124-125, 138-139, as a moving from implicit belief to formal statement, 124, 126-127, 164 n. 216, as a necessary evolution guided by the original revealed idea, 126, as a via media between extremes, 123-125. See also *Revelation; Theology.*

Doubt, 50-51, 153-154; as incompatible with objective faith, 19, 58-59 n. 53, 186; as necessarily accompanying faith, 18, 34; as unreasonable and non-intellectual, 50, 153-154; grace as rendering it difficult to, 186; grace as subduing irrational, 154, 197 n. 52; its relation to difficulties, 50-51, 65 n. 129 and n. 140, 66 n. 144, 153-154. See also *Certainty.*

Dulles, Avery, 164 n. 214.

Elements of Logic (Whately), 1-2, 12 n. 4, 93.

Elements of Rhetoric (Whately), 64 n. 124.

Elements of the Philosophy of the Human Mind (Stewart), Newman's reading of, 60-61 n. 84, 158 n. 70.

Empiricism, 19-23; and phenomenalism, 96-97, 156-157 n. 32; as

n. 60, and the regress of justifying inferences, 92, 107-108, 159 n. 88; its object, 8-10, 20, 78-79, 84 n. 6, 87 n. 45, 99-100, 105-106, 136-137; its reflexivity, 117-118, 149-150, 162 n. 159, 170 n. 372; natural, of God, 25 n. 33, 26 n. 37, 37, 177-178, 187, 197 n. 47.

Kordig, Karl R., 166 n. 289.

Körner, Stephen, 87 n. 41.

Kuhn, Thomas S., on normal and extraordinary science, 167 n. 296; on the method of science, 137, 167 n. 292.

Lectures on Justification (Newman), 30-31, 180.

Lectures on the Present Position of Catholics in England (Newman), xii, 109, 110, 154, 160 n. 101.

Lectures on the Prophetic Office of the Church (Newman), *see Via Media of the Anglican Church,* vol. 1.

Lee, Henry, 86 n. 28.

Letter to Pusey (Newman), *see Certain Difficulties Felt by Anglicans in Catholic Teaching,* vol. 2.

Letter to the Duke of Norfolk (Newman), *see Certain Difficulties Felt by Anglicans in Catholic Teaching,* vol. 2.

Lewis, C. I., on certainty and probability, 101.

Liberal education, and faith, 198 n. 58; as enlarging the mind, 81-82.

Liberalism, Newman's definition of, 2, 12 n. 10; the emergence of a new, 2-4.

Limits of Religious Thought, The, Henry Mansel's Bampton lectures, 67 n. 160; Newman's evaluation of, 54.

Locke, John, xiii, 5-11, 17-19, 23-24 n. 1, 37, 68-75, 77-83, 148, 180-181; and Descartes, 9-10, 15 n. 63, 68-70, 84 n. 10 and n. 14; and Deism, 24 n. 14; and empiricism, 7-11, 84 n. 5, 86-87 n. 40, 89 n. 98; and his English predecessors, 70-72, 85 n. 17 and

n. 18; and the analytic/synthetic distinction, 85 n. 20; contrasted with Newman, 7, 88 n. 69, 88-89 n. 80, 89 n. 93, on abstraction, 8-9, 76-79, on faith, 10-11, 14 n. 38, 32, 36-37, 181-182, on knowledge, 8-10, 79-83, 88 n. 65; his ambiguity when discussing ideas, 75; his ambiguity when discussing the function of sagacity and illation (judgment), 80-81, 84 n. 8 and n. 10, 88 n. 79, 89 n. 83 and n. 87; his begging the question against divine faith, 180-181; his confusion of assent and inference, 148; his correspondence with Sergeant, John, 86 n. 28; his correspondence with Stillingfleet, William, 72; his criticism of Descartes on intuition, 69-70, 84 n. 14; his critics, 72, 86 n. 28, 87 n. 45; his inconsistency when discussing the certainty of faith, 17-19; his influence at Oxford and in England, 5-6, 14 n. 32; his opinion of Descartes, 10, 15 n. 63, 68; his private notes on certainty, 18, 89 n. 83; his skepticism in matters of fact, 71-72, 75, 86 n. 31; on assent, as uncertain but unavoidable, 73, 75, 86 n. 35; on certainty, as assurance, 86 n. 35, 186, as clarity, 71; on enthusiasm, 18, 24 n. 17, 36-37, 62 n. 104, 75; on faith, 17-19, as an assent to what is revealed, 17-19, as an opinion (probable), distinct from knowledge (certain), 18, 24-25 n. 19, 71-72, 74, as assured ("certain"), 17, 19, 32, 86 n. 35, 186, as ultimately reasoned, 1, 11, 17-18; on ideas, as incapable of development, 164 n. 219, as innate, 69, as real, 69-70, 74, as simple or complex (abstract), 72, as the objects of knowledge, 8-9, 20, 68-70, 84 n. 6, 87 n. 45, 136-137, of substances, 72-73; on inference from regular observance, 151; on intuition as irresistable belief, 73-74; on knowledge, and linguistic convention, 87 n. 41, 160 n. 101, and logical certainty, 19, 69, 90-91, 92, 186, as intuition, 69, as the perception of the connection between ideas, 24 n. 15, 69-70, 84 n. 5 and n. 14, 88 n. 79, 151; on nature, 72; on nominal knowledge of general essences, 71, 85 n. 20, 85-86 n. 26; on sensations, as knowledge, 74-75, as unexplained conviction, 75; on the justification of existential knowledge, 72-75. *See also Empiricism; Faith; Ideas; Knowledge; and the titles of his individual works.*

Logic, 94; improper, a habit of the mind dealing with truth and certainty, 94; inexorable, Froude's ambiguous use of the term, 128; proper, an instrumental art drawing premises to their inevitable results, 47, 94. *See also Inference.*

Logic and Scientific Discovery (Popper), 135-136.

Logic of testimony, 168 n. 339, 181-182, 190-191; a logic of accepting the word of another, distinct from proving the conclusion of premises, 11, 181-182, 190-191, 194, 201 n. 150; and the nature of divine faith, 29, 61 n. 87, 61-62 n. 88; and the object of divine faith, 57 n. 20, 175.

Loss and Gain (Newman), 50, 178.

Malcolm, Norman, compared with Newman on certainty and error, 99, 157 n. 41.

Mansel, Henry L., 67 n. 160, 88 n. 65; his notes in his edition of Aldrich's *Artis Logicae Rudimenta* compared with Newman on verisimilitude, 64 n. 123; Newman's reading of, 54.

Mascall, Eric, 163 n. 178, 200 n. 113.

Masham, Lady Demaris, her letter to Jean Le Clerc on Locke and Descartes, 15 n. 63.

Method, of philosophy, as grounded in common experience, 9-10, 144; of science, 110-112, 129-132, 135-137, as grounded in particular experiments, 142-143; of theology,

as grounded in revelation, 143-145, 188-190.

Method of Science (Sergeant), 86 n. 28.

Meynell, Charles, 54, 107; his warning Newman against becoming a "hypothetical realist," 105-106.

Mill, John Stuart, Newman's reading of, 93, 156 n. 16 and n. 22; on causality as universal regularity, 93-94; on imagination, 93-94; on propositions as real or verbal, 93.

Milner, Joseph, his attack on reason in religion, 1, 11 n. 1.

Monophysites, Newman's recognition of a via-media in the, 123.

Motives of credibility (motiva credibilitatis), *see Judgment of credibility.*

Movements of Religious Thought in Britain during the nineteenth century (Tulloch), 13 n. 20.

Murray, John C., 168 n. 339.

Mystery, 168 n. 339; and certain but obscure faith, 34, 58 n. 45, 145-146, 193, 195; and certain but obscure knowledge, 11, 79-80, 122-123, 128, 145, 148, 152, 154; distinct from "nonsense," 168 n. 339.

Natural History of Religion (Hume), 21.

Nature of Things, The (Quinton), 96-97, 155-156 n. 12, 158 n. 65 and n. 68.

Newman, John Henry, xi-xiii, 1-11, 19-23, 28-56, 75-83, 90-95, 98-155, 173-195, 201-202 n. 155; and Aristotle, 113, 161 n. 132, 164 n. 213, 172 n. 428; and Butler, 2-3, 12 n. 11, 66 n. 142 and n. 143; and empiricism, 5-11, 19-23, 75-77, 82-83, 97, 155, 172 n. 429; and evangelicalism, 1, 11-12 n. 3, 13 n. 22; and fideism, 42-43, 61 n. 86; and Gambier, J. E., 169-170 n. 365; and informal rationalism, 13 n. 17, 38-40, 43, 46, 53, 55, 65 n. 136, 180; and Keble, 3-4, 13 n. 20, 57 n. 25; and Mansel, H. L., 54, 63-64 n.